Innovation and Entrepreneurship within Health Education

Recognizing the growing significance of innovation and entrepreneurship in the field of health education, this novel volume discusses digital skills, collaborative learning and contemporary curricular challenges in order to foster innovative and entrepreneurial mindsets.

Against the backdrop of an evolving healthcare system characterized by the delivery of consumer-led, data-driven, targeted healthcare solutions, the chapters in the book spotlight entrepreneurship as a vital component of the New Health Economy and the role of education in supporting entrepreneurship and innovation among medical professionals and trainees. Citing international perspectives on curriculum initiatives in various educational settings, the book presents case studies of health entrepreneurship frameworks, startups and the idea of an entrepreneurial healthcare ecosystem that supports networking, professional development and technological advancement.

Supporting the use of entrepreneurship strategies for educational purposes within medical education settings, this book will be of interest to scholars, researchers, faculty and postgraduate students in the fields of health education, curriculum studies, technology in education, medical education and entrepreneurship.

Jeff Wilkesmann is Professor, Faculty of Applied Natural Sciences and Industrial Engineering, Technical University of Deggendorf, Germany and former Education and Collaboration Lead, European Institute of Innovation and Technology, EIT Health Germany.

Contemporary Pedagogies of Medical and Health Professions' Education

Series editors: Paul Crampton and John Tredinnick-Rowe

This novel series will focus on innovation and best practice in relation to curriculum design and teaching methodologies within the environments of medical schools, ultimately aiming to promote innovation in medical education. Books in the series offer cutting-edge examples of pedagogical techniques and practises through case studies and rigorous scholarship, and reflect subjects that medical schools are adapting in order to drive innovation such as the increasing role of patient-centred medicine or the expanding use of technology in medical curricula.

Themes identified in the series have international relevance given the similarities around educating medical students and their interaction with other clinical professions, and showcase novel research methodologies and frameworks to aid teaching and learning and preparedness of the next generation of clinical professionals.

Books in the series include:

Pedagogies of Biomedical Science
A Holistic Approach to Integrating Pedagogy across the Curriculum
Edited by Donna Johnson

Pedagogies of Widening Participation in Medical Settings
Addressing Under-representation through Partnership and Professionalism
Edited by Louise Alldridge

Innovation and Entrepreneurship within Health Education
International Perspectives on Multidisciplinary Collaboration and Digital Skills
Edited by Jeff Wilkesmann

For more information about the series, please visit: Contemporary Pedagogies of Medical and Health Professions' Education - Book Series - Routledge & CRC Press

Innovation and Entrepreneurship within Health Education

International Perspectives on Multidisciplinary Collaboration and Digital Skills

Edited by Jeff Wilkesmann

Routledge
Taylor & Francis Group
LONDON AND NEW YORK

First published 2026
by Routledge
4 Park Square, Milton Park, Abingdon, Oxon OX14 4RN

and by Routledge
605 Third Avenue, New York, NY 10158

Routledge is an imprint of the Taylor & Francis Group, an informa business

British Library Cataloguing-in-Publication Data
A catalogue record for this book is available from the British Library.

ISBN: 978-1-032-94049-6 (hbk)
ISBN: 978-1-032-94047-2 (pbk)
ISBN: 978-1-003-56865-0 (ebk)

DOI: 10.4324/9781003568650

Typeset in ITC Galliard
by KnowledgeWorks Global Ltd.

To my family Jarod, Kylie, Liliana & Tata

To my former colleagues at EIT Health for all the help and support, especially Montse, Céline, Katarina, Sigrid, Jean-Marc, Christian, Nandor and Kurt

Contents

Editor and Contributors

Lisa Auweiler is a psychologist and research assistant at the teaching and research area of Occupational Health Psychology at RWTH Aachen University, Germany. Her doctoral thesis and research interests are psychosocial risk assessment and digital training evaluation.

Malte Busch is the team leader of the Joint Innovation Hub Heilbronn at the Fraunhofer Institute. His areas of expertise include innovation management, systemic stakeholder analysis, the transfer of research findings into companies and organizations and policy consulting. He has been involved in international MBA and MA programs for several years.

Rainer Busch is a professor at Ludwigshafen University of Business and Society. His teaching and research focus is on strategic international management, market entry strategies, networks and ecosystems and the integration of artificial intelligence in management. He has successfully developed MBA programs, combining theoretical expertise with practical approaches.

Paul Coyle is the Director of the Entrepreneurial Mindset Network, a global community of practice, with special interest groups for the application of the entrepreneurial mindset in business, education, healthcare and social entrepreneurship. Paul is an expert in the entrepreneurial mindset, innovation, entrepreneurship, leadership and organizational change.

Constanze Duhme, PhD, is an experienced transfer and innovation manager and researcher with a strong background in life sciences and medical research. She currently works at the Medical Faculty of the University of Cologne and previously served as a transfer scout at the Gateway Excellence Start-up Center of the University of Cologne and as an innovation manager at the industry association BioRiver. Her research career includes postdoctoral roles in liver regeneration and stem cell and cancer research at leading institutions.

Maria Dutarte has been Executive Director of the European Patients' Academy on Therapeutic Innovation (EUPATI) since 2020. She previously worked for the European AIDS Treatment Group (EATG), coordinating patient involvement in several training initiatives and scientific projects. She also worked at the French National Research Center for Scientific Research (CNRS), International AIDS Society (IAS), The Global Fund to Fight AIDS, Tuberculosis and Malaria and The International Foundation for Science (IFS). Her educational background is in International Education and Communications.

René T. Eiswirth is at the Department of Process and Chemical Engineering, Technical University Mannheim, Mannheim, Germany. MSc in Chemical Engineering, Doctor of Engineering, worked for an international chemical company, since 2015 at Technical University Mannheim, teaching and research in the field of process engineering and chemical engineering.

Karina Fisch, PhD in Educational Sciences at the University of Regensburg, with expertise in didactics focused on innovative teaching formats using new media. Her research interests include learning transfer, blended learning formats, digital learning preferences and hybrid teaching.

Sabine Fischer holds a PhD in economics and specializes on analyzing, explaining and predicting behavior and decision-making, as well as designing and evaluating behavioral interventions across various fields. Her current work focuses on eliciting preferences for learning scenarios and implementing instructional designs to enhance learning efficiency.

Caroline IJkema is a passionate healthcare innovation and digital transformation expert, specializing in designing and implementing digital solutions that bridge technology and patient-centered care to drive measurable outcomes. She brings extensive experience to her work, leading projects that support new care models, drive value-based healthcare and foster stakeholder collaboration.

Berta Jover is committed to bringing innovation to the healthcare sector to bring the best care to patients. Working at Amgen in Barcelona, Berta is leading the implementation of value-based solutions such as telemedicine tools in hospitals around Spain.

Kevin Kastner is at CeMOS Research and Transfer Center, Technical University Mannheim, Mannheim, Germany. MSc in Medical Engineering, Research in Virtual Engineering, Digital Twins, Smart Immersive Environments and XR approaches in Education, Industry, Biomedical or Healthcare.

Marc Kley has worked in the field of spin-off coaching since 2001. Marc is currently the CEO of the Gateway Excellence Start-up Center at the University of Cologne. He has built an environment to support research-based spin-offs from ideation to market entry. As part of this, Marc has initiated a group of transfer scouts to foster spin-off activities from research. His list of publications includes several articles on innovation management, business modeling and ecosystem building.

Marta Lago Arenas is a service designer and human-centered innovation leader with over 15 years of experience in health and care. She has worked with global biotech companies like Amgen and Boehringer Ingelheim, focusing on designing, implementing, and scaling innovative healthcare solutions - digital and non-digital- to improve outcomes, enhance care, and drive transformation. Passionate about making healthcare ecosystems more humane and equitable, Marta now leads Care Systems Transformation programs at The Care Lab in Barcelona and teaches care-centered design at the University of Applied Sciences and Arts in Lucerne, Switzerland.

Jessica Lang is professor of Occupational Health Psychology at RWTH Aachen University, Germany. Her applied research aims at identifying job-specific stressors and their systematic assessment. Her research findings resulted in online training for leaders, employees and occupational safety and health specialists, bringing research knowledge on psychosocial risk assessment and health promotion into practice.

Elke Langbein is a researcher and part of Team ELDA at the Technical University of Munich, Department Health and Sport Sciences. Her research and teaching expertise span accessibility in new technologies and educational formats in universal design for all, participation, inclusion, diversity and cocreation.

Richard Latzel holds a PhD in sport science and professor at the Deggendorf Institute of Technology, specializing in applied sport sciences with a focus on training sciences. With extensive experience in high-performance sports, his research interests include load monitoring and control, performance diagnostics and the energetics of exercise. Prof. Latzel is a member of the Deutsche Basketballärzte e.V. and the National Strength and Conditioning Association (NSCA).

João O. Malva is a Research Coordinator and leads the Institute of Pharmacology and Experimental Therapeutics at the Faculty of Medicine of the University of Coimbra. He has served as President of the Portuguese Society for Neuroscience (2007–2011) and coordinates the quadruple helix-based regional network Ageing@Coimbra. João O. Malva is a principal researcher and coordinator of relevant ageing-related EU projects including Horizon 2020 Teaming for Excellence Multidisciplinary Institute of Ageing (MIA-Portugal), EIT Health Ageing PhD School and Horizon Europe Excellence Hubs CHAngeing.

Christian May is the owner of MayConsult, a consulting firm specializing in international innovation project management, with a focus on Japanese and Chinese companies. He also has extensive experience teaching in international MBA programs, particularly in business simulations, combining technical expertise with intercultural competence.

Marita Mehlstäubl is experienced in setting up innovation support in academic systems and has worked for many years in research management positions at universities and for the Fraunhofer Society. She is currently the head of transfer scouts at the Gateway ESC. Previously, she built up the innovation center at the German Sports University Cologne. She has a background in physical chemistry research.

Eva Nefen is the Senior Director International MBA at the University of Economics and Society/Graduate School Rhein-Neckar. As one of the leaders in the university's internationalization efforts, she is dedicated to building and maintaining global networks, combining academic excellence with intercultural collaboration.

M. Cristina Polidori is Full Professor and Head of Ageing Clinical Research as attending physician of Internal Medicine and Geriatrics at the Dpt. II of Internal Medicine of the University Hospital of Cologne. She is Master of Philosophy, Professor of Physiological Chemistry, Professor of Ageing Medicine and CECAD PI. Dr. Polidori is former Marie-Curie and Harvard University Fellow, Honorary Fellow of the Royal College of Physicians of London, member of the Academic Board and Clinical Guidelines Committee of the European Geriatric Medicine Society as well as President Elect of the German Society of Gerontology and Geriatrics.

Julian Reichwald is since 2020 Professor for Business Informatics (Digital Business Technologies), Technical University Mannheim, Mannheim, Germany. Teaching and Research topics in specific fields of digital transformation and digital twins. Head of the Virtual Engineering Competence Center, Group Lead of Digital Transformation at CeMOS Research and Transfer Center, Technical University Mannheim. Diploma degree and PhD in business informatics, especially in distributed grid computing environments.

Martina Reitmaier-Krebs holds a PhD in educational science and head of the Division of innovative teaching at the Deggendorf Institute of Technology, specializing in the field of digital media. Her research interests include blended learning formats and digital examinations. Dr. Reitmaier-Krebs is a member of Gesellschaft für Informatik e.V. and Gesellschaft für Medien in der Wissenschaft (GMW).

Borja Sañudo is a PhD in sports sciences and professor at the Department of Physical Education and Sport at the University of Seville. His primary research focuses on using technology to improve health habits in various populations, leveraging tools like wearable sensors and mobile applications to promote active lifestyles. He is the Director of the TAPAS network, which applies innovative wireless and networked technologies to prevent disease and enhance health outcomes in both clinical and community settings. Borja has led multiple large-scale trials and contributed extensively to the study of physical activity and technology-driven interventions.

Ulrich Traegner is at the Department of Chemical- and Process Engineering, Technical University Mannheim, Mannheim, Germany. PhD in Environmental Engineering from the University of Illinois, employment in the chemical industry, since 2009 at Technical University Mannheim, teaching and research in chemical products development, process simulation and sustainable technologies.

Philipp Wiedemann is at the Department of Biotechnology, Technical University Mannheim, Mannheim, Germany. Biologist, PhD in Molecular Neuropharmacology, employment in the biopharmaceutical industry, since 2007 at Technical University Mannheim, teaching and research in cell culture processes and process monitoring.

Jeff Wilkesmann is a PhD in biochemistry and the former Education and Collaboration Lead at the European Institute of Innovation and Technology, EIT Health Germany. Former lecturer at the University of Applied Sciences Mannheim and at the Baden-Wuerttemberg Cooperative State University Mannheim and appointed as Professor for Bioengineering at the Deggendorf Institute of Technology in 2024.

Anne-Christin Zobel is a graduate in Health Sciences from the Technical University of Munich. She collaborated with the IDHEApp team on her bachelor's thesis, titled "The Impact of Digital Technological Devices on Healthy Behavior in Young People with Intellectual Disabilities: A Systematic Review."

Series Editor Foreword

Our intention with this book series is to explore fresh approaches, highlight points of difference and examine situations in which academics have sought to innovate around problems and develop more effective solutions for teaching future healthcare workers.

More specifically, we have taken this fresh approach partly because of the many clinical professions experiencing crises in recruitment. Central government responses to this have involved increasing school places or placing great emphasis on increasing staff health and well-being during core and foundation training. *Contemporary Pedagogies of Medicine and Health* focuses on innovation and good practice in relation to curriculum design and teaching. Books in the series are segmented into two core types.

1 Pedagogies of individual subjects taught as part of a curriculum
   - E.g., Pedagogies for Biomedical Science
2 Pedagogies of topics or themes within clinical curriculums
   - E.g., Pedagogies of Widening Participation

In addition to texts on individual curriculum areas, the series will include books on themes that might emerge in several areas across a curriculum – for example, introducing social justice concerns, ethics or gender-related issues in medicine. A common feature of both formats is the variety of voices in chapters that create balanced monographs and do not shy away from presenting differing stakeholder opinions or subjects. The series creates a space for critique and voicing of multiple points of view, which we believe is fundamental in driving meaningful progress in curriculum development. To this end, we welcome works coauthored with patients and students.

The international relevance of the series is driven by the fact that many problems in medical and healthcare education are consistent across borders (global) and include increasing recruitment, retention of staff, sustainable delivery, technological advancement, preservation of well-being and so on. As a result, the series content is highly internationally relevant because it focuses on concerns that transcend national boundaries. Similarly, innovations and new approaches are required in all locations to continue to deliver high-quality education.

Consequently, the need to develop pedagogy within healthcare education to facilitate changes in teaching clinical subjects is a pressing current concern. The Lancet Commission, in their report on medical education, opined that medical school curricula were currently not fit to meet societal demands and were "*outdated and static*". This series offers a space for clinical tutors and academics to showcase how medical schools (and so curricula) can be made fit for the 21st century through the dissemination of evidence-based pedagogies for instruction, for which there is clearly a demand in terms of societal pressure but also a regulatory requirement.

The series' scope is broad and encourages submissions from underserved clinical subjects in terms of research and scholarship on education and pedagogy. We envisage cross-cutting themes in healthcare education and medical subjects, but look to offer opportunities for specialisms that receive less limelight to showcase innovations; projects in allied healthcare and other clinical professions are very welcome. Moreover, there is scope for books to focus on new teaching methodologies present across different areas of medicine and other clinical subjects combined.

We believe this series will interest anyone involved in the development of healthcare professions because of the salience (and need) of education, workforce and regulatory developments as we all attempt to increase the quantity and quality of trainees entering a health service.

Universities worldwide possess a wealth of knowledge, skills and equipment that can be used to develop services and products, particularly in clinical subjects and engineering. However, while many academics are good at producing ideas for novel techniques and products, it is very unusual that they are trained to be able to exploit the resources at their fingertips within their institutions. Training in management or other skills is common for clinical academics and healthcare researchers, but much more could be done to support them on an entrepreneurial journey, during which they learn to turn their world-class research into innovations that can benefit patients. Prof. Wilkesmann's book acts as a guide for educational activities in this area of professional development. This is a severely underserved subject that has great potential to flourish. Most institutions have resources for product development on par with large corporations that staff can access at almost no cost. However, there is virtually no guidance on how institutions can support innovative product discovery in their academic staff. As with other books in this series, it is filled with workable examples from a wide range of subjects on exactly how this can be done. It draws from international authors in different institutions.

Jeff and his coauthors have created a book that is a first in its field and, hopefully, will act as a stepping stone for universities and colleges to learn to exploit the vast potential of their staff to contribute to commercial life.

From Paul Crampton and John Tredinnick-Rowe

February 2025

Note for the Reader

All chapters herewith presented have been written by their respective authors. Partial developments and corrections have been performed with the assistance of AI-based tools for translation and writing refinement purposes. All authors confirm that they have independently verified the content's originality, accuracy and integrity in alignment with Taylor & Francis's policies on AI usage in academic publishing.

Preface

Kurt Höller

Innovation and entrepreneurship in health education are transforming the future of healthcare, addressing global challenges and creating opportunities for new solutions. EIT Health Germany has, since its creation in 2017, played a pivotal role in this evolving landscape as a catalyst for change, fostering collaboration between academia, industry and policymakers. As one of Europe's largest health innovation networks, EIT Health has always provided a trusted and dynamic environment where stakeholders can exchange knowledge, develop pioneering ideas and bring impactful solutions to the healthcare sector. By facilitating interdisciplinary cooperation and empowering the next generation of healthcare entrepreneurs, EIT Health has launched numerous initiatives, putting itself at the forefront of shaping a more resilient and innovative health ecosystem.

Entrepreneurship is more than just launching startups – it is about cultivating a mindset of innovation, adaptability and problem-solving. In health education, fostering entrepreneurial thinking equips students and professionals with the skills to navigate complex healthcare landscapes, integrate emerging technologies and address unmet medical needs. This book explores how education, research and business development intersect to drive meaningful change and emphasizes the importance of structured training, funding access and digital transformation in healthcare entrepreneurship. Through insights from experts across various disciplines, it underscores the critical role of collaboration and cross-sector partnerships in advancing health innovation.

The international dimension of this work is essential. EIT Health has built a pan-European network of innovators, educators and healthcare professionals, which enables seamless knowledge exchange and strengthening of the entrepreneurial ecosystem across borders. By providing a safe and trusted space for stakeholders to share ideas and achievements, EIT Health has always ensured that innovation thrives in an open, supportive and inclusive environment. This network is a bridge between established institutions and emerging entrepreneurs and a driving force in shaping future healthcare policies, educational methodologies and market-driven innovations. This international and trustworthy setting is visible in the selection of experts and contributors to this book.

The book idea emerged from very nourishing webinars organized by EIT Health Germany with the help of different partners and stakeholders during the corona pandemic, with the firm conviction that it should be transformed into a book. This book is a tangible result of common efforts and goodwill and serves as a valuable resource for anyone engaged in health education, innovation and entrepreneurship. It offers fresh perspectives on the current state, existing gaps and future directions of health entrepreneurship in Europe, highlighting best practices and emerging trends. Beyond documenting experiences and insights, this project opens new possibilities for collaboration and dialogue, fostering strong relationships between healthcare experts, educators and entrepreneurs. I am convinced this work will inspire further engagement, shape new educational models and contribute to a stronger, more innovative European health environment, where knowledge, trust and collaboration continue to drive progress.

Kurt Höller is Senior Director Digital Affairs in the Healthcare Vertical Market team at Siemens AG and held different positions at EIT Health from its inception, including vice chairman of the supervisory board of EIT Health Germany, Director of Business Creation, interim Director of Education and interim COO at EIT Health e.V., Managing Director EIT Health Services & Investments GmbH and Managing Director EIT Health Germany-Switzerland CLC GmbH.

Introduction

Jeff Wilkesmann

Lifelong learning opportunities for professionals in the health area are needed globally and continuously. A myriad of possibilities for health education topics in various fields are found nowadays, going beyond (but not excluding) classical university classroom experience. With the integration and help of the different stakeholders – members from universities, private firms belonging to the small and medium-sized enterprise (SME) sector and research institutions – we have been able to gather an update on a selection of diverse health and education topics. This book integrates the right ingredients for successful entrepreneurialism in health and the healthcare system, how to arrange for collaborative learning and the importance of digital skills in healthcare. Beyond this, the book offers an overview of the current challenges in pharmaceutical production and the importance and challenges when building an incubator and accelerator interlinked with a university. It also includes a psychological assessment as a road to promoting and achieving healthier working conditions.

Innovation and entrepreneurship in health education are essential for preparing future healthcare professionals to tackle global health challenges, technological advancements and evolving patient needs. Integrating entrepreneurial thinking, digital health solutions, and interdisciplinary collaboration into medical and health-related curricula fosters a proactive approach to problem-solving and healthcare transformation.

This book fills a gap that involves the association of the knowledge triangle: education, research and business in the health area. The literature in this area is scarce, and there is an eager young audience capturing the essence of these elements in a rather non-continuous way (webinars, workshops, etc.).

Across the different chapters, the state-of-the-art of current trends and advancements are discussed, including the importance of entrepreneurial curriculum integration. Currently, different higher-education institutions (HEIs) have introduced healthcare entrepreneurship courses, business incubators and design-thinking methodologies into everyday activities. The use and impact of artificial intelligence (AI), generative AI (GenAI), big data, telemedicine and wearable health tech is increasingly being taught in medical and public health programs, and several chapters provide concrete examples.

DOI: 10.4324/9781003568650-1

This book also reflects the importance of interdisciplinary collaboration. The original idea of this book concerned how to maximize the benefits of partnerships between medical, engineering, and business schools and how to encourage cross-sector innovation. During the corona pandemic, many online activities guided by the European Institute of Innovation and Technology (EIT Health Germany) successfully converged into the need to diffuse valuable content generated by the different stakeholders. Thus, a group of professors, managers and entrepreneurs, all leaders and experts in their fields, came together and proposed a first draft of this book.

Also discussed in the chapters are different models related to experiential learning. Innovation days, startup competitions and simulation-based training provide hands-on entrepreneurial experience. The reader will also find a discussion of the key stakeholders that need to be engaged to develop a successful healthcare entrepreneurial ecosystem that bridges traditional coursework and theoretical education, hands-on entrepreneurial activity and connections with industry, investors and users/patients. Furthermore, case studies of the incubators, accelerators and startups within the Academy and related educational programs implementing these health entrepreneurship frameworks are also found throughout many of the chapters.

Innovation and entrepreneurship are becoming increasingly important in the field of health education. In our mission to explore the connection between health education and entrepreneurship, we have identified some gaps. There is a clear lack of standardized entrepreneurial training, and there is a considerable student population unprepared for commercializing innovations. Biomedical and health science (in general) education has shown the tendency to remain highly traditional, often prioritizing clinical training over innovation. This book may weaken the resistance toward change in traditional curricula. Another challenge to be tackled is that although access to technological advancements has increased, not many institutions comprehensively teach AI, blockchain and digital therapeutics.

It is clear that optimization of educational models is required to include a new wave of entrepreneurship and Third Mission of HEIs. This book also aims to identify and describe ideal educational practices for fostering innovative and entrepreneurial mindsets in health education. According to the literature, entrepreneurship is generally viewed as a positive component in health education programs.[1]

There is presently a shift evolving in the healthcare system characterized by the delivery of targeted healthcare solutions guided by consumer needs, with digital solutions and data-driven models. Entrepreneurship is considered a vital component of this so-called New Health Economy shift. The protagonists of this shift in strengthening health systems are in general entrepreneurs of SMEs and startups. The new global policy initiatives are to promote entrepreneurship and innovation in healthcare sectors, and **education is the first step**.

Much is being done within healthcare organizations to foster innovations inside hospitals, clinics and universities (i.e., intrapreneurship or innovation within existing structures). The content of this book helps the further evolution of entrepreneurship strategies for educational purposes, and expands views on how to enhance entrepreneurship education and skills development, and how to promote awareness and networking in the different communities.

To bridge the existing gaps, among the clear products of this book is the intent to standardize entrepreneurial training across health disciplines. HEIs must steadily integrate – sooner rather than later – structured courses on business models, investment strategies and health economics. The incorporation of AI, machine learning and digital health innovation topics into curricula will enhance future healthcare solutions. Furthermore, the stronger the ties between academic institutions, startups and healthcare companies are, the bigger the direct benefit for students gaining real-world experience. Finally, the expansion and flexibility of learning pathways are important elements that have spread widely. Micro-credentialing and online platforms (massive open online courses, or MOOCs) are allowing healthcare students (and also a broader community of learners) to gain entrepreneurial and digital health skills at their own pace.

The book is especially dedicated to individuals interested in the healthcare entrepreneurial ecosystem, including academic institutions, hospital systems looking to engage entrepreneurship and students in the fields of medicine, healthcare, natural sciences, biotechnology and medical technology, among others. Healthcare trainees need greater exposure to innovation and entrepreneurial skills, so they can improve the healthcare system and develop new approaches that can benefit patients, and ultimately, society.

Innovation and entrepreneurship in health education are critical for the future of healthcare. Although progress has been made in digital health integration, experiential learning and interdisciplinary approaches, significant gaps remain in standardized entrepreneurial training, funding access and regulatory navigation. The future of health education will require a structured, technology-driven and industry-connected approach, ensuring that the next generation of healthcare professionals is equipped to lead transformational changes in the industry. This book contributes to the further development of entrepreneurship strategies for educational purposes, the enhancement of entrepreneurship education and skills development and the promotion of awareness and networking in the different communities. A compilation of lessons learned is therefore provided to develop a thriving healthcare entrepreneurial ecosystem that engages all stakeholders. As an asset, the book's content shall also serve as inspiration for further partnership opportunities to develop similar educational and entrepreneurial systems elsewhere.

Note

1 Suryavanshi, T., Lambert, S., & Chan, T. (2019). P126: Entrepreneurship in healthcare and health education: A scoping review. *Canadian Journal of Emergency Medicine*, 21(S1), S109–S110. https://doi.org/10.1017/cem.2019.317

1 Multidisciplinary Education to Support Healthy Lifestyles and Disease Management

Health and Longevity in the 21st Century

M. Cristina Polidori and João O. Malva

Introduction: Life course journey to healthy aging

In 1946, the World Health Organization (WHO) defined health as "a state of complete physical, mental and social well-being and not merely the absence of disease or infirmity" (WHO, 1948). Despite controversies, this definition is accepted and consolidated. However, simultaneously with its publication, a biomedical model of illness was developed and increasingly operationalized, culminating in Disease-Related Groups and relative procedures, codes and reimbursement systems. The biomedical model of illness was founded in the mid-19th century, when most diseases were acute and therefore responded well to the one mechanism–one disease–one therapy method. Since then, the world population has undergone unique changes that strongly challenge it – most impressively, population expansion and aging. The journey through time from the WHO definition of health, to the proposed biopsychosocial model of disease (Engel, 1977), to the description of the effects of the comprehensive geriatric assessment (CGA; Rubenstein et al., 1981), to the published International Classification of Functioning, Disability and Health (WHO, 2001) and the CGA clinical guidelines published in Europe, is shown in Table 1.1.

Further important steps in understanding of health and aging in their current context are the publication of the Integrated Care for Older People (ICOPE)

Table 1.1 Development in the holistic approach to health and aging after the WHO Definition of Health

Year	*Multidimensional definition/model/instrument of health/health care*
1948	WHO definition of health
1977	Engel, Biopsychosocial model of disease
1981	Rubenstein, comprehensive geriatric assessment (CGA)
2001	WHO, International Classification of Functioning, Disability and Health
2019	WHO, Integrated Care for Older People (ICOPE)
2020–2030	United Nations Decade of Healthy Aging
2024	First official CGA clinical guidelines in Europe
	WHO, Integrated Care for Older People (ICOPE, 2nd Edit.)

DOI: 10.4324/9781003568650-2

guidelines (WHO, 2019; WHO, 2024). These guidelines offer "evidence-based direction on: (*i*) comprehensive assessment of health status in an older person; (*ii*) delivery of the integrated health care that will enable an older person to maintain their physical and mental capacities, and/or to slow or reverse any declines in these; and (*iii*) delivery of interventions to support caregivers". The guidelines aim to support healthcare professionals in clinical settings by identifying declines in physical and mental abilities and implementing effective measures to prevent or slow their progression. The guidelines also serve as a valuable resource for shaping national policies. Moreover, they can guide the integration of healthy aging interventions into essential health benefit packages to promote universal health coverage.

Despite all these efforts, it cannot be ignored that health is still approached and understood as the absence of disease. *Intrinsic capacity* is a recent term defined by the WHO to highlight the health of older people from a functional rather than disease-based perspective. It defines healthy aging as "the process of developing and maintaining the functional ability that enables wellbeing in older age" (WHO, 2015). The concept of functional ability encompasses all the health-related attributes that enable people to be and to do what they have reason to value. This life course construct comprehends functional ability as determined by (*i*) the intrinsic capacity (i.e., the composite of all the physical and mental capacities of an individual), (*ii*) the environment (i.e., all the factors in the extrinsic world that form the context of an individual's life) and (*iii*) the interactions between the two. Within this frame, the maintenance of intrinsic capacity is recognized as the central concept of a unique demographic change in which the world population is positively characterized by increased and steadily increasing life expectancy at birth, but negatively characterized by the effects of overweight. These key challenges are the consequence of improved health care and technologies on one side, and on the other side, easy access to low-cost, high-calorie foods as the predominant source of disease risk, with most chronic disorders worldwide being associated with lifestyle-related chronic conditions such as cardiovascular diseases, diabetes, dementia, cancer and osteoporosis. In other words, as baby boomers become aging boomers, a gap within global health system reactions is created. Therefore, even the SARS-Cov-2 pandemic as an acute illness could not be efficiently counteracted because the affected population is substantially different from that affected by other pandemics of the past: the highest COVID-19 mortality rates involved aged and obese individuals (WHO COVID-19 Dashboard; https://data.who.int/dashboards/covid19/cases?n=c).

Considering this evidence, education is the most fundamental key to effective human solidarity (from Latin *solidum*, "whole sum"). To achieve its full potential as a whole sum, education actions need to be fully integrated to close important gaps (Table 1.2).

All these gaps are fundamentally facilitated by neglecting health as a lifelong process that includes personality, values, biography and culture as determinants. Educating the workforce for age-attuned health care is, therefore, a central academic task in contemporary societies. It targets not only (future)

Table 1.2 Important gaps to consider for education actions to be implemented and how EIT Health Aging PhD School addresses them

Gap type identified	*Explanation*	*EIT Health Aging PhD School approach*
The health care–life expectancy gap	The dialogue between longevity research and medical interventions must be informed by ethics and avoidance of futility to provide adequate evidence to industry and policymakers.	EIT Health promotes multidisciplinary and cross-sector dialogue based on a quadruple helix approach to support innovative solutions for aging societies: (*i*) science / knowledge; (*ii*) public authorities and health care; (*iii*) innovation, entrepreneurship and industry; (*iv*) civil society
The community–academy gap	High-performance science and medicine must inform community actions to improve self-competence and self-empowerment toward healthy lifestyles as early as during childhood.	EIT Health Ageing PhD School students and alumni actively participate in science awareness events to inform citizens about the added value of aging and health research.
The medical–demographic gap	Students and trainees of healthcare disciplines are provided with knowledge useful in the management of challenges of our time through person-centered, goal-oriented, value-based concepts based on strongest know-how of organ medicine.	EIT Health Ageing PhD School supports a new generation of health professionals, health managers and decision makers provided by multidisciplinary and cross-sector training. The curriculum is embedded with a strong component of soft skills, including communication and leadership skills.
The discipline-to-discipline-to-innovation gap	Professionals across disciplines must be exposed to interaction to achieve real-life innovation and entrepreneurship.	EIT Health Ageing PhD School supports the international mobility of PhD students to support real-life innovation and entrepreneurship competencies in the wide European space. The multidisciplinary nature of the PhD School curriculum supports open-minded scientific and professional approaches, moving out of a silo mindset and supporting innovation and co-creation.
The aging science – biology of aging to health care gap	More interaction between basic scientists and physicians is needed to inform experimental models of the hallmarks of aging through the highly heterogeneous aging phenotypes	By promoting bridges between different science, innovation and entrepreneurship domains; encouraging social and healthcare sectors to move toward integrated care approaches; and nurturing a culture of transferrable skills and hands-on and co-creation approaches, EIT Health Ageing PhD School has been highly successful in bridging the biology of aging with health care to support knowledge transfer to the market and human health/social care interventions.

geriatricians but most medical and nonmedical healthcare practitioners (HCPs), including nurses, therapists, psychologists, social workers and spiritual carers. All such practitioners are exposed to global challenges and opportunities within digital transformation, climate change, medical technological progress and migratory processes (United Nations, n.d.a.). These phenomena are deeply interwoven and mutually influence the interactions, educational response and effects on learning outcomes; consequently, trainers and educators need to reach a consensus on a curriculum that is feasible and sustainable. Age-related biological and physiological changes are better understood than in the past, but manifestations and phenotypes in clinical practice are multifaceted, non-specific and often atypical. This already challenging picture is further complicated by the fact that older people are often excluded from clinical studies. Especially multimorbid and frail patients – the receivers of the largest portion of healthcare resources and pharmacological therapies – are systematically excluded from research (Buffel du Vaure et al., 2016; He et al., 2020). These patients belong to the oldest-old population, which is most rapidly expanding.

The acute disease–multimorbidity educational gap has been known for many years (Holman, 2004), but chronic illness is still not primarily addressed in usual care. Indeed, the limits of implementation science, which require on average 17 years to transfer innovation into practice, are evident and dangerous (Rubin, 2023). All the aforementioned gaps (Table 1.1) force the system into steadily producing new concepts of health, rather than systematically adopting and consolidating existing evidence.

Environmental health

Environmental pollution is still posing a massive existential threat to human health (Lavezzi & Ramos-Molina, 2023), notwithstanding the ambitious goals and actions set out globally (e.g., United Nations Sustainable Development Goals [UN SDGs]) and in Europe (European Green Deal, European Commission, n.d.a.). Although air pollution is a well-recognized factor causing an increase in premature death and morbidity (Juginović, 2023), noise and artificial light pollution, as well as natural light, are now also being associated with adverse human health (Bonanni et al., 2023) ranging from individual discomfort to the alteration of circadian rhythm (Cao et al., 2023). The onset of the European Human Exposome Network (n.d.) has encouraged exploration of the linkages between the systematic and synergistic exposure to these environmental stressors and the development of noncommunicable diseases (NCDs) in humans. NCDs are the leading cause of death globally, and are responsible for about 90% of all deaths in the WHO European region (Global Health Observatory, WHO, n.d.b.). NCDs (i.e., cancer, mental health, cardiovascular, respiratory and metabolic diseases, including relevant comorbidities such as kidney diseases) are multifactorial disorders promoted by several well-established and modifiable risk factors, such as increased blood pressure, overweight and obesity and hyperglycemia and hyperlipidemia. In addition, taking into consideration the role that the oral cavity plays in the contact between the individual's body and the environment (including food, water and air supply), the WHO Global Oral Health Status Report (WHO, 2022) highlighted the alarming state of oral health worldwide and called for urgent action by integrating oral health into NCDs and universal health coverage initiatives. It is well known that several environmental risk factors contribute to NCDs, and air pollution is the most studied. However, the need to disentangle the impact of the complex interactions between the human body and environmental exposure throughout life (exposome) on human health is time-critical.

Pollution, linked to human behaviors, inevitably affects most people in Europe and worldwide. A 2015 assessment attributed 16% of total yearly global premature mortality to pollution-related disease, approximately 9 million people (Fuller et al., 2022). Annually, 13% of deaths (630 000) in the WHO Europe region are attributable to environmental stressors, and a report from the European Environment Agency (EEA) (European Parliament, 2023) concluded that 90% of deaths are attributable to NCDs that are strongly affected by pollution, including asthma, cardiovascular problems and cancer. Living and working in a health-promoting environment may prevent the onset and development of different NCDs. On the other side, the simultaneous and synergistic exposure to several environmental stressors may trigger physiological frailty and contribute to the development of NCDs. Moreover, policies and recommendations on occupational exposure limits lack a specific focus on pollutants of emerging concern (e.g., black carbon, sand particles, artificial light pollution and changes in daily natural light exposure associated with changes in cloud cover). However, a general systematic approach to reducing environmental exposure that can provide multiple co-benefits to human health is still missing (WHO, 2023).

One Health approach of healthy aging

Growing evidence highlights the close interconnections between planetary health, ecosystem health and human health (Antó, 2024; Sinclair, 2019). In fact, the *One Health* approach opens new windows to better understand the intimate connections linking key environmental stressors, specifically environmental pollutants, with human health, which is particularly relevant and impactful for age-related metabolic syndrome and chronic conditions in older adults.

In the last decades, agriculture and animal farming became highly intensive, pushed by demographic and economic pressure to increase food production at low cost. To avoid exhaustion of productive soils, more and more chemicals have been added to the intensive agriculture and animal farming pipelines, including the use of fertilizers, pesticides, herbicides and antibiotics, among other drugs and other industry-based chemicals. The wide and uncontrolled use of popularized chemicals, including antibiotics, pesticides and herbicides, has introduced difficult-to-metabolize compounds and their bioaccumulation in the soil, food chain and ultimately humans through air, water and food contamination (Ferrante et al., 2023).

Access to low-cost agroindustry-based food came with increased environmental contamination and human exposure to pollutants. New scientific evidence highlights the association between human exposure to environmental pollutants and the development of a plethora of health conditions associated with metabolic syndrome and progression of chronic age-related diseases in humans (Otaru et al., 2024).

At the cellular and molecular levels, these diseases share common features including mitochondrial dysfunction, increased oxidative stress, a strong inflammatory component, impaired autophagy and increased cell senescence (Guo et al., 2022). Importantly, contaminated food or water enters animal and human bodies through the gastrointestinal system, where it first and directly impacts the gut microbiome. The gut microbiota is directly affected by environmental pollutants, with effects on microbial cell viability, changes in microbiota composition and metabolism (Lindell et al., 2022). Therefore, in addition to their direct absorption from the gut into the blood stream, environmental pollutants may cause major modifications in the luminal gut fluid composition mediated through microbiome-associated secondary metabolism and production of bioactive molecules that affect the host physiology. Some of these bacterial-derived molecules have toxic properties, leading to disruption of the gut–immune barrier, chronic inflammation and insulin resistance (Prasad et al., 2022).

It is now evident that there is a close connection between lifestyle, including physical exercise and food habits, and exposure to environmental health determinants, including environmental pollutants, and its global impact on human health. To live and age healthier, there is a need to promote a culture of healthier lifestyles and respect for the environment. This is strongly embedded in the "blue zones" (Buettner & Skemp, 2016), where lifestyles and healthy environments support human health and longevity. We are part of the intricate network of living organisms on Earth. We are actors and beneficiaries of the Global Health and One Health approach, which may inspire the adoption of new behaviors that are part of the Mediterranean diet culture and other lifestyle practices inspired by blue zones. We, as a society, can embrace ancestral heritage lifestyle habits and adapt them to the modern socioeconomic and cultural contexts of our time. It is urgent that we change the way we live, adopt healthier standards of human health and respect Mother Nature. Educating the society at large on these principles is mandatory, and a requirement of our time, if we are to have sustainable good health and longevity for all.

Empowering the workforce

Education on healthy aging and well-being is based upon a multidisciplinary team approach that requires various *transversal skills*. These are based on emotional intelligence and integrate self-esteem, empathy, self-control, active listening, interpersonal communication/relationships and teamwork as well as the competence to work and decide alone as well as in teams. Transversal skills are often labeled as *21st-century skills, soft skills, non-cognitive skills* or *skills* in general (Erstad and Siddiq, 2023) (Figure 1.1).

The Feasibility Study of Health Workforce Skills Assessment was conducted to enhance the support of health workers to perform and conduct personalized care (OECD, 2018), and describes *shared competency frameworks.* Shared competency frameworks are meant to guide teaching and learning (i.e., educational methods and learning objectives) so that professionals across disciplines are provided with long-lasting instruments to successfully practice in their respective fields of personalized care. As a new approach to education emphasizing skills for life-long learning, shared competency frameworks serve to avoid segmentation and fragmentation of professions. For medicine, the

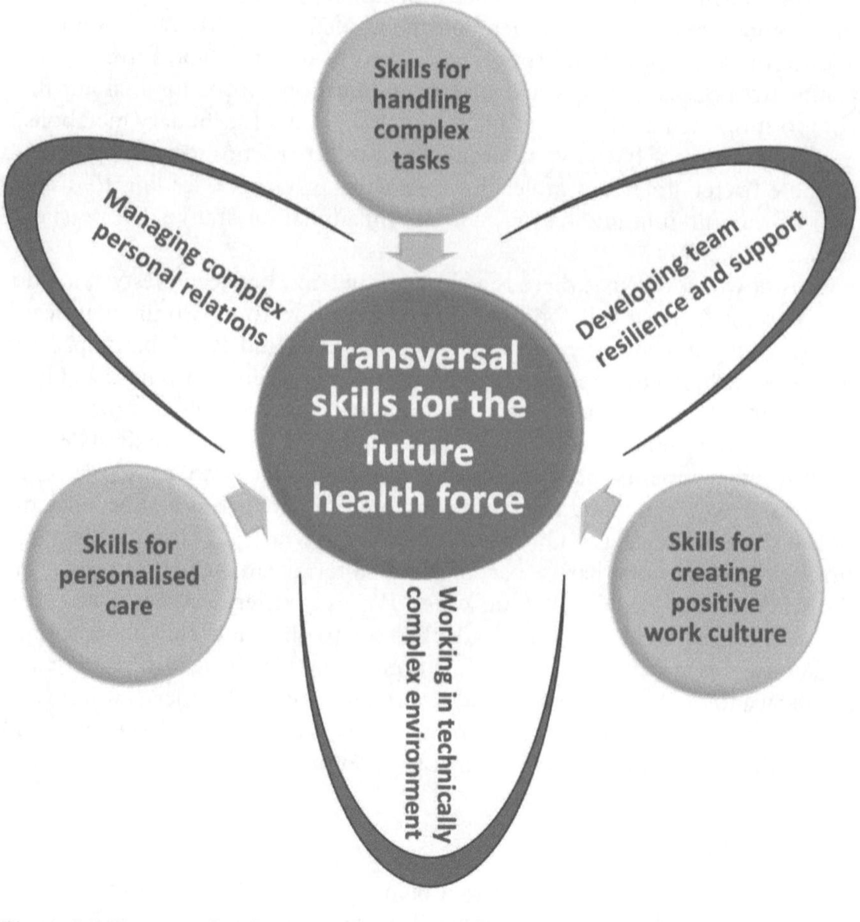

Figure 1.1 Transversal skills required for integrated and people-centered care (inspired by "Feasibility Study of Health Workforce Skills Assessment: Supporting Health Workers Achieve personalized Care", OECD, 2018).

World Federation of Medical Education (WFME) is actively engaged in establishing a global competency framework for the discipline.

Students and trainees must be equipped with the competencies and capabilities to enable health and well-being as well as intrinsic capacity maintenance, independent of their future specialization. The European Higher Education Area (EHEA) has published a framework describing a skill gradation with relative specific learning outcomes for undergraduate training (European Commission, 2008). The three key transversal skills for the health and social workforce include ***inter-professional/socio-emotional skills***, ***creative thinking*** and ***learning to learn***. In this sense, learner-centered training approaches, giving structured space for reflection rather than traditional or teacher-centered training environments, may further support the development of transversal skills. Active learning, deep learning and understanding based upon increased student responsibility for the learning journey (EHEA framework) (Carrió & Rosa, 2022) constitute an educational paradigm shift of great potential for 21st-century society. These learning principles are also the basis of the European University for Well-Being (EUniWell), which was selected for membership as a European University Alliance in 2020. As a result of the Seed Funding Program, the EUniWell Winter and Summer Schools, Open Lecture Series and Research Incubator, are enlarging participation of student and staff communities in the topic of well-being. Through the development of common infrastructures, strategies and roadmaps, a sustainable European University involves students at each step of the design and development processes to ensure that they are aligned with student needs and maximize their impact.

Concerning geriatric care, the EU COST action called PROGRAMMING (Promoting Geriatrics in the Countries where it is still emerging) aims at identifying "a pragmatic set of possibilities for continuous professional education in Geriatric Medicine (GM), that will be globally endorsed, to propose to stakeholders and policymakers across Europe, to facilitate or trigger change at each national level towards a minimum but substantial integration of principles of Geriatric Medicine in the attitudes and practices of practitioners and would eventually prepare the ground for more extended changes in countries where Geriatric Medicine is still emerging" (PROGRAMMING, 2025).

Finally, exchange platforms and surveys are ongoing to foster synergies among established educational programs such as the European Academy for Medicine of Ageing (EAMA)/EuGMS and the online "Train the Trainers" e-Training. In Gerontology and GERiatrics (e-TRIGGER)/IAGG together with the above cited more recent ones including the 2025 kick-off edition of the UEMS European Geriatric Medicine Specialty Exam (EGEMSE).

Empowering the population: Inform

After the first wave of the COVID-19 pandemic, during which the severity of the disease in certain countries was attributed to a lack of basic education of the inhabitants, a literature review of educational trajectories, health and aging well demonstrated that alongside genetics, the affective and educational family environment, as well as the general environment, interact significantly starting from the very first days of life (Frangos et al., 2023). Thus, epigenetics ("An epigenetic trait is a stably heritable phenotype resulting from changes in a chromosome without alterations in the DNA sequence," Berger et al., 2009, p. 781 plays a major role in the determination of health and disease in the first 1,000 days of life as well as in the characterization of gender. Other factors, such as socio-economic level, parental education and schooling in urban or rural areas, also play a major role in the differential acquisition of health literacy. This determines adherence (or lack thereof) to healthy lifestyles, risky behaviors and substance abuse, but also compliance with hygiene rules and adherence to vaccines and treatments. The combination of all these elements and lifestyle choices facilitates the emergence of metabolic disorders (obesity, diabetes), which promote cardiovascular and kidney damage, and neurodegenerative diseases, explaining that the less well-educated have shorter survival and spend more years of life in disability. After demonstrating the impact of the educational level on health and longevity, the members of this inter-academic group proposed specific educational actions at three levels: (1) teachers and health professionals, (2) parents and (3) the public, emphasizing that these crucial actions can only be carried out with the unfailing support of state and academic authorities (Frangos et al., 2023). Within the framework of the 17 UN SDGs, a population's self-empowerment is as multifaceted and multilayered as determinants of one-health and well-being themselves (Figure 1.2) (WHO, 2023). Demographic aging resulting in a rapidly increasing older population in cities worldwide is accompanied by the rising population of frail people living in cities. For people with physical disabilities, the urban built environment is often a challenge (WHO: World Health Organization, n.d.b). Designing a safe and barrier-free urban environment is of vital importance (Buffel & Phillipson, 2016) for these groups to effectively conduct an independent, self-determined and self-empowered life.

Doctoral Networks: Innovation and entrepreneurship and science outreach in PhD training

Demographic changes and population aging impose tensions on care systems and drive the need to develop new organization models to face emerging challenges and ensure sustainability. Accordingly, there is a growing need for new professionals equipped with practices based on science excellence, a holistic view of integrated care, nurtured by transferrable and soft skills practices to inspire educating citizens on healthy aging and well-being.

The One Health approach understands human health in a more complex and integrated context, where broader animal health and ecosystem health are key determinants of human health and are especially relevant for advanced age-related chronic diseases (Ferrucci & Fabbri, 2018). The training approach of PhD students calls for innovative practices like those implemented by the PhD network EIT Health Ageing PhD School. The holistic approach in health-related PhD training, adopted by EIT Health Ageing PhD School, considers

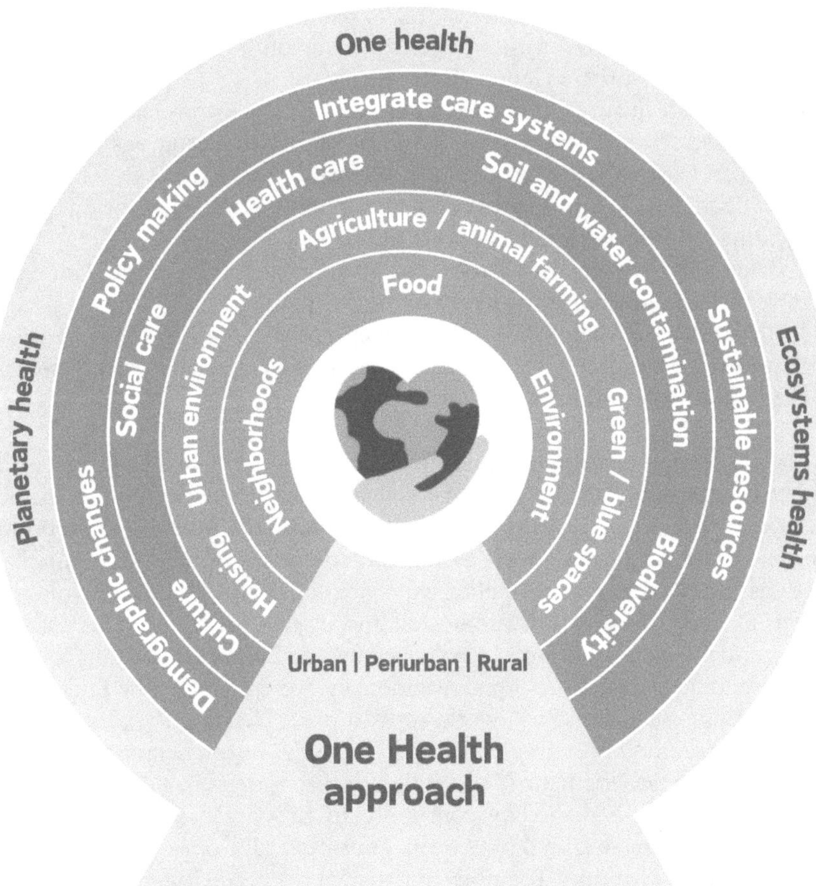

Figure 1.2 Multifaceted and multilayer determinants of (one) health and well-being (Inspired by WHO, 2023).

the need to support a new generation of scientists, professionals and business leaders. Solid PhD projects based on science excellence that include strong elements of international and cross-sector mobility will encourage innovation and the spirit of the student entrepreneur to foster knowledge translation and societal impact. To achieve this, innovative research projects should be supported by an educational portfolio of courses and hands-on training, and learning-by-doing secondments under intensive mentorship to empower students with transferrable skills, through a cross-sector training program between academia and industry. The training modules may contribute to the following training objectives:

- Train PhD students on the One Health approach with an integrated and multidisciplinary perspective that emphasizes the interconnected impact of environmental health, animal health and planetary health on overall human health and well-being, with a particular focus on improving the quality of human aging; **holistic view.**

- Provide high-quality, structured doctoral training in diverse and international research environments at some of the most prestigious centers for health and aging research in Europe; **scientific excellence.**
- Provide international and cross-sector training opportunities for unique secondments; **international networking.**
- Provide PhD students with tools for personal development and transferrable skills; **adaptability to new and better jobs.**
- Instill students with innovation and entrepreneurship spirit; **value creation.**
- Support short and long-term development of career plans; **successful careers and leadership**.

On the economic front, the innovative approach in doctoral training has the potential to promote innovation and create new business opportunities, including new job opportunities in start-ups and increasing risk investments to bridge the innovation gap from bench to market. Identification of specific markers for diseases linked to environmental exposure could pave the way for new solutions in health care, health promotion and disease prevention. This creates the potential for new products to be developed and introduced to the market, helping people live healthier lives. Additionally, we emphasize the importance of translating research into real-world applications, extending the contributions outside a laboratory. Fostering partnerships between researchers and businesses will lead to the development of technologies that address health and environmental challenges, and directly contribute to the Green Charter principles (European Commission, n.d.b), Green Transition (European University Association, n.d.), Healthier Together Initiative (European Commission, 2021), and the United Nations Challenges for the decade (United Nations, n.d.b). Table 1.2 shows the important educational gaps identified by the EIT Health Ageing PhD School and approaches employed to bridge the respective gaps.

Conclusion

Due to the rapid demographic, societal, climatic and technological transitions of our time, (one) health and aging in well-being and auto-determination are challenged by substantial implementation gaps of measures needed. These implementation gaps are likely to be increasingly positively filled by education and training actions of multidisciplinary and networking nature. Exposing young generations of students and trainees to interwoven health-influencing factors beyond single disciplines and enabling them to embrace complexity and multidimensionality in health sciences and medicine will deliver a competent workforce able to use transversal skills. At the same time, enabling citizens to achieve self-empowerment and improved health and digital literacy will accelerate the paths to one health at all societal levels.

Acknowledgments

Financial support acknowledged to EU funded projects Horizon Europe, Widera Excellence Hubs, CHAngeing, grant agreement 101087071 and EIT Health (EIT Health Ageing PhD School).

References

Antó, J. M. (2024). Human health and the health of planet earth go together. *Journal of Internal Medicine. 295*(5), 695–706. doi: 10.1111/joim.13774

Berger, S. L., Kouzarides, T., Shiekhattar, R., & Shilatifard, A. (2009). An operational definition of epigenetics. *Genes & Development. 23*(7), 781–783. doi:10.1101/gad.1787609

Bonanni, A., Basile, M., Montone, R. A., & Crea, F. (2023). Impact of the exposome on cardiovascular disease. *European Heart Journal Supplements. 25*(Supplement_B), B60–B64. https://doi.org/10.1093/eurheartjsupp/suad069

Buettner, D., & Skemp, S. (2016). Blue zones: Lessons from the World's longest lived. *American Journal of Lifestyle Medicine. 10*(5), 318–321. doi: 10.1177/1559827616637066

Buffel, T., & Phillipson, C. (2016). Can global cities be 'age-friendly cities'? Urban development and ageing populations. *Cities. 55*, 94–100. http://dx.doi.org/10.1016/j.cities.2016.03.016

Buffel du Vaure, C., Dechartres, A., Battin, C., Ravaud, P., & Boutron, I. (2016). Exclusion of patients with concomitant chronic conditions in ongoing randomised controlled trials targeting 10 common chronic conditions and registered at ClinicalTrials.Gov: A systematic review of registration details. *British Medical Journal Open. 6*(9), e012265. https://doi.org/10.1136/bmjopen-2016-012265

Cao, X., Wang, L., Selby, C. P., Lindsey-Boltz, L. A., & Sancar, A. (2023) Analysis of mammalian circadian clock protein complexes over a circadian cycle. *Journal of Biological Chemistry.* 299(3), 102929. doi: 10.1016/j.jbc.2023.102929

Carrió, M., & Rosa, N. (2022). *Learning strategies to promote transversal skills on health and social care studies: a methodological guide.* Available from: https://repositori-api.upf.edu/api/core/bitstreams/dd81193d-b966-4b10-9f6e-ec256b825ab3/content

Engel, G. L. (1977). The need for a new medical model: A challenge for biomedicine. *Science.* 8, 129–136. doi: 10.1126/science.847460

Erstad, O., & Siddiq, F. (2023). Educational assessment of 21st century skills—Novel initiatives, yet a lack of systemic transformation. In R. J. Tierney, F. Rizvi, K. Ercikan (Eds.), *International encyclopedia of education* (pp 245–255, Fourth Edition). Elsevier. Doi: 10.1016/B978-0-12-818630-5.09038-2

European Commission, (n.d.a) *The European green deal*, retrieved January 3, 2025 from https://commission.europa.eu/strategy-and-policy/priorities-2019-2024/european-green-deal_en

European Commission, (n.d.b) *Directorate-general for education, youth, sport and culture Marie Skłodowska-Curie actions, MSCA Green Charter.* Retrieved January 3, 2025 from https://marie-sklodowska-curie-actions.ec.europa.eu/about-msca/msca-green-charter

European Commission (2008). *The European qualifications framework for lifelong learning (EQF).* Office for Official Publications of the European Communities. DOI 10.2766/14352 https://ehea.info/media.ehea.info/file/Framework_for_qualifications/69/0/EQF-LLL-2008_596690.pdf

European Commission (2021). *Healthier together initiative*, https://health.ec.europa.eu/non-communicable-diseases/healthier-together-eu-non-communicable-diseases-initiative_en

European Human Exposome Network (n.d.) retrieved January 3, 2025 from: https://www.humanexposome.eu/

European Parliament (2023) *Report on non-communicable diseases (NCDs)*. https://www.europarl.europa.eu/doceo/document/A-9-2023-0366_EN.pdf

European University Association (n.d.) *Green transition*, retrieved January 3, 2025 from: https://www.eua.eu/our-work/topics/green-transition.html

Ferrante, M., Rapisarda, P., Grasso, A., Favara, C., & Conti, G. O. (2023). Glyphosate and environmental toxicity with "One Health" approach, a review. *Environmental Research. 235*, 116678. doi: 10.1016/j.envres.2023.116678

Ferrucci, L., & Fabbri, E. (2018). Inflammageing: Chronic inflammation in ageing, cardiovascular disease, and frailty. *Nature Reviews Cardiology*, *15*(9), 505–522. doi: 10.1038/s41569-018-0064-2

Frangos, E., Barriguete-Mélendez, A., Debré, P., Gutiérrez Robledo, L. M., Parodi, A. L., & Michel, J. P. (2023). Life course education, health, and ageing well: A short inter-academic report. *Gerontology*, *69*(7), 799–808. doi: 10.1159/000529869

Fuller, R., Landrigan, P. J., Balakrishnan, K., Bathan, G., Bose-O'Reilly, S., Brauer, M., ... & Yan, C. (2022). Pollution and health: A progress update. *The Lancet Planetary Health*, *6*(6), e535–e547.

Guo, J., Huang, X., Dou, L., Yan, M., Shen, T., Tang, W., & Li, J. (2022). Aging and aging-related diseases: From molecular mechanisms to interventions and treatments. *Signal Transduction and Targeted Therapy*, *7*(1), 391. https://doi.org/10.1038/s41392-022-01251-0

He, J., Morales, D. R., & Guthrie, B. (2020). Exclusion rates in randomized controlled trials of treatments for physical conditions: A systematic review. *Trials*, *21*(1), 228.

Holman, H. (2004). Chronic disease—the need for a new clinical education. *Jama*, *292*(9), 1057–1059. doi: 10.1001/jama.292.9.1057.

Juginović, A. (2023). Zolpidem, but lemborexant more consistently, showed self-reported and objective benefits compared with placebo in insomnia patients with sleep duration of less than 6 hours per night. *Journal of Clinical Sleep Medicine*, *19*(3), 429–430. doi: 10.5664/jcsm.10458

Lavezzi, A. M., & Ramos-Molina, B. (2023). Environmental exposure science and human health. *International Journal of Environmental Research and Public Health*, *20*(10), 5764. doi: 10.3390/ijerph20105764

Lindell, A. E., Zimmermann-Kogadeeva, M., & Patil, K. R. (2022). Multimodal interactions of drugs, natural compounds and pollutants with the gut microbiota. *Nature Reviews Microbiology*, *20*(7), 431–443. doi: 10.1038/s41579-022-00681-5

OECD (2018), *Feasibility study on health workforce skills assessment: Supporting health workers achieve person-centred care*, OECD Health Policy Studies, OECD Publishing, https://www.oecd.org/en/publications/feasibility-study-on-health-workforce-skills-assessment_e631bd14-en.html

Otaru, S., Jones, L. E., & Carpenter, D. O. (2024). Associations between urine glyphosate levels and metabolic health risks: Insights from a large cross-sectional population-based study. *Environmental Health*, *23*(1), 58. doi: 10.1186/s12940-024-01098-8

Prasad, M., Gatasheh, M. K., Alshuniaber, M. A., Krishnamoorthy, R., Rajagopal, P., Krishnamoorthy, K., & Jayaraman, S.. (2022). Impact of glyphosate on the development of insulin resistance in experimental diabetic rats: Role of NFκB signalling pathways. *Antioxidants*, *11*(12), 2436. doi: 10.3390/antiox11122436

PROGRAMMING - PROmoting GeRiAtric Medicine in countries where it is still eMergING (2025) https://cost-programming.eu/

Rubenstein, L. Z., Abrass, I. B., & Kane, R. L. (1981). Improved care for patients on a new geriatric evaluation unit. *Journal of the American Geriatrics Society*, *29*(11), 531–536. doi: 10.1111/j.1532-5415.1981.tb03357.x

Rubin, R. (2023). It takes an average of 17 years for evidence to change practice—the burgeoning field of implementation science seeks to speed things up. *Jama*, *329*(16), 1333–1336. doi: 10.1001/jama.2023.4387
Sinclair, J. R.(2019). Importance of a one health approach in advancing global health security and the sustainable development goals. *Revue scientifique et technique. 38*(1):145–154. doi: 10.20506/rst.38.1.2949
United Nations (n.d.a). *Sustainable Development Goals*. Retrieved January 3, 2025. https://sdgs.un.org/goals
United Nations (n.d.b). *United Nations challenges for the decade*. https://www.un.org/sustainabledevelopment/decade-of-action/
World Health Organization (n.d.a). *Global health observatory*. Retrieved January 3, 2025, from: https://www.who.int/data/gho
World Health Organization (n.d.b). *The WHO age-friendly cities framework - age-friendly world*. Retrieved January 3, 2025, from https://extranet.who.int/agefriendlyworld/age-friendly-cities-framework/).
World Health Organization (1948). *Summary report on proceedings minutes and final acts of the international health conference* held in New York from 19 June to 22 July 1946. WHO. https://iris.who.int/handle/10665/85573
World Health Organization (2001). *International classification of functioning, disability and health: ICF*. https://iris.who.int/handle/10665/42407
World Health Organization (2015). *World report on ageing and health*. https://www.who.int/publications/i/item/9789241565042
World Health Organization (2019). *Integrated care for older people (ICOPE): guidance for person-centred assessment and pathways in primary care*. https://iris.who.int/handle/10665/326843.
World Health Organization (2022). *Global Oral health status report: Towards universal health coverage for Oral health by 2030*. World Health Organization. https://www.who.int/publications/i/item/9789240061484.
World Health Organization (2023). *Generating and working with evidence for urban health, policy brief*. https://iris.who.int/bitstream/handle/10665/373753/9789240084032-eng.pdf?sequence=1
World Health Organization. (2024). *Integrated care for older people (ICOPE): guidance for person-centered assessment and pathways in primary care*, 2nd ed. World Health Organization. https://iris.who.int/handle/10665/380175

2 (Bio-)Pharmaceutical Production and Extended Reality Aided Education

Philipp Wiedemann, Kevin Kastner, René Eiswirth, Julian Reichwald and Ulrich Trägner

Introduction and background

Innovation in health education has many aspects, several of which are highlighted in this book. This chapter deals with one particular challenge in health education, namely, the preparation of future professionals for occupational activities in the field of (bio-)pharmaceutical production. Although this topic has a strong technological focus in the context of this chapter, the methodology presented here can easily be applied to many other health-related areas, such as the full range of hospital operations. In all such applications, the qualification of personnel is key to their success. Often, this qualification takes place in a university environment, which is the setting of this chapter's contents: The authors of this contribution are all members of Technical University Mannheim and teach in Bachelor (BSc) and Master of Science (MSc) courses, among others on (bio-) pharmaceuticals, medical and pharmaceutical process engineering and (medical) information technology. We all face the challenge of having to transfer complex, difficult-to-teach matters to students, and it is crucial for next-generation professionals to be up-to-date on technological development, from both a methodological and a scientific perspective.

As an example, it would be important for young professionals in biotechnological or pharmaceutical production to not only know the science and theory behind industrial-scale processes when leaving the university, but to also have a solid understanding of real-world production principles, equipment and processes at the actual industrial scale. Nevertheless, this can hardly ever be taught in a small-scale academic laboratory setting. It is impossible for most universities to run a (bio-) pharmaceutical production plant. Furthermore, although field trips to operational industrial-sized process sites are informative to a certain extent, access to details and the equipment itself is usually prohibited. In other words, it is relatively straightforward to teach the science behind pharmaceutical production, be it chemical or biotechnological, in a classroom setting. It is also straightforward to perform small-scale experiments in a teaching laboratory. However, preparing future pharma-professionals, operators and managers for the technological and operational challenges of a large-scale application of this science- and lab-based knowledge is difficult; how does a

DOI: 10.4324/9781003568650-3

10-mL experiment help understand how to run a 10.000-L production vessel? Such preparation needs different, cutting-edge teaching methods.

We have tried to bridge this gap by employing several extended reality (XR) methods, predominantly virtual reality (VR). These technologies have been implemented into our curriculum and are currently employed on a routine basis every semester. XR has tremendous potential in (health) education because it immerses the student in the topic – here, large-scale pharmaceutical production. First, this immersion sparks a high degree of identification with the topic and enables contextualization of otherwise extremely difficult-to-teach matters. Second, the technology opens up the possibility of virtually bringing complex production-scale equipment right into the (XR-equipped) university. This allows visualization of an industrial-scale environment and teaching principles at the actual real-world scale. In the following, we highlight our attempt to improve education through XR.

In this context, our most advanced use case is the employment of a state-of-the-art, five-wall cave automatic virtual environment (CAVE) to visualize an industrial-scale cell culture production plant for biopharmaceutical processes. Such processes are an interdisciplinary endeavor of science and engineering involving molecular genetics, cell biology and mechanical as well as process engineering. In most cases, animal, yeast or bacterial cells are recombinantly equipped with DNA for the biopharmaceutical protein to be produced and are then stored in frozen form. In the actual production process, they are thawed, cultivated and the cultures are enlarged up to the desired production scale; for example, in the case of animal cells, 10–20,000 L. Every cell needs to be supplied with nutrients, metabolic waste products must be carried away, and the desired protein product must be safeguarded and taken to harvest. It instantly becomes clear that these processes are tremendously complex, particularly on a large scale, where they must be automated and controlled. Cell science and genetics can be taught in the classroom and lab – the large scale is visualized in the CAVE.

XR technology

XR is an umbrella term that encompasses immersive technologies, including VR, augmented reality (AR) and mixed reality (MR), which blend physical and virtual environments (Dörner, Broll, Grimm & Jung, 2019, p. 22f; Wölfel, 2023, p. 20ff). This technology aims to manipulate human sensory perception by creating multiple simultaneous stimuli, which is known as "immersion". True immersion is achieved when a person interacts in XR as naturally as they would in the real world (Dörner et al., 2019, p. 56; Kastner et al., 2023). These technologies enable users to experience and interact with digital elements in simulated or enhanced reality. VR creates a completely immersive digital environment where users are transported to a different reality. It usually involves wearing a headset that covers the user's field of view, blocking out the physical world. AR overlays digital information onto the physical world in real time. Unlike VR, AR does not replace the real world but enhances it by adding computer-generated visuals, sounds, or data. MR is a blend of VR and AR, where physical and digital objects coexist and interact in real time. It allows users to manipulate real and virtual objects simultaneously, creating a hybrid environment.

A CAVE can be used for this, for example. CAVE systems are stationary VR installations that use projection systems to display virtual content. The image is usually projected from behind or as a front projection; newer systems use light-emitting diode (LED) technology, which can replace projectors. A CAVE setup consists of one to six projection surfaces: a single side is the simplest setup – also known as a "Powerwall" – whereas six projection surfaces represent the most immersive version. The projection size ranges from the size of a television screen to several meters in length to create a strong sense of presence and immersion for users (see Figure 2.1). In both cases, users

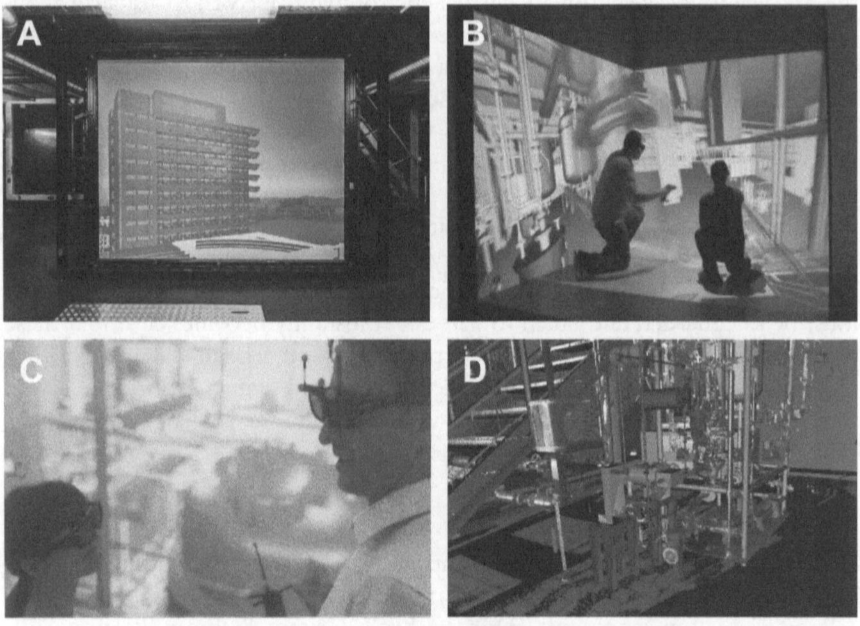

Figure 2.1 CAVE at Technical University Mannheim. A: Overview from behind the projection screens – the five-wall CAVE cube with only the back projection visible. B: In operation – projection (top projection not operated); users can move inside the CAVE physically and by operating the flystick (in the right hand of the left user). Distortions caused by the edges of the projection walls are not visible when wearing shutter glasses. C: Teaching – direct interaction of users in the CAVE. D: Example of the teaching subject complexity. B, C, D, please note: Pictures are taken with a standard camera only for documentation purposes. Projections appear different when wearing shutter glasses in the CAVE. All pictures courtesy of Technical University Mannheim.

wear shutter glasses that are tracked by the CAVE's optical tracking system so that the projection always looks smooth and realistic to the tracked user. For example, the edges of the walls of the "CAVE cube" in which the users move around are determined by hidden calculations – users do not see any distortions of, for example, pipes that run across numerous projection surfaces (i.e., walls of the cube). Users can move in the CAVE physically and also by using a manual "flystick". The flystick enables the user to move in all six directions and around bends without physical movement of the whole body and head; the movement of the projection is calculated based on moving the hand with the flystick in any direction. The flystick not only facilitates movement in all six directions; it also serves as an important interaction tool between the user and the CAVE environment. It allows the user to interact with virtual objects and manipulate them seamlessly. Using the flystick, users can select, move and change the virtual objects in real time. This capability fosters a more intuitive and dynamic relationship with the virtual world and enables effective exploration and experimentation within the CAVE.

CAVE systems are especially well-suited for collaborative applications and allow groups of users to explore and discuss virtual scenarios together. This setup fosters natural communication, similar to a real conversation, making it ideal for fields like architecture, engineering, or training, where group discussions and model reviews are essential.

However, CAVE systems come with technical and organizational challenges. Because they are customizable, setup and maintenance are complex and require specialized knowledge. Hardware and software requirements are significantly higher than for head-mounted displays (HMDs, see below); powerful computers with multiple, synchronized Graphics Processing Units (GPUs) are needed to render graphics in real time, which often requires clusters and stable network connections. The complex infrastructure of projectors or LED walls, spatial design and computational power also leads to high initial, management and maintenance costs.

HMDs are a more cost-effective and flexible alternative that can be used almost anywhere. Their hardware requirements are usually less significant because the graphics are mainly processed directly on the device. Some variants can connect to a PC for higher performance, and hybrid models can switch between both depending on the use case. Additionally, as shown in Kastner et al. (2024), smartphones can also be used. However, HMDs are typically single-user devices, so each person experiences the virtual world individually, making them versatile for applications such as gaming, entertainment, training and therapy, but not as much for group discussions and team learning.

There are different types of HMDs, ranging from fully immersive VR headsets to optical see-through systems. Although VR HMDs completely isolate users from the real environment, MR headsets overlay the physical world with virtual objects. AR glasses, for example, can project technical instructions or navigation instructions into the real environment, making them ideal for displaying digital information in real space.

Because HMDs are designed for individual use, communication is more limited compared to Powerwall or CAVE systems and often requires additional technical solutions for collaboration. Furthermore, the interaction is typically limited to audio because realistic avatar expressions and movements are still challenging and often lack the authenticity of face-to-face interactions (Mayer et al., 2023).

We operate a fully equipped five-wall CAVE and two Powerwalls. We also use MR-HMDs and XR data goggles for practical training in certain technical skills, such as checking the status of the current valve or how to operate the system. Because our prime teaching expertise is in group learning, which necessitates space for and interaction of participants, in the following, we concentrate on using a CAVE and a Powerwall for teaching graduate students in (bio)pharmaceutical production.

Educational concept: Embedding XR in the curriculum

In the following, we describe the embedding of cutting-edge XR technologies into curricular activities to improve their educational value. In this advanced use case, we implemented a state-of-the-art five-wall CAVE in a Master of Science (MSc) program: 8 credits, 7 h per week over a 15-week semester (15% XR), in a Level 4 module on Advanced Animal Cell Technology (i.e., biopharmaceutical processes). Additional elements of the module are a lecture and a laboratory practical course. The main learning objectives of the lecture are to know biopharmaceutical concepts; understand the combination and importance of genetic engineering, cell biology and process technology for biopharmaceutical process development and production; understand the needs and problems of a cell culture production process; and fit a biopharmaceutical process and its development in the larger setting of plant design and economics. Therefore, the lecture lays the foundation for understanding the scope of the topic, the theoretical background and the principles applied. It covers a broad range of subjects, starting with the pharmaceutical ingredient and its Critical Quality Attributes (CQAs), moves on to the cell cultivation means for producing the ingredient and ends with typical reactors and production plants. Logically following on from there, the main learning objectives of the laboratory course are to apply cell cultivation techniques to relevant questions of cell culture process design, obtain an understanding of the structure and organization of development projects and strengthen student skills of carrying out temporally focused laboratory projects.

The lectures are assessed using a standard written exam. Although this might be criticized, in our experience, transfer questions on an MSc level demanding full command of the scope of the lectures are a very purposeful form of assessment. Simple repetitive questions are avoided, and the exam is open book. Furthermore, the module is fully taught in English. This allows students to become familiar with writing concise English text and is an additional benefit for professional activities in the pharma/biotech field, which operates mostly in English. The laboratory course is assessed using a poster session. This approach avoids writing yet another lab report and prepares students for a scientific career. Lectures occur throughout the semester, and the practical happens in the second half, which leaves enough time for students to become familiar with the theoretical background before hands-on work.

The "elephant in the room" is obvious: All this might be carefully tuned, but does not prepare for mastering a pharmaceutical production system on an industrial scale – and yet, this is what a significant number of graduates will encounter in their career. The missing piece is a means to visualize this kind of environment, to allow hands-on experience of (at least) moving in and understanding an industrial setting (if not working in it). This is where VR comes into play: In each semester, we utilize the five-wall CAVE to fill this gap. The main learning objectives are twofold: (1) to become familiar with VR principles, so that students can move around in a VR setting and understand the differences between VR and other plant visualization principles and (2) to understand the principal setup of a large-scale biopharmaceutical production plant, including the ability to discriminate between its different operational units.

Through application of this technology, students can move through a full-scale biopharmaceutical production plant equipped with all the necessary piping and reaction vessels. This environment is very complex. Technological specialist terms like plant layout, accessibility, traffic pathways, cleaning in place and human–machine interface are brought closer to learners on the fly. The VR sessions happen late in the semester, after the theoretical foundations have been laid. This allows students, for the first time, to examine all the entire complicated interplay of the different aspects of a biopharmaceutical plant, formerly only known through "dissecting" and learning separate details. Importantly, students are not only asked to move around the plant and become familiar with the overall layout, but it is mandatory to tackle questions, which is only possible by moving in and understanding the industrial setup. Instructors are always present to provide guidance. The instructors should ideally be familiar with the CAVE technology and have a fundamental understanding of the visualized topic. This enables a very direct identification with the subject. The immersive experience helps students learn the "bits and pieces" in the lecture and practical course combined. The CAVE is the culmination of the module and, in our opinion, a compelling educational means to prepare students for their future professional start in this field. In the CAVE environment, we have the opportunity to present the full potential of digitalization in general and to even discuss advanced aspects of life-cycle considerations in product development, process design and production.

Quality assurance: Evaluation

The Technical University Mannheim uses a digital, anonymous evaluation system for all teaching activities. It consists of a questionnaire that students are asked to complete every semester. Although there is a range of prepared forms applicable to different forms of teaching, such as lectures, laboratory courses and seminars, there is the possibility to amend and tailor questionnaires for specific needs. Standard questions concern, for example, the average time spent for preparation, the compliance, the scientific level of the unit, and so on. Evaluation results are discussed with the respective group of students and are also forwarded to the faculty. If necessary, action is taken.

For the case study presented here, we added specific questions to understand if the students attribute an additional value to this educational unit over standard teaching forms. Although there is not enough room here to display all the results (many of them are answers in prose), some are highlighted below.

As an overall indicator, we ask, "How important was it that you yourself moved around in the biopharmaceutical plant (rather than looking at a projection by a lecturer/during a lecture; 1: not important; 10: very important)?" The answer across six semesters with an average group size of 13 students was 9.1 (SD 0.9), clearly pointing toward the additional benefit of the technology. A second general indicator is the question "Do you feel motivated to study in this field (highly, fairly, a little bit, not at all)?" The answers across the same six semesters showed that 64% of students were "highly motivated" and 33% were "fairly motivated", hinting again at the educational value of this teaching unit.

Additional questions demand specific comments. As an example, we ask about a potential additional benefit of a CAVE over three-dimensional (3D) projection (Powerwall) that we use as a comparison: "One aim was to get an insight into Virtual Reality. Was it reached? Which differences do you see between VR and 'simple' 3D projection?" Typical (if not statistically proven) example answers:

- "The CAVE was way more exciting than the 3D projection. It also helped to get a better view on the spatiality i.e. the proportions".
- "Yes, VR really gives you a feel for the space, for example, how much space has been left between the pipes. The simple 3D projection did that, too, but not to the same extent".

Of course, not all results were positive. The two most prominent points of concern that became clear through the evaluation, but partly already during the sessions, were the following:

1 *Dizziness*: Several students reported dizziness; some even had to leave the CAVE environment. The reasons were mostly related to movement that was too quick or too dramatic in the CAVE. This is also connected to the second point.
2 *Flystick operation abilities*: As explained above, movement in the CAVE and Powerwall is facilitated by using a flystick. If the person operating the flystick is not experienced, movements can be very dramatic and cause the problem above; furthermore, working in the VR environment is hampered.

Conclusion

Here we present, to the best of our knowledge, the first report on embedding XR technology into the comprehensive education of health professionals regarding (bio-)pharmaceutical production. The focus of our contribution is on a practical use case of XR technologies to enable the teaching and in-depth understanding of complex (bio-)pharmaceutical product development and production processes.

Why does it work? As described in this chapter, the special learning environment supports all aspects of successful learning and understanding. For instance, the CAVE technology and large Powerwalls allow collaborative observation of real but virtual processes in high quality in a group setting of observers. The guided communication and explanations within a group of peer members automatically catalyze the memorization and understanding (Jadin, 2013); in this case, of complex biopharma processes. For example, a person taking on the role of plant designer, operator or maintenance manager links the images in the VR environment to real-life narratives. The effect is a deeper memorization and understanding of complex matters.

At this point, we would like to emphasize that the content itself, discussed and presented in VR environments, is of utmost importance. The selection of the proper end-user devices is the second step. In our applications, we observed a high readiness of the students to "dive into" the XR learning environment. This may have something to do with the younger generation's broader experience of modern media (Gamberini et al., 2008).

Choosing between CAVE systems, Powerwalls and VR headsets depends largely on the specific application needs. CAVE systems offer a high level of immersion and are ideal for group applications where social interaction and shared experiences are important. However, they require precise calibration and specialized tracking systems for a realistic VR experience and are more costly to operate. Powerwalls provide a flexible midway approach, offering a large projection area that is particularly useful for (marketing) presentations and simulations focused on visualization and teamwork.

VR headsets stand out for their high mobility and individual freedom of movement, making them ideal for single-user applications and flexible use. They also allow interaction with physical objects and can guide users, for instance, through a pharmaceutical facility using an avatar (Kastner et al., 2023). However, they come with performance limitations because onboard systems are generally less powerful than PC-connected models. Comfort remains a factor as well, because some HMDs can weigh over one kilogram, which is much heavier than the lightweight shutter glasses used in CAVE or Powerwall systems. VR headsets are also limited in terms of social interaction.

Ultimately, the choice of the best XR technology depends on the required levels of immersion, flexibility and user experience, with each system offering unique advantages. At our university, we are happy to use several XR devices for teaching purposes. We are convinced that a low-threshold entry into the virtual world is the key to entering the more complex realm of global digitalization.

References

Dörner, R., Broll, W., Grimm, P., & Jung, B. (Eds.). (2019). *Virtual und augmented reality (VR/AR)*. Springer Berlin Heidelberg. https://doi.org/10.1007/978-3-662-58861-1

Gamberini, L., Barresi, G., Majer, A., & Scarpetta, F. (2008). A game a day keeps the doctor away: A short review of computer games in mental healthcare. *Journal of Cyber Therapy & Rehabilitation, 1*(2), 127–145.

Jadin, T. (2013). Multimedia und Gedächtnis. Kognitionspsychologische Sicht auf das Lernen mit Technologien. In M. Ebner & S. Schön (Eds.), *L3T: Ein Lehrbuch für Lernen und Lehren mit Technologien*. 2, 1–10. Auflage. https://doi.org/10.25656/01:8346

Kastner, K., Lehmann, J., Wuehler, F., Amann, S., Beisheim, N., Raedle, M., & Reichwald, J. (2023). Leveraging transdisciplinary engineering through the coalescence of digital twins and XR-technologies. In *Advances in transdisciplinary engineering* (pp. 343–352). IOS Press. https://doi.org/10.3233/atde230628

Kastner, K., Miguel-Alonso, I., Mayer, A., Chardonnet, J.-R., Bustillo, A., Ovtcharova, J., Eiswirth, R., & Reichwald, J., (2024). Evaluating the Effectiveness of Avatar-Based Collaboration in XR for Pump Station Training Scenarios. In *IEEE 3rd German Education Conference (GECon)* (pp. 1–7). IEEE 2024 – doi: 10.1109/GECon62014.2024.10734032, https://hal.science/hal-04768790/document

Kastner, K., Wuehler, F., Kolb, F., Reichwald, J., Raedle, M., & Eiswirth, R. (2024). ARCTIC: Empowering transdisciplinary engineering education through immersive augmented reality experiences. *Advances in Transdisciplinary Engineering* (pp. 136–145). IOS Press. https://doi.org/10.3233/ATDE240853

Mayer, A., Kastner, K., Reichwald, J., Chardonnet, J.-R., & Ovtcharova, J. (2023). Comparing Avatar and Face-to-Face Collaboration in VR Education: Concept and Preliminary Insights. In *2023 IEEE 2nd German Education Conference (GECon)* (pp. 1–5). https://doi.org/10.1109/gecon58119.2023.10295113

Wölfel, M. (2023). *Immersive Virtuelle Realität*. Springer. https://doi.org/10.1007/978-3-662-66908-2

3 Innovation in Health Education

Integrating Blended Learning and Digital Assessment into Program Design – A Best-Practice from Applied Sport Sciences

Richard Latzel, Karina Fisch, Martina Reitmaier-Krebs and Sabine Fischer

Introduction

The evolution of the modern workplace has brought significant changes to health education, underscoring the need for digital and remote work skills. Today's health professionals, especially those in high-performance sports contexts, frequently balance responsibilities that require flexibility and digital proficiency. For instance, members of medical support staff – such as physiotherapists and strength and conditioning (S&C) coaches – are often required to provide remote support to injured athletes while traveling with their teams. The athlete receiving care may remain at home, engaging in remote rehabilitation sessions facilitated by technology.

Additionally, developments in telemedicine and media literacy have expanded the demand for digital skills across healthcare and sports professions, requiring health professionals to navigate varied digital platforms and ensure secure handling of sensitive data. This shift is particularly relevant in high-performance sports, where technologies that enable remote diagnostics, data collection and analysis are becoming central. Using cloud-based applications, for example, coaches and S&C professionals can access and interpret data from anywhere, providing timely feedback that directly supports an athlete's recovery and training needs.

Other factors driving the need for innovation in health education include the increasing internationalization of academic programs, growing visa-related challenges faced by international students and the persistent shortage of skilled professionals in health and sports sciences. Higher-education institutions aiming to prepare graduates for these evolving demands should emphasize the development of adaptable, remote work competencies. This focus on creating flexible, tech-savvy environments ensures that students gain the skills needed to thrive in a digitally integrated health landscape and maintain productivity and focus regardless of their physical location.

DOI: 10.4324/9781003568650-4

Innovation in teaching

Modern educational institutions face the challenge of adapting to a diverse student population with varying needs, including demands for spatial and temporal flexibility. To address these needs, three primary teaching models are now widely employed: face-to-face teaching with digital enrichment, e-learning and blended learning. These models are designed to foster a competitive edge while catering to different student profiles, such as international and part-time students, and to support an inclusive approach to diverse learning preferences.

Traditional in-person teaching remains prevalent but has increasingly been enhanced with digital tools. This enrichment may include interactive online elements, such as polling programs or virtual whiteboards, and supplemental virtual courses that run alongside in-person sessions. In these virtual spaces, students access resources like documents, links, learning videos and recorded lectures. To deepen understanding, activities like forums, quizzes and group projects can be incorporated, promoting interaction, communication and collaboration among students.

E-learning provides a fully virtual experience where all course activities occur online. This model is typically reserved for specific groups, such as international students who may face visa-related delays. It encompasses live online sessions through platforms like Zoom or Teams and additional tools for interaction and collaboration within a virtual course environment, such as Moodle. These platforms enable fully remote learning and support students who may otherwise be unable to attend in-person sessions.

In contrast, blended learning combines in-person and online components, creating a cohesive learning experience that incorporates both modes (Kunze & Frey, 2021, p. 71). Through this approach, certain aspects of in-person teaching are replaced with virtual elements, such as Moodle-based courses or live online sessions, allowing for a versatile configuration that may include hybrid teaching or recorded sessions.

To create optimal learning conditions, it is essential to understand and accommodate individual student preferences and needs and develop tailored learning scenarios that maximize engagement and retention within diverse student groups.

Online learning

Online learning offers essential flexibility and enables students to access materials from any location at any time. This mode is particularly valuable for students who may face geographical or scheduling constraints. By providing both synchronous (live) and asynchronous (self-paced) modules, online learning supports diverse learning styles and empowers students to review and revisit complex content at their chosen pace. Although fully online formats may be less suitable for highly practical disciplines, they remain beneficial as a supplemental learning method, particularly when integrated into broader learning frameworks (Liu et al., 2016; Vallée et al., 2020).

Hybrid formats

Hybrid learning, which combines in-person and remote participation, provides students with flexible access to course content while retaining the interpersonal benefits of classroom interaction. This model is especially advantageous for international students who may face visa delays and for working professionals balancing studies with professional commitments. Hybrid formats maintain a higher level of student engagement by allowing for both physical presence and virtual participation, fostering a supportive learning community. Research has shown that hybrid models are effective in addressing the diverse needs of health education students by promoting both accessibility and a sense of community (Balakrishnan et al., 2021; Eiben et al., 2018).

Blended learning

Blended learning integrates in-person instruction with live online sessions, effectively combining the benefits of both formats to support applied learning. Rather than relying solely on self-paced modules, programs might also emphasize live, synchronous online sessions, which allow students to engage directly with instructors and peers. These approaches have demonstrated significant improvements in knowledge acquisition, underscoring their effectiveness in health education settings (Vallée et al., 2020).

By combining structured, interactive, in-person learning with flexible online components, blended learning provides an ideal solution for fields that require both theoretical and practical competencies (Liu et al., 2016; Vallée et al., 2020).

Challenges and solutions

Successfully integrating in-person and online phases in a blended or hybrid learning model can be challenging for educators. Pedagogical design is critical for ensuring the seamless connection between these phases, yet many educators encounter barriers, such as unfamiliarity with digital platforms and course-building tools like Moodle. Tutorials, peer support and training resources can alleviate these challenges and promote greater comfort with digital teaching (Chidzonga et al., 2022).

The shift to a digitally enhanced curriculum also requires significant investment in online material creation. When designed strategically, these materials can be reused across semesters, allowing educators to dedicate more time to enhancing teaching quality or conducting further research (Handke & Schäfer, 2012; Kunze & Frey, 2021). For example, educators in health education might spend substantial time creating video demonstrations or interactive modules on remote diagnostics, but these resources can be used repeatedly with new student cohorts.

For students, the blended format introduces challenges in self-directed learning, particularly in online and hybrid environments where developing strong self-discipline is essential. Clear guidance on technical tools, effective learning strategies and structured support can significantly enhance student engagement and improve course outcomes (Chidzonga et al., 2022; Saber et al., 2022). Students also develop practical digital skills that are relevant to modern health professions, such as setting up environments conducive to focused learning – skills that directly transfer to remote work settings in telemedicine, hybrid workplaces, or consulting roles.

The challenge of facilitating remote monitoring and data collection in online or hybrid learning extends beyond sports science and finds relevance in general health education. Many health programs now incorporate patient monitoring technologies that require knowledge of equipment setup, data privacy and secure communication channels. Addressing these challenges is critical in preparing students for a technology-driven workforce, where remote engagement skills are increasingly essential.

In hybrid learning, technical issues – such as inadequate audio-visual equipment or limited instructor experience with digital tools – can hinder learning experiences. Addressing these barriers requires both technical resources and active, interactive teaching methods to foster student participation. This demand for advanced resources and support systems points to the importance of specialized facilities, such as the Digital Teaching Lab at Deggendorf Institute of Technology (DIT), which will be explored further in the Best Practices section.

Innovation in examination

With the rise of digital transformation in higher education, digital exams have become integral to adapting assessment methods in health education. Several formats have emerged to meet diverse needs, including digital exams for remote and in-person settings, competency-based portfolio assessments and digital tools for academic integrity checks.

Digital exams

Digital exams can be implemented as remote, proctored exams or as computer-based, in-person exams. Remote exams offer flexibility and enable students to complete assessments from a location of their choice while monitored through online proctoring (Times Higher Education, 2023). This flexibility has proven especially beneficial for international students awaiting visas or students balancing personal responsibilities. However, remote exams also present technical and academic integrity challenges, such as ensuring reliable internet access and preventing dishonest practices. Proctoring tools and adaptive settings, such as randomized question order and restricted browser options, help maintain exam integrity.

Computer-based in-person exams

For computer-based in-person exams, students are provided with uniform devices and software, which promotes consistency and reduces technical discrepancies. This format combines the efficiency of digital assessments with the controlled environment of traditional exams, allowing educators to leverage various question formats, from multiple-choice to complex matching and essay responses. It is also more adaptable to specialized applications and software, which enhances the capability to test practical knowledge with real-time feedback.

Competency-oriented portfolio assessments

Portfolio assessments provide a flexible, competency-based examination method designed to evaluate students' skill development over time rather than through a single test. By incorporating varied submissions, such as written assignments, presentations and group projects within a module, portfolios allow students to demonstrate ongoing learning and growth. Research highlights that portfolios effectively support competency-based education by fostering self-reflection, goal-setting and continuous feedback, adhering closely to the principles of John Biggs' Constructive Alignment model, which emphasizes structuring assessments to achieve specific learning outcomes (Biggs, 1996; Heymann, 2004).

In practice, portfolios are particularly advantageous for heterogeneous student groups because they enable tailored assessment strategies. Portfolios are especially effective in evaluating competencies that require high levels of practical application and reflective skills. Benefits of this approach include providing formative feedback, encouraging continuous improvement and offering students opportunities to highlight their individual strengths through varied assessment types. However, managing portfolios requires careful planning, including realistic timelines and alignment with other course deadlines. For instructors, effective workload management may also involve integrating automated grading where applicable to streamline the assessment process.

Objective Structured Clinical Examination (OSCE)

The OSCE, originally developed and widely used in medical education, has recently found applications in other health-related fields, including sports sciences. The OSCE format involves multiple stations where students perform specific tasks – such as patient assessments, clinical decision-making and communication exercises – with each station designed to evaluate essential skills in a controlled and objective manner (Harding, 2017; Jefferies, 2022; University of Washington, 2024). Although OSCEs traditionally use trained actors to simulate patients, in our program, previously trained sports science students take on the role of patients or athletes. This approach not only allows examinees to develop and demonstrate their communication skills, but also fosters peer learning in interactions that closely simulate real-world professional scenarios.

The application of OSCEs in sports sciences is particularly innovative because this field traditionally relies on theoretical assessments and physical performance evaluations. By integrating OSCEs, sports science programs can assess competencies in the technical and interpersonal skills that are crucial for health professionals. For example, an OSCE station might involve students demonstrating injury assessment techniques, explaining treatment plans to "patients", or interpreting performance metrics – competencies that are vital for careers in high-performance sports. This approach ensures that students acquire not only theoretical knowledge, but also the hands-on and communication skills necessary for applied sport science roles.

The OSCE model aligns well with competency-based learning goals in health education because it emphasizes the demonstration of skills over memorization. By adapting OSCEs to assess both technical and communication skills in sports science, educators support a more holistic and practice-oriented approach to assessment and ensure that students are thoroughly prepared for the interpersonal and practical demands of professional roles.

Plagiarism detection for theses

To uphold academic integrity in final theses, digital plagiarism detection tools, such as Ouriginal (https://www.ouriginal.com/de/), are employed to verify originality systematically. These tools, often integrated within learning management systems, enable instructors to scan submissions for potential unoriginal content. This process not only safeguards academic standards but also provides constructive feedback by highlighting specific areas for further review. Instructors can efficiently review flagged sections, which facilitates a thorough and transparent evaluation while supporting students in developing responsible research practices.

AI and digital literacy

The integration of artificial intelligence (AI) and digital tools into academic work has provided students with essential support in refining and structuring their theses. Beyond AI, access to digital content and online resources also enables students to develop skills crucial for modern work environments, including remote collaboration and self-directed learning. These tools facilitate stronger research foundations, enhance clarity and coherence, encourage focused engagement with content and support students in producing high-quality academic work while upholding rigorous academic standards (Latzel & Glauner, 2024; Pinzolits, 2023).

However, the widespread availability of AI and digital resources calls for an emphasis on responsible, ethical use. In program design, these competencies can be effectively cultivated through a blended learning approach that embeds digital engagement and ethical considerations across existing modules. This integration allows students to develop an understanding of these tools as supplementary aids rather than replacements for critical analysis and original thought (Chubb et al., 2022; Tang et al., 2023).

In today's evolving work culture, where remote work and digital communication are becoming increasingly common, educational programs must ensure students are equipped with the digital and ethical skills necessary to navigate this landscape responsibly. Integrating these considerations into program structure and assessment policies helps students develop a balanced, ethical approach to technology use and prepares them for both academic and professional challenges.

Best practices: Master in Applied Sport Science

The Master in Applied Sport Sciences at DIT represents an advanced model of blended learning, designed to accommodate diverse learning preferences and professional needs. Through a carefully structured blend of live online sessions, in-person practical experiences and the support of a state-of-the-art Digital Teaching Lab, this program exemplifies a best-practices approach for modern health education. By considering the unique needs of students – from international backgrounds to those requiring flexible study options – this program demonstrates a commitment to both educational excellence and accessibility.

Student learning preferences and program design

Understanding and responding to student needs has been foundational in designing the blended structure of this Master's program. An internal survey conducted in 2023 revealed that 80% of students desired online components, with a significant portion preferring a predominantly in-person format supplemented by online options (Referat Digitale Lehre, 2023). This data indicated a strong demand for blended learning that balanced face-to-face interaction with digital flexibility. By aligning the program structure with these preferences, DIT ensures an inclusive learning environment that offers flexibility while maintaining academic rigor.

This preference for digital integration reflects broader trends in higher education, where blended formats are increasingly favored due to their adaptability and student-centered approach (Chubb et al., 2022; Vallée et al., 2020). By embedding digital and in-person components, the program supports varied learning styles and allows students to engage with course material in a way that best suits their needs.

Addressing diverse student needs

The program's design considers the diverse backgrounds and responsibilities of its students. Many international students, for instance, face delays in obtaining visas, which can prevent immediate in-person participation. The program's blended format addresses this challenge by enabling international students to join live online sessions until they can attend in person. Similarly, although the Master's program is not designed for part-time study, the blended format allows working students to manage their responsibilities while pursuing their degree. These digital accommodations make it feasible for students to pursue their education while managing professional or personal obligations, and provide flexibility that supports various needs without affecting their academic progress.

A unique aspect of this program is its requirement for students to engage in high-performance sports internships. Given the regional limitations on such opportunities, students may need to relocate to gain hands-on experience. The option to complete parts of their coursework remotely allows students to pursue practical experience in high-performance environments without sacrificing academic progress.

Blended learning format

The program's blended learning approach combines the flexibility of digital learning with the engagement of in-person interactions, which creates a comprehensive educational experience tailored to the demands of modern health and sports education. Each semester, the program includes four to five intensive blocks of face-to-face classes, each lasting three to five days. These in-person sessions focus on applied skills, with preparatory live online and hybrid sessions conducted beforehand.

Before each in-person block, students engage in online sessions covering foundational theory, ensuring they are well-prepared for hands-on activities when they arrive on campus. For example, in a module on diagnostics and training in sports, online sessions might cover the physiology of lactate production, introduce testing protocols and organize team roles. Addressing these foundational elements in advance allows the in-person sessions to focus fully on applied learning; students can immediately conduct tests, collect data and gain practical experience with sports science equipment without needing time for preliminary setup.

The program also introduces students to the use of digital tools for remote data collection and analysis – a critical skill in both sports science and broader health settings. In high-performance sports, for example, coaches often support athletes remotely using wearable devices that track metrics such as heart rate and variability, which are then analyzed through cloud-based applications. This approach is increasingly common across health fields, where professionals rely on remote monitoring for ongoing assessments, whether in managing patient recovery, monitoring cardiovascular health, or tracking progress in physical rehabilitation.

In team sports, where youth athletes often participate in multiple teams with varied training loads, remote access to data provides sports scientists and coaches with a comprehensive view of each athlete's performance and overall physical load. This challenge of balancing multiple training sources is mirrored in other health disciplines; for instance, healthcare professionals working with patients in diverse rehabilitation settings may monitor exercise compliance or manage recovery via remote tools. This integration of remote accessibility of the program prepares students to work confidently with these digital systems and enables them to make data-driven decisions irrespective of location.

Live online sessions for theoretical foundations

Theoretical content is delivered through interactive live online sessions, offering students the opportunity to engage in real-time learning from wherever they are. These sessions incorporate various digital tools that enhance both individual participation and collaborative learning. For instance, breakout rooms facilitate small-group discussions, allowing students to work closely with peers on targeted topics, whereas tools like Mentimeter (https://www.mentimeter.com/de-DE) and polling software are used to gather instant feedback, conduct polls and spark interactive discussions on complex topics. Group presentations are also integrated into these sessions, fostering teamwork and communication skills as students present findings or case studies virtually.

Beyond individual student engagement, the live online format enables easy access to guest speakers who might otherwise face logistical challenges. Invited experts from various locations can log in remotely to provide valuable insights without the need for extensive travel. This setup reduces both the time and financial costs associated with travel, which is especially advantageous for venues with remote geographical locations (like Deggendorf). Moreover, by avoiding long-distance travel, this format contributes to environmental sustainability by reducing carbon emissions associated with transportation.

Hybrid sessions

Some sessions are conducted in a hybrid format, allowing students to join either from campus or remotely. The Digital Teaching Lab at DIT enables these hybrid sessions to function as an immersive and collaborative environment, where both in-person and online students can actively participate in real time. Equipped with high-definition video, advanced audio systems and interactive screens, the lab creates a cohesive classroom experience for everyone involved.

An added feature of the Digital Teaching Lab is the presence of two specialized soundproof booths, similar to silent phone booths found in open office spaces. These booths are designed to minimize outside noise and create an ideal setting for groups of students working collaboratively. This setup is particularly advantageous in hybrid scenarios where some students are physically present in the classroom while others participate remotely. The booths allow mixed-location groups to work together seamlessly, facilitating communication and collaboration without disrupting the rest of the class.

Face-to-face practical sessions

Although online sessions establish the theoretical framework, face-to-face sessions are essential for developing practical skills specific to applied sports sciences. Physical attendance is required because these classes provide hands-on experience with sports science equipment, techniques for data collection, measurement methods and other discipline-specific practices. Through direct interaction with instructors, peers and specialized instruments, students gain the applied competencies necessary to meet the program's goals in sports sciences.

The blended model of the Master's program embodies a responsive, adaptable learning environment that accommodates diverse needs without sacrificing the quality of education. By offering a combination of synchronous online and in-person sessions, students receive comprehensive training that aligns theoretical knowledge with practical skills.

Student and educator experiences

Feedback from the program's quality improvement survey has highlighted the value of the blended learning approach. Many students indicated they would not have been able to participate if the program had been fully in-person, citing travel, work obligations and the need for scheduling flexibility. The blended format allows students from diverse backgrounds to balance their studies with personal and professional commitments, making the program more inclusive.

The structure of the live online sessions also encouraged students to develop critical skills for digital and remote work. As part of the online learning experience, students learned how to set up and manage their own environments to maintain focus, a skill essential for success in remote work settings, such as teleworking or hybrid workplaces. This aspect of the program fosters a level of self-discipline and adaptability that prepares students for the demands of today's digitally connected world.

Educators have noted that the blended format enables them to implement a diverse range of teaching methods, suited to both online and in-person contexts. This flexibility enriches the learning experience and increases student engagement because instructors can tailor their approaches to suit each format effectively.

Additionally, the blended learning model offers unique support for students participating in internships, particularly in high-performance sports. Because high-performance internships often require relocation or extended placements, the option to attend sessions remotely allows students to gain hands-on experience without compromising their academic progress. This approach maximizes learning opportunities and ensures that students can fulfill both their academic and professional aspirations.

Conclusions

The Master's Program in Applied Sport Sciences at DIT illustrates how a thoughtfully designed blended learning model can meet the needs of modern students by offering both flexibility and academic rigor. By integrating digital resources, responding to diverse student backgrounds and balancing theoretical and practical competencies, the program sets a benchmark for inclusive and adaptive education in health sciences. This approach not only addresses the immediate demands in health education but also prepares students for a technology-driven, global work environment.

Through its student-centered design and innovative use of blended learning, this best-practice model shows how higher education can evolve to support dynamic, well-rounded learning experiences. As institutions continue adapting to meet new challenges, DIT's program stands as an example of how program design can enhance accessibility, foster academic excellence and equip students with the skills needed to thrive in a connected, digital world.

References

Balakrishnan, A., Puthean, S., Satheesh, G., M. K, U., Rashid, M., Nair, S., & Thunga, G. (2021). Effectiveness of blended learning in pharmacy education: A systematic review and meta-analysis. *PLOS ONE*, *16*(6), e0252461. https://doi.org/10.1371/journal.pone.0252461

Biggs, J. (1996). Enhancing teaching through constructive alignment. *Higher Education*, *32*(3), 347–364. https://doi.org/10.1007/BF00138871

Chidzonga, M. M., Haruzivishe, C., Chikwasha, V., & Rukweza, J. (2022). Health professions faculty's perceptions of online teaching and learning during the COVID-19 pandemic. *PLOS ONE*, *17*(11), e0276170. https://doi.org/10.1371/journal.pone.0276170

Chubb, J., Cowling, P., & Reed, D. (2022). Speeding up to keep up: Exploring the use of AI in the research process. *AI & Society*, *37*(4), 1439–1457. https://doi.org/10.1007/s00146-021-01259-0

Eiben, A., Mazzola, R., & Hasseler, M. (2018). Digitalisierung in der wissenschaftlichen Weiterbildung im Bereich Gesundheit und Pflege. *Zeitschrift Hochschule und Weiterbildung (ZHWB)*, *2018* (1), 31–37 Seiten. https://doi.org/10.4119/ZHWB-240

Handke, J., & Schäfer, A. M. (2012). *E-Learning, E-Teaching und E-Assessment in der Hochschullehre: Eine Anleitung*. Oldenbourg Wissenschaftsverlag Verlag. https://doi.org/10.1524/9783486716849

Harding, D. (2017). The objective structured clinical examination (OSCE) explained. *The British Medical Journal*, *j3618*. https://doi.org/10.1136/sbmj.j3618

Heymann. (2004). Besserer Unterricht durch Sicherung von "Standards"? Pädagogik, 6–9.

Jefferies, C. (2022). *What is an OSCE?* https://geekymedics.com/what-is-an-osce/ last consulted on Dec. 2024

Kunze, L., & Frey, D. (2021). Digitale Lehre an der Hochschule: Warum Blended Learning so gut funktioniert. In M. Frey, & Uemminghaus (Eds.), *Innovative an der Hochschule* (pp. 69–86). Springer Berlin Heidelberg. https://doi.org/10.1007/978-3-662-62913-0_4

Latzel, R., & Glauner, P. (2024). Artificial intelligence in sport scientific creation and writing process. In C. Dindorf, E. Bartaguiz, F. Gassmann, & M. Fröhlich (Eds.), *Artificial intelligence in sports, movement, and health* (pp. 15–29). Springer Nature Switzerland. https://doi.org/10.1007/978-3-031-67256-9_2

Liu, Q., Peng, W., Zhang, F., Hu, R., Li, Y., & Yan, W. (2016). The effectiveness of blended learning in health professions: Systematic review and meta-analysis. *Journal of Medical Internet Research*, *18*(1), e2. https://doi.org/10.2196/jmir.4807

Pinzolits, R. F. J. (2023). AI in academia: An overview of selected tools and their areas of application. *MAP Education and Humanities*, *4*(1), 37–50. https://doi.org/10.53880/2744-2373.2023.4.37

Referat Digitale Lehre. (2023). *Lehre an der THD. Ergebnisse der Studierendenbefragung 2023.* Technische Hochschule Deggendorf. https://ilearn.th-deg.de/pluginfile.php/769349/mod_book/chapter/11564/Studierendenbefragung_2023.jpg

Saber, H., Abdul Manaf, R., Basman, A. T., Sanip, S., Lee, P. Y., Kamalludeen, R., Ibrahim, R., & Amin-Nordin, S. (2022). Challenges and barriers of blended learning among Asian health sciences students: A pilot study. *Education in Medicine Journal*, *14*(1), 1–16. https://doi.org/10.21315/eimj2022.14.1.1

Tang, A., Li, K., Kwok, K. O., Cao, L., Luong, S., & Tam, W. (2023). The importance of transparency: Declaring the use of generative artificial intelligence (AI) in academic writing. *Journal of Nursing Scholarship, 12938.* https://doi.org/10.1111/jnu.12938

Times Higher Education. (2023). *Digital assessment and examination needs to adapt to ensure its future success.* https://www.timeshighereducation.com/campus/digital-assessment-and-examination-needs-adapt-ensure-its-future-success last consulted on Dec. 2024

University of Washington. (2024). *OSCE: General information.* https://education.uwmedicine.org/curriculum/exams/osce/ last consulted on Dec. 2024

Vallée, A., Blacher, J., Cariou, A., & Sorbets, E. (2020). Blended learning compared to traditional learning in medical education: Systematic review and meta-analysis. *Journal of Medical Internet Research*, *22*(8), e16504. https://doi.org/10.2196/16504

4 Technological Innovations for a Healthier Life

A Chance for Young People with Intellectual Disabilities

Anne-Christin Zobel, Elke Langbein and Borja Sañudo

Introduction

Digital technologies hold immense educational potential, especially in promoting healthy habits among people with Intellectual Disabilities (pwID). By offering accessible, dynamic and interactive resources, these tools can facilitate the acquisition of knowledge about healthy lifestyles, develop practical skills and foster autonomy in health-related decision-making. In educational contexts, technology enables the adaptation of content to individual needs while creating inclusive learning environments that motivate users to actively engage in their own well-being. Repetition, positive reinforcement and visual learning are particularly effective in promoting sustainable and beneficial routines (Kalemkuş, 2024).

In 2024, a group of experts came together in a European project called IDHEApp: Using Technologies to Promote Healthy Lifestyles in Adolescents with Intellectual Disabilities. This transnational initiative addresses health inequalities among pwID by implementing online lifestyle intervention strategies. Evidence shows that access to internet-enabled devices in pwID is often lower than in the general population. Even when these tools are available, they typically require the support of caregivers or peers for setup, which limits self-efficacy and empowerment (Alfredsson Ågren et al., 2018, 2019). IDHEApp aims to empower pwID to lead self-determined, healthier lives by introducing accessible educational technology tools. The initiative focuses on upskilling users with accessible and engaging methods. Short messages provide actionable steps for achieving health recommendations, while gamification features, such as challenges and quizzes, foster engagement and help reinforce knowledge. Progress is visually highlighted using wearables and digital technologies, providing users with motivation and a sense of achievement. Although adolescents with ID are the primary focus, IDHEApp also includes their supporters (family, mentors, coaches, professional caregivers). By equipping supporters with digital and educational resources, including mobile apps and online training modules, the project empowers educators, health professionals and mentors to effectively use these tools to support adolescents with ID in

DOI: 10.4324/9781003568650-5

improving their healthier lifestyle. Ultimately, IDHEApp raises awareness of healthy living, provides digital resources to enhance the lives of pwID and assesses the current use and acceptance of technology in health management for this population. This initiative is crucial for identifying tailored, digital health solutions specifically designed for young pwID and exploring practical ways to implement these innovations (IDHEApp, n.d.).

A step toward digital inclusion

Information and communication technology (ICT) requires essential skills for operating digital tools that serve as a gateway to education, social interaction and numerous opportunities. However, individuals without these skills risk exclusion from the increasingly digital world. PwID are particularly vulnerable because rapid advancements in ICT often fail to accommodate their needs. Poorly designed systems and interfaces create additional barriers to participation, compounding existing challenges (Dekelver et al., 2015). Addressing these disparities requires technological adaptations and inclusive strategies to enable equitable participation.

Despite their widespread adoption of digital tools, significant gaps remain. Although smartphone usage among adolescents in Germany has reached 99% (Robert Koch-Institut, 2020), it is significantly lower among pwID. Studies indicate that only 68% of the Swedish participants own smartphones (Johansson et al., 2020). Among 415 students with ID, only 33% use smartphones independently, while 63% have access at home but do not possess one (Arun & Jain, 2022).

This digital divide has broader implications for health and well-being. Increased screen time (ST) and reduced physical activity (PA) correlate with rising noncommunicable diseases (NCDs) (World Health Organization, 2023). Adults (18 to 64 years) with ID engage in only 17.5% to 33% of the recommended PA levels (Jacob et al., 2023) and spend approximately 67% of their day (495 min) in sedentary activities (Chow et al., 2018). These trends exacerbate health risks and have prompted the proliferation of apps targeting health, fitness and nutrition.

This raises an important question: How can we ensure that pwID are included in this digital health revolution, particularly from an educational perspective? Tailored technologies are essential for fostering inclusion and promoting learning opportunities that encourage healthier lifestyles. A well-designed app for pwID could serve as an educational tool, empowering them to acquire knowledge about nutrition and PA, develop essential skills and take an active role in managing their health independently.

Balance between screen time and physical activity

The Robert Koch Institute's miniKIM study in 2018 reported that approximately 40% of children in Germany aged 6–13 years own a smartphone, highlighting the pervasive influence of digital services on young people's lives

(Robert Koch-Institut, 2020). The increased availability of screen-based media has contributed to a significant increase in screen time (ST), resulting in prolonged sedentary behavior. Evidence demonstrates a clear dose–response relationship between ST and metabolic syndrome (MetS). Each additional hour of ST increases the risk of MetS by 21% (OR, 1.21; 95% CI: 1.08–1.35) (Khan et al., 2019). Adolescents who exceed two hours of daily ST are twice as likely to develop MetS compared to their peers with lower ST (adjusted OR = 2.20; 95% CI: 1.04–4.67). These trends are exacerbated by declining PA levels, particularly since the COVID-19 pandemic shifted many activities online (Musa et al., 2022). The World Health Organization (WHO) recommends at least 60 min of moderate-to-vigorous PA daily for adolescents (World Health Organization, 2020). Only 20% of those aged 11–17 years meet these guidelines, and less than half of adults remain sufficiently active (Guthold et al., 2020). For pwID, these statistics are even more concerning. Research shows that most fail to meet recommended PA levels (Diaz, 2020; Sundahl et al., 2016). Further, research shows that children and adolescents with ID spend approximately 70% (204 min/day) of their after-school time (5 h coming from school until going to bed) in a sedentary state (Yuan et al., 2022). This places pwID at a higher risk of NCDs and mortality compared to the general population (Coppus, 2013).

Life expectancy for pwID in England and Wales has improved from an average of 51 years (1980s) to slightly more than 60 years (2010s), while mortality rates remain significantly higher compared to the general population. Overall, these data show a reduction in age-standardized mortality rates for pwID in groups of young (10–20 years) and older adults (over 70 years) (Emerson et al., 2014).

Adequate PA and a healthy diet provide a solid foundation for a healthy life and have a significantly positive impact on reducing mortality risk (Diaz, 2020). As the role of technology in daily life grows, it is worth considering its dual potential: although excessive ST is linked to sedentary behaviors, digital health solutions may present opportunities to promote PA and healthy habits. Emerging evidence suggests that well-designed health technologies can positively influence behavior, encourage increased PA and improve nutrition (Goodyear et al., 2017; Monroe et al., 2015; Schoeppe et al., 2016, p. 20). The success of these interventions often depends on personalized goal setting (Schoeppe et al., 2016, p. 20) and the incorporation of performance-based feedback (Langarizadeh et al., 2021). Adapting digital health tools to the specific needs of pwID could provide innovative pathways for improving health.

Tailored digital innovations

Digital participation opens new opportunities and possibilities for pwID and offers a powerful educational source to enhance their quality of life, foster digital independence and promote health. It enables social inclusion through technology and utilizes health apps to support physical and mental well-being. Connected devices (wearables, smartphones) play a key role by providing regular reminders about PA or healthy eating, which helps users establish and maintain health-promoting routines. Tailored digital solutions designed to enhance access and promote active participation in the digital world are essential to fully realizing these benefits. However, some barriers persist. PwID often encounter challenges in accessing and effectively using digital technologies, limiting their ability to fully benefit from these innovations.

Over the last decade, mobile devices have increasingly been utilized for population monitoring, improving clinical practices and advancing public health (Parmenter et al., 2022). Additionally, digital technologies are emerging as vital tools for delivering health-related behavior change interventions to pwID (Sanudo et al., 2024).

Research on digital participation reveals that the application of digital technologies to promote health among pwID is primarily limited to specific areas. Rather than evaluating their direct impact on health behavior, these technologies are often employed as tools to facilitate health promotion (Baumann et al., 2022; Haymes et al., 2015). Addressing digital inclusion requires focusing on three key dimensions: access to digital technologies, participation through digital technologies and participation in digital technologies (Borgstedt & Möller-Slawinski, 2020; Bosse, 2016).

Access to digital technologies

Ensuring access to digital technologies and necessary infrastructure is fundamental to successfully integrating digital innovations. Equally important is digital competence, which includes the knowledge and skills needed to operate and use these technologies effectively. Educational resources such as training and instructional materials play a vital role in facilitating comprehensive use. Simplified interfaces and customizable features, such as text-to-speech functions or visual aids, enhance accessibility and usability. These elements are essential to bridging the "digital gap" (Borgstedt & Möller-Slawinski, 2020; Bosse, 2016).

Participation through digital technologies

Digital technologies provide pwID with opportunities to connect with peers, foster independence and enhance well-being. These tools support communication, facilitate education and promote social inclusion. For instance, a tailored health app can enable participation through technology and encourage healthier lifestyles.

Participation in digital technologies

Access alone is insufficient; active involvement in the development process is essential. Including pwID in designing digital solutions ensures that the resulting technologies address their needs and function effectively in real-life settings. To achieve this, developers and designers must engage with the target group throughout the implementation process, testing and validating the technology to ensure it meets practical requirements. Only by involving pwID can genuinely inclusive and accessible technology be created.

From theory to application

Several studies explore the use of digital technologies for health promotion among young pwID. Although these studies vary in the types of digital interventions and health-related behaviors they target, they offer insights into the applicability of these technologies and their potential impact on health behaviors in pwID. This section provides an overview of the technologies used and, where evaluated, describes their influence on health behaviors.

Zoom

Zoom has been used to offer exercise sessions for young pwID over 12 weeks (Guerrero et al., 2023; Prieto et al., 2023). Zoom-supported exercise sessions, conducted three times a week for one hour each, aim to improve balance and leg strength of young people with Down syndrome. Although improvements in balance and leg strength were observed, the study does not explicitly address whether these results were attributable to the technology itself. In contrast, Prieto et al. (2023) compared the effects of a digital sports intervention via Zoom with an in-person intervention conducted by trainers. In a parent-mediated sports program for children with autism, the in-person group showed the most significant improvements in fundamental motor skills, the online group showed moderate improvements and the control group exhibited minimal change. However, the impact of technology was not unexamined.

Mobile fitness and nutrition applications

A mobile application called *Nutrition Ninja* delivers a nutrition intervention combined with behavior change training to promote healthier eating habits, focusing on increasing fruit and vegetable (FV) intake and reducing consumption of unhealthy snacks and sugary beverages (Kral et al., 2023; Lee et al., 2022; Michalsen et al., 2023). Results showed no significant differences in eating habits between intervention groups, suggesting participants' eating behaviors are independent of group affiliation. Lee et al. (2022) compared two fitness apps: *Puzzle Walk*, a gamified behavior-change app with a reward system, and the freely available *Google Fit*. Accelerometers were used to measure daily steps and general activity. Michalsen et al. (2023) evaluated multiple apps for promoting PA among pwID. The primary app, *Aktiv Fritid*, features an activity planner with individualized solutions, goal-setting possibilities, and accessible interfaces. Simplified visuals, easy-to-read text and text-to-speech options ensure usability. The second app, *Sorterius*, an augmented reality game inspired by *Pokémon Go*, is designed to increase PA by linking walking activities to meaningful goals.

App usage evaluation

Not all studies report the impact of technology use on behavior. Kral et al. (2023) reported that participants with low initial FV intake who engage actively with the technology increase their FV consumption by 1.5 servings/day. Michalsen et al. (2023) reported qualitative data indicating that participants and caregivers found *Activ Fritid* easy to use. However, most participants required caregiver support to register activities, with only one of nine participants using the app independently. This highlights the importance of cognitive abilities in determining independent technology use. The augmented reality app *Sorterius* received positive feedback for its reward system, which enhances motivation by linking walking activities to engaging goals.

Online health platform

The *POWERforID* platform supports weight management through computer-generated health strategies based on questionnaire responses. It provides resources such as health materials, website-based assistance in weight management and PA suggestions (Neumeier et al., 2021). However, this study did not evaluate the platform's acceptance or usability and focused solely on medical data like weight and body mass index (BMI).

Testing various technologies demonstrates that digital innovations can enhance the daily lives and health of pwID. Digital tools such as Zoom and mobile apps encourage regular participation in PA and lead to a healthier life. Motivation emerges as a key factor, with gamified elements and rewards systems, such as those in *Puzzle Walk* and *Sorterius*, positively influencing activity levels.

Developing personalized, user-friendly applications tailored to individual needs is crucial. Simple interfaces and symbols enhance usability and reduce reliance on caregivers. Adapting technologies to users' cognitive and practical abilities fosters independence. Thorough preparation and involving stakeholders, including caregivers and pwID, are essential for effective implementation.

These studies highlight the importance of user-friendly design and the need to consider the unique requirements of the target group. Integrating digital health measures into daily life offers an opportunity to establish long-term healthy behaviors and improve the quality of life. Although many technologies still require support for use, growing digital competence and a focus on tailored technologies can enhance usability, acceptance and independent use of technology.

IDHEApp project

This chapter illustrates that technology plays a significant role in the lives of young pwID. The IDHEApp project focuses on the ages 12–24 years. To ensure their inclusion, it is essential to prioritize the accessibility and usability of digital tools and leverage their potential to enhance the well-being and health of pwID.

Accessibility

Designing a mobile application for pwID requires prioritizing accessibility through user-friendly interfaces and specific functional elements tailored to their needs (Dekelver et al., 2015). Following the "Design for All" principles, several key elements ensure accessibility (Borblik et al., 2015):

- *Flexibility*: The app adapts to a wide range of preferences and abilities, allowing adjustments like font size for readability, voice commands, screen readers and symbols for those with limited literacy.
- *Simplicity and intuition*: The app is simple to use and easy to understand. Clear navigation paths and feedback mechanisms enable users to interact with confidence and independence.

The IDHEApp health app project focuses on creating an accessible application that promotes a healthy lifestyle among adolescents with ID. By incorporating user-friendly designs and easy-to-read content, the app fosters independence and builds digital competencies.

Usability

The primary goal is to enable pwID to use the app independently with minimal assistance from caregivers. The mobile tool is designed with simple, intuitive navigation and clear menus, ensuring users can navigate quickly and effortlessly (Figure 4.1). An integrated help feature addresses potential issues related to understanding and promotes independence. The user interface consists of a simple and consistent structure (Dekelver et al., 2015). Research highlights that pwID value clarity and prefer technologies that do not overwhelm them (Borgstedt & Möller-Slawinski, 2020).

Information and communication

Ensuring the app's content is understandable requires effective communication and visual clarity, including a high contrast between text and background. Easy language is particularly important for pwID, using short, easily understandable sentences of eight to ten words. A legible font, customizable in style and size, supports readability. Technical jargon and overly long or complex texts are avoided, with titles kept short and simple. To minimize cognitive load and enhance better understanding, related images are included (Dekelver et al., 2015). Providing examples and explanations for specific words ensures comprehension. A text-to-speech function further supports users by reading text aloud, compensating for challenges with written language (Borgstedt & Möller-Slawinski, 2020).

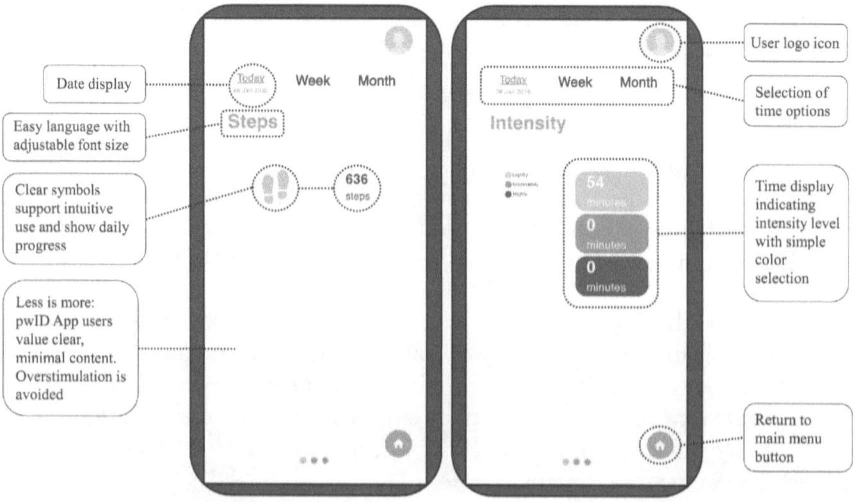

Figure 4.1 Screenshots of the IDHEApp. Presentation of the current level of steps made in 1 day.

Promoting motivation

To realize the primary goal of a health app and significantly enhance health, motivational elements such as gamification are incorporated. Features such as progress indicators, coupled with a reward system, motivate users to maintain their efforts (Michalsen et al., 2023). Real-time goal setting and self-monitoring are included, along with tips and feedback to provide positive reinforcement regarding target behaviors (Langarizadeh et al., 2021).

Personalization

Predefined performance levels might not be suitable for all users. Personalization that allows individual adjustments to meet diverse needs is crucial (Michalsen et al., 2023). The Menu function of the mobile tool is adjustable, enabling it to adapt to the user's requirements (Dekelver et al., 2015). As illustrated in Figure 4.2, the main screen features challenges and options for daily, weekly and monthly goals, which allows users to tailor the app to their personal needs. This ensures that the app remains accessible and continues to motivate a broad user base.

Guidance and support

As with many fitness apps, the more interactive and illustrative the exercises are, the better users can understand, execute and remember them. Videos and images that clearly explain the steps enhance comprehension. Including videos

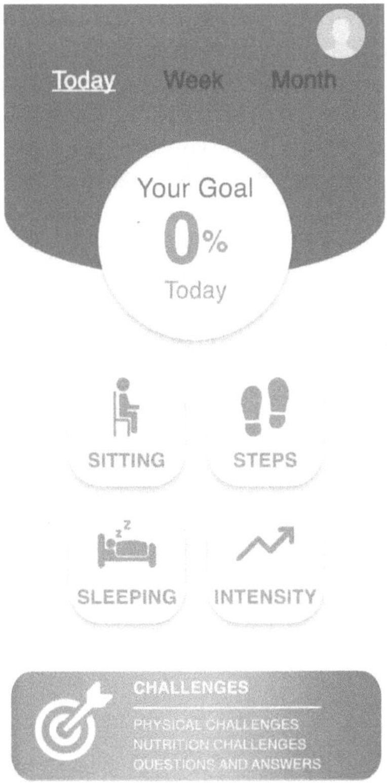

Figure 4.2 Main screen of the IDHEApp with challenges for daily/weekly/monthly goals.

featuring pwID performing exercises helps users better follow the movements, relate to the demonstrators, and increase their motivation while reducing barriers.

Evaluation

Integrated feedback systems allow users to continuously evaluate the app's usability and thus enable ongoing adjustments and improvements. In the IDHEApp project, several steps ensure that the app is accessible and user-friendly for pwID. The app content and instructions are rendered in easy-to-read formats that simplify language and visuals to aid comprehension.

Additionally, IDHEApp organizes focus groups involving young pwID who actively participate in the design and testing process, which provides valuable insights into their needs and preferences. These contributions help refine the app, making it more effective and inclusive. The IDHEApp project also conducted a randomized controlled study to investigate differences in healthy lifestyles between a focus group and a control group. The focus group received advice for a healthier lifestyle through written educational activity cards, daily gamified challenges promoting healthier nutrition, reduced sedentary time and increased PA. All of these benefits are delivered via the app, along with the possibility of controlling them using a wearable connected to the app. In contrast, the control group only received written educational activity cards and used the wearable for activity tracking without daily challenges.

Research shows that pwID use technology for independent living (alert buttons, mobility) and communication (Palmer et al., 2012). For pwID, digital participation also means social integration, leisure activities and a tangible improvement in quality of life. However, digitization presents challenges. Financial constraints create significant barriers because acquiring digital technologies can be costly and unaffordable for some individuals with limited financial resources. This leads to growing inequality in access to digital resources. Limited access to technology can result in social exclusion, especially because many interactions increasingly occur with the help of digital tools (WhatsApp, Messenger, Instagram).

Overall, it becomes clear that digitization brings both opportunities and challenges. Promoting participation and integration through digital technologies is vital for enriching and simplifying the lives of pwID. Addressing ethical, social and cultural dimensions is essential to ensure inclusion and equitable access in the digital age.

Conclusions

Although evidence of the influence of digital devices on healthy lifestyle behaviors of pwID remains limited, current findings suggest that digital technology interventions could positively influence health behaviors in this population. Measurable changes in medical data, such as reduction in body weight or BMI, are observed as outcomes of these interventions (Bundeszentrale für gesundheitliche Aufklärung, 2021; Corey et al., 2024; Neumeier et al., 2021). Addressing these research gaps is essential to fully harnessing the potential of digital health tools and ensuring their effectiveness for pwID.

Digital innovations present unique opportunities to enhance quality of life, improve educational access and encourage digital independence for pwID. Easy-to-access applications serve as powerful educational tools that deliver health messages through engaging and user-friendly methods, such as easy-to-understand text, visually appealing content and interactive features such as individual and group challenges. By combining accessibility with educational elements, these tools promote learning and empower individuals to adopt healthier behaviors and develop essential life skills. The success of these technologies relies on their usability, accessibility and alignment with the specific needs of pwID.

The development of accessible digital solutions, as demonstrated in the IDHEApp project, underscores the importance of prioritizing usability and user-centered design in promoting a healthy lifestyle among pwID. A key educational focus of the app is providing users with tailored learning opportunities to acquire essential knowledge and skills for leading healthier lives.

These are age-specific and interest-driven educational goals. Younger users are offered engaging and interactive content on basic health principles, while older users can access practical tools for applying this knowledge, such as personalized goal setting, activity tracking and nutritional guidance. Although the groundwork has been laid, the next step involves transitioning from design and testing to implementation and intervention. This phase evaluates the real-world impact of the application on health outcomes and technological independence, and its effectiveness as an educational tool. The findings provide critical insights into the role of digital technologies in empowering pwID through both health promotion and education, paving the way for future advancements in this field.

Acknowledgments

We would like to express our sincere gratitude to Daniela Schwarz for connecting with Jeff Wilkesmann, which has provided the opportunity to contribute to this book project. Furthermore, we would like to express our deep gratitude to the European IDHEApp team for insights into this topic.

References

Alfredsson Ågren, K., Kjellberg, A., & Hemmingsson, H. (2018). Access to and use of the Internet among adolescents and young adults with intellectual disabilities in everyday settings. *Journal of Intellectual & Developmental Disability*, *45*(1), 89–98. https://doi.org/10.3109/13668250.2018.1518898

Alfredsson Ågren, K., Kjellberg, A., & Hemmingsson, H. (2019). Digital participation? Internet use among adolescents with and without intellectual disabilities: A comparative study. *New Media & Society*, *22*(12), 2128–2145. https://doi.org/10.1177/1461444819888398

Arun, P., & Jain, S. (2022). Use of smart phone among students with intellectual and developmental disability. *Journal of Psychosocial Rehabilitation and Mental Health*, *9*(4), 447–452. https://doi.org/10.1007/s40737-022-00279-3

Baumann, H., Fiedler, J., Wunsch, K., Woll, A., & Wollesen, B. (2022). mHealth interventions to reduce physical inactivity and sedentary behavior in children and adolescents: Systematic review and meta-analysis of randomized controlled trials. *JMIR mhealth and uhealth*, *10*(5), e35920. https://doi.org/10.2196/35920

Borblik, J., Shabalina, O., Kultsova, M., Pidoprigora, A., & Romanenko, R. (2015, 06–08 July). *Assistive technology software for people with intellectual or development disabilities: Design of user interfaces for mobile applications [Conference session]* In 2015 6th International Conference on Information, Intelligence, Systems and Applications (IISA), Corfu, Greece. https://doi.org/10.1109/IISA.2015.7387976

Borgstedt, S., & Möller-Slawinski, H. (2020). *Digitale Teilhabe von Menschen mit Behinderung*. SINUS Markt- und Sozialforschung GmbH. https://www.sinus-institut.de/media-center/studien/digitale-teilhabe-von-menschen-mit-behinderung-trendstudie

Bosse, I. (2016). *Teilhabe in einer digitalen Gesellschaft - Wie Medien Inklusionsprozesse befördern können*. Bundeszentrale für politische Bildung. https://www.bpb.de/themen/medien-journalismus/medienpolitik/172759/teilhabe-in-einer-digitalen-gesellschaft-wie-medien-inklusionsprozesse-befoerdern-koennen/

Bundeszentrale für gesundheitliche Aufklärung. (2021, January). *Inklusion und Gesundheitsförderung*. Bundeszentrale für gesundheitliche Aufklärung. https://leitbegriffe.bzga.de/alphabetisches-verzeichnis/inklusion-und-gesundheitsfoerderung/

Chow, B. C., Choi, P. H. N., & Huang, W. Y. J. (2018). Physical activity and physical fitness of adults with intellectual disabilities in group homes in Hong Kong. *International Journal of Environmental Research and Public Health, 15*(7), 1370. https://doi.org/10.3390/ijerph15071370

Coppus, A. M. (2013). People with intellectual disability: What do we know about adulthood and life expectancy? *Developmental Disabilities Research Reviews, 18*(1), 6–16. https://doi.org/10.1002/ddrr.1123

Corey, J., Tsai, J. M., Mhadeshwar, A., Srinivasan, S., & Bhat, A. (2024). Digital motor intervention effects on physical activity performance of individuals with developmental disabilities: A systematic review. *Disability and Rehabilitation, 47*(10), 1–16. https://doi.org/10.1080/09638288.2024.2398148

Dekelver, J., Kultsova, M., Shabalina, O., Borblik, J., Pidoprigora, A., & Romanenko, R. (2015). Design of Mobile applications for people with intellectual disabilities. In A. Kravets et al. (Eds.) *Creativity in Intelligent Technologies and Data Science* (Vol. 535, pp. 823–836). https://doi.org/10.1007/978-3-319-23766-4_65

Diaz, K. M. (2020). Leisure-time physical activity and all-cause mortality among adults with intellectual disability: the National Health Interview Survey. *Journal of Intellectual Disability Research, 64*(2), 180–184. https://doi.org/10.1111/jir.12695

Emerson, E., Glover, G., Hatton, C., & Wolstenholme, J. (2014). Trends in age-standardised mortality rates and life expectancy of people with learning disabilities in Sheffield over a 33-year period. *Tizard Learning Disability Review, 19*(2), 90–95. https://doi.org/10.1108/tldr-01-2014-0003

Goodyear, V. A., Kerner, C., & Quennerstedt, M. (2017). Young people's uses of wearable healthy lifestyle technologies; Surveillance, self-Surveillance and resistance. *Sport, Education and Society, 24*(3), 212–225. https://doi.org/10.1080/13573322.2017.1375907

Guerrero, K., Umagat, A., Barton, M., Martinez, A., Ho, K. Y., Mann, S., & Hilgenkamp, T. (2023). The effect of a telehealth exercise intervention on balance in adults with down syndrome. *Journal of Applied Research in Intellectual Disabilities, 36*(2), 385–393. https://doi.org/10.1111/jar.13068

Guthold, R., Stevens, G. A., Riley, L. M., & Bull, F. C. (2020). Global trends in insufficient physical activity among adolescents: A pooled analysis of 298 population-based surveys with 1.6 million participants. *The Lancet Child & Adolescent Health, 4*(1), 23–35. https://doi.org/10.1016/S2352-4642(19)30323-2

Haymes, L. K., Storey, K., Maldonado, A., Post, M., & Montgomery, J. (2015). Using applied behavior analysis and smart technology for meeting the health needs of individuals with intellectual disabilities. *Developmental Neurorehabilitiation, 18*(6), 407–419. https://doi.org/10.3109/17518423.2013.850750

IDHEApp (n.d.). *IDHEApp - Technology to promote healthy lifestyles in adolescents with intellectual disabilities*. https://idheapp.eu/de/

Jacob, U. S., Pillay, J., Johnson, E., Omoya, O. T., & Adedokun, A. P. (2023). A systematic review of physical activity: Benefits and needs for maintenance of quality of life among adults with intellectual disability. *Front Sports Act Living, 5*, 1184946. https://doi.org/10.3389/fspor.2023.1184946

Johansson, S., Gulliksen, J., & Gustavsson, C. (2020). Disability digital divide: The use of the internet, smartphones, computers and tablets among people with disabilities in Sweden. *Universal Access in the Information Society, 20*(1), 105–120. https://doi.org/10.1007/s10209-020-00714-x

Kalemkuş, F. (2024). Trends in instructional technologies used in education of people with special needs due to intellectual disability and autism. *Journal of Research in Special Educational Needs*. https://doi.org/10.1111/1471-3802.12723

Khan, M. A., Shah, S. M., Shehab, A., Ghosal, S., Muhairi, S. J., Al-Rifai, R. H., Al Maskari, F., Alkaabi, J., & Nauman, J. (2019). Screen time and metabolic syndrome among expatriate adolescents in the United Arab Emirates. *Diabetes & Metabolic Syndrome*, *13*(4), 2565–2569. https://doi.org/10.1016/j.dsx.2019.07.006

Kral, T. V. E., O'Malley, L., Johnson, K., Benvenuti, T., Chittams, J., Quinn, R. J., Thomas, J. G., Pinto-Martin, J. A., Levy, S. E., & Kuschner, E. S. (2023). Effects of a mobile health nutrition intervention on dietary intake in children who have autism spectrum disorder. *Frontiers in Pediatrics*, *11*, 1100436. https://doi.org/10.3389/fped.2023.1100436

Langarizadeh, M., Sadeghi, M., As'habi, A., Rahmati, P., & Sheikhtaheri, A. (2021). Mobile Apps for weight management in children and adolescents; An updated systematic review. *Patient Education and Counseling*, *104*(9), 2181–2188. https://doi.org/10.1016/j.pec.2021.01.035

Lee, D., Frey, G. C., Cothran, D. J., Harezlak, J., & Shih, P. C. (2022). Effects of a gamified, behavior change technique-based Mobile app on increasing physical activity and reducing anxiety in adults with autism spectrum disorder: Feasibility randomized controlled trial. *JMIR Formative Research*, *6*(7), e35701. https://doi.org/10.2196/35701

Michalsen, H., Henriksen, A., Pettersen, G., Hartvigsen, G., Wangberg, S., Thrane, G., Jahnsen, R., & Anke, A. (2023). Using mobile health to encourage physical activity in individuals with intellectual disability: A pilot mixed methods feasibility study. *Frontiers in Rehabilitation Sciences*, *4*, 1225641. https://doi.org/10.3389/fresc.2023.1225641

Monroe, C. M., Thompson, D. L., Bassett, D. R., Fitzhugh, E. C., & Raynor, H. A. (2015). Usability of mobile phones in physical activity–related research: A systematic review. *American Journal of Health Education*, *46*(4), 196–206. https://doi.org/10.1080/19325037.2015.1044141

Musa, S., Elyamani, R., & Dergaa, I. (2022). COVID-19 and screen-based sedentary behaviour: Systematic review of digital screen time and metabolic syndrome in adolescents. *PLoS One*, *17*(3), e0265560. https://doi.org/10.1371/journal.pone.0265560

Neumeier, W. H., Guerra, N., Hsieh, K., Thirumalai, M., Ervin, D., & Rimmer, J. H. (2021). POWERSforID: Personalized online weight and exercise response system for individuals with intellectual disability: A randomized controlled trial. *Disability and Health Journal*, *14*(4), 101111. https://doi.org/10.1016/j.dhjo.2021.101111

Palmer, S. B., Wehmeyer, M. L., Davies, D. K., & Stock, S. E. (2012). Family members' reports of the technology use of family members with intellectual and developmental disabilities. *Journal of Intellectual Disability Research*, *56*(4), 402–414. https://doi.org/10.1111/j.1365-2788.2011.01489.x

Parmenter, B., Burley, C., Stewart, C., Whife, J., Champion, K., Osman, B., Newton, N., Green, O., Wescott, A. B., Gardner, L. A., Visontay, R., Birrell, L., Bryant, Z., Chapman, C., Lubans, D. R., Sunderland, M., Slade, T., & Thornton, L. (2022). Measurement properties of smartphone approaches to assess physical activity in healthy young people: Systematic review. *JMIR mHealth and uHealth*, *10*(10), e39085. https://doi.org/10.2196/39085

Prieto, L. A., Meera, B., Barry, A., Swarup, G., Asmus, J., Ku, B., Roth, K., Foley, J. T., & Columna, L. (2023). A randomized parent-mediated physical activity intervention for autistic children. *Autism Research*, *16*(7), 1450–1461. https://doi.org/10.1002/aur.2969

Robert Koch-Institut. (2020). *Verfügbarkeit von Bildschirmmedien [Fact sheet]*. https://www.rki.de/DE/Content/Gesundheitsmonitoring/Studien/Adipositas_Monitoring/Verhaeltnisse/PDF_Themenblatt_Familie_Bildschirmmedien.pdf?__blob=publicationFile

Sanudo, B., Sanchez-Trigo, H., Dominguez, R., Flores-Aguilar, G., Sanchez-Oliver, A., Moral, J. E., & Oviedo-Caro, M. A. (2024). A randomized controlled mHealth trial that evaluates social comparison-oriented gamification to improve physical activity, sleep quantity, and quality of life in young adults. *Psychology of Sport and Exercise*, *72*, 102590. https://doi.org/10.1016/j.psychsport.2024.102590

Schoeppe, S., Alley, S., Van Lippevelde, W., Bray, N. A., Williams, S. L., Duncan, M. J., & Vandelanotte, C. (2016). Efficacy of interventions that use apps to improve diet, physical activity and sedentary behaviour: A systematic review. *International Journal of Behavioral Nutrition and Physical Activity*, *13*(1), 127. https://doi.org/10.1186/s12966-016-0454-y

Sundahl, L., Zetterberg, M., Wester, A., Rehn, B., & Blomqvist, S. (2016). Physical activity levels among adolescent and young adult women and men with and without intellectual disability. *Journal of Applied Research in Intellectual Disabilities*, *29*(1), 93–98. https://doi.org/10.1111/jar.12170

World Health Organization. (2020, November). *Guidelines on physical activity and sedentary behaviour*. https://www.who.int/publications/i/item/9789240015128

World Health Organization. (2023, July). *Assessing national capacity for the prevention and control of noncommunicable diseases: Report of the 2021 global survey*. https://www.who.int/publications/i/item/9789240071698

Yuan, Y., Ding, J., Wang, C., Zhang, S., Wang, Y., Liu, Y., & Liu, J. (2022). The after-school sedentary behavior status among children and adolescents with intellectual disabilities. *Front Psychiatry*, *13*, 1049180. https://doi.org/10.3389/fpsyt.2022.1049180

5 New Perspectives in Digital Health for Patient Engagement in Cardiovascular Prevention

The Rehab+ Experience

Marta Lago Arenas, Caroline IJkema and Berta Jover

Introduction: Enabling patient empowerment to address care after a heart attack

> *"When I am stressed, it feels like an internal unrest, and I think 'could it be another attack?'"*
>
> *"The worry sticks with you, always."*
>
> (Post myocardial infarction patient, Germany 2017)

One million people suffer from a myocardial infarction each year in Europe. Without the right support, many of them will fail to come to terms with the lifestyle improvements that are so necessary to lower the risk of a next event. Patients who have experienced a cardiovascular event are at high risk of experiencing another, and each subsequent event is likely to be more severe (Raymond et al., 2014). Cardiovascular disease continues to be the main cause of death in Europe, with 1.8 million deaths and approximately €282 billion in expenses each year (Wilkins et al., 2023; Luengo-Fernandez et al., 2023).

Cardiac rehabilitation programs have proven efficient in helping patients recover from a heart attack, educate them into an improved lifestyle and lower their cardiovascular risk. However, their reach is limited: on average, only roughly one-third of all eligible patients access cardiac rehabilitation programs in the European Union (EU) (Brouwers et al., 2020). The causes of the limited access are diverse and complex. Physical distance from rehab centers and difficulty in dedicating the time to the program due to care burden or work obligations are common reasons for patients abandoning or not joining these programs. Also, their duration, six weeks on average, could be too short to have a sustainable impact on lifestyle in the long term. COVID-19 compounded these factors, making access to these services difficult, and most rehabilitation units had to close or limit their involvement. The pandemic sharpened the urgency for healthcare systems in Europe to provide support and education that is closer to patients and fosters their autonomy.

DOI: 10.4324/9781003568650-6

Rehab+ was created as a response to this challenge: a digitally enabled program to future-proof high-quality cardiac rehabilitation, making it accessible to many patients in the immediate aftermath of a heart attack. Rehab+ is a digital cardiac rehabilitation solution that supports patients in the 12-month journey after a myocardial infarction (MI). It helps patients as they transition back to their daily lives and educates them in building their ability to stay engaged with their health. This approach helps patients adopt and establish long-lasting healthier lifestyles and thereby manage their cardiac risk to prevent a next heart attack. Its ultimate goal is to enable the person to transition from a passive recovery mindset into an active mindset for chronic self-care.

Conveniently delivered through an app for patients and a web-based dashboard for caregivers, Rehab+ provides regular support from a human coach who helps patients assess their lifestyle and set their personal lifestyle objectives to reduce their cardiac risk. Through the app, patients can track their progress toward their goals, receive educational content addressing their personal needs and situation and access community support via group sessions.

From its inception and throughout the development and implementation process, the program was focused on understanding the patient's needs and pain points in a very difficult phase of their life and addressing them with a suitable solution. Hence, at every step, patients and caregivers cocreated the solution via regular patient interviews and working sessions, applying a human centered design approach. Beyond patients, the participatory approach extends to rehabilitation teams: the transition from conventional rehab to a digitally based education service such as Rehab+ is complex. Continuous co-creation with the teams and reflective practice during implementation helped to identify and overcome hurdles, constantly enrich the program and make it more robust for future implementations.

Rehab+ was codeveloped by a diverse consortium of healthcare players, including hospitals (Zuyderland, Vall d'Hebron, Virgen de la Victoria), a digital health provider (Liva Healthcare), a university (CARIM, from Maastricht University) and an industrial partner (Amgen). With the support of the EIT Health in Education Award grant in 2021, the consortium has been driving the implementation of Rehab+ in clinical practice in four centers, and performing a scientific evaluation of its impact on health outcomes as compared with conventional rehabilitation services.

Rehab+ was developed during 2019 and 2021 and implemented from 2022 onwards. The scientific evaluation, currently ongoing, is testing the impact of the program on patients' cardiovascular health and quality of life. This evaluation is comparing it to the golden standard of face-to-face rehabilitation programs – a hard requirement for considering the incorporation of telerehabilitation to the standard of care for post-MI patients. The results of this study will be the subject of a scientific publication.

This chapter focuses on the many learnings that the cocreation, implementation and evaluation brought about, and the implications for future health education programs. This text is based on a synthesis of documentation produced to bring Rehab+ to life, as well as the reflections and experience of the people involved, including the authors, lead cardiologists, rehabilitation nurses and coaches, clinical investigators, technologists, designers, patients and caregivers, and the privacy and compliance experts. We will delve into the following topics:

- A collaborative effort in a diverse consortium
- Reframing post-MI care: from acute recovery to training for a new life
- Rehab+ as program, service and digital platform
- Learnings from implementation in clinical practice
- Impact evaluation
- A reflection on Rehab+ and the transformation of healthcare education
- Future perspectives: Rehab+ and establishing digital rehabilitation at scale

A collaborative effort in a diverse consortium

Rehab+ was conceived and brought to life by a diverse consortium of organizations with the support of EIT Health (European Institute of Innovation and Technology for Healthcare). Each organization brought its own set of priorities and capabilities in the space of patient engagement and cardiovascular secondary prevention, and came together to design and implement a program with the common goal of improving accessible care for people having suffered a heart attack.

- Amgen, a global biotech company with a base in California, established a strategic focus on cardiovascular secondary prevention in Europe, as well as a commitment to value-based healthcare.
- Liva Healthcare, a digital health startup based in Copenhagen, developed a digital platform to enable efficient coaching and behavioral change.
- Zuyderland Hospital in the Netherlands has prioritized digital transformation. Prof. Dr. Arnoud Van't Hof, interventional cardiologist, championed an ongoing effort to transform post-MI pathways by introducing digitally enabled services to enhance care and improve outcomes.
- The University Hospital of Virgen de la Victoria in Malaga (Spain) and Hospital Vall d'Hebron in Barcelona (Spain), led by their head of interventional cardiology Dr. Gomez Doblas and cardiologist Dr. Jordi Lozano, respectively, sought to improve the reach of their cardiac rehabilitation programs and alleviate the ever-growing waiting lists. They are keen pioneers in piloting digital health solutions to improve care and outcomes.
- The Cardiovascular Research Institute of Maastricht University (CARIM), a leading research institution for cardiovascular preventative health, completed the consortium from an academic perspective and led the evaluation.

EIT Health offered a suitable framework for collaboration, enabling a diverse group of organizations to come together and make Rehab+ a reality.

Without this overarching scheme, it would have been very difficult to coordinate organizations with different priorities, urgencies and processes. Having been granted the EIT Health Education Award 2021, the consortium came together to implement and conduct a clinical evaluation of the Rehab+ program, with the endorsement of the Spanish and Dutch Societies of Cardiology (SEC and DS, respectively) and Farca, a patient association in Malaga, Spain.

Challenges (and blessings) of COVID-19

In early 2020, as the future partners co-created Rehab+ and prepared for its implementation, the pandemic hit. COVID-19 brought about a double-edged new reality, making it more urgent and challenging at the same time. On the one hand, the pandemic imposed remote support of patients: many rehabilitation efforts were paused or delayed in the first wave in 2020, because patients were kept away from hospitals except for essential interventions. Hence, health centers accelerated efforts to implement telemedicine solutions.

On the other hand, the attention of centers in the first wave and in severe phases of subsequent waves, was necessarily on short-term urgencies. Prevention programs, although in line with strategic health objectives, suffered as hospital resources were repeatedly assigned to address the peaks in demand caused by the pandemic (Scherrenberg et al., 2021).

Another challenge faced in the consortium was moving the collaboration fully to the digital realm. Cocreation and field research with patients, caregivers and rehabilitation teams moved online. The impact of this shift was profound in methodology as well as collaboration dynamics. We can say that the creation of Rehab+ was, in itself, a prototype in digital transformation.

Reframing post-MI care: From acute recovery to training for a new normal

Inspired by growing knowledge of e-health interventions to improve health behaviors (Brandt et al., 2018), Rehab+ was created to tackle a critical question: **how can patients overcome fear after a heart attack and be empowered to improve and maintain their lifestyle?**

Achieving such a change in behavior demands a profound shift in people's mindset, from acute recovery to proactive management of cardiovascular risk as a chronic condition (Ryan & Deci, 2000). Early dialogue and research with patients and caregivers (sustained along the design and implementation process) inspired a new solution paradigm:

- From providing point-care to support along the patient journey
- From prescribing care to cocreating care with patients
- From an intensive rehab period to training for a new normal

The Rehab+ concept was inspired by this paradigm and designed together with patients and caregivers in Switzerland, Spain and the Netherlands. It followed an iterative, care-centered approach that included workshops, in-home

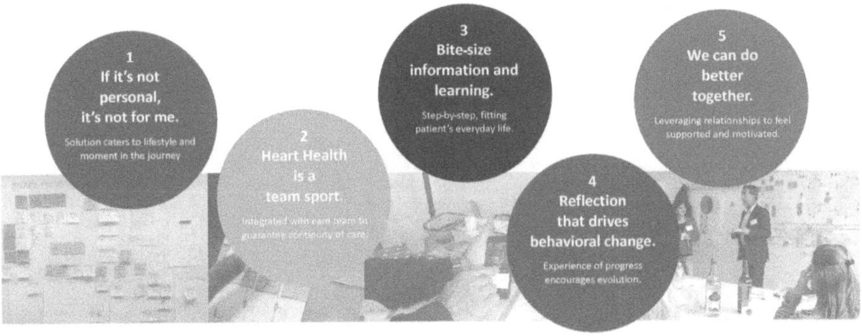

Figure 5.1 Research-based requirements for engaging patients post-heart attack (Source: Amgen and The Care Lab).

visits, in-depth interviews and group conversations in the design process led by Amgen and The Care Lab, a design organization specializing in health and care. As a result, a set of requirements (Figure 5.1) helped outline a "minimum desirable product" to ensure a successful patient experience: personalized content and interactions, connection with healthcare teams, integration in the care pathway and a flexible, step-by-step learning program. The Liva Healthcare platform, with proven results in helping chronic diabetes patients (Komkova et al., 2019), offered an optimal base to develop a clinically efficient solution toward these requirements defined by patients.

Rehab+ as program, service and digital platform

Rehab+ was conceived as a program, a service and a platform to offer a cohesive experience (Figure 5.2).

- *As a Program*: Rehab+ is a 12-month cardiac rehabilitation program focused on lifestyle changes and health education with periodic coaching sessions. It empowers patients to set and maintain their health goals while facilitating physical and emotional recovery.
- *As a Service*: Rehab+ offers a personalized experience by blending digital tools with real-life coaching structured around a guiding service blueprint. Integrated into post-MI care pathways, patients receive continuous support from trained coaches, who provide expert advice tailored to individual needs.
- *As a Digital Platform*: Rehab+, through the platform from Liva Healthcare, facilitates remote monitoring, self-tracking and communication between patients and healthcare providers. The platform can also integrate wearable devices and offers real-time feedback, ensuring a personalized and adaptable rehabilitation process.

Rehab+ features two interfaces: a mobile app for patients and a web-based dashboard for coaches. Ease-of-use in both cases ensures seamless access to critical information and support.

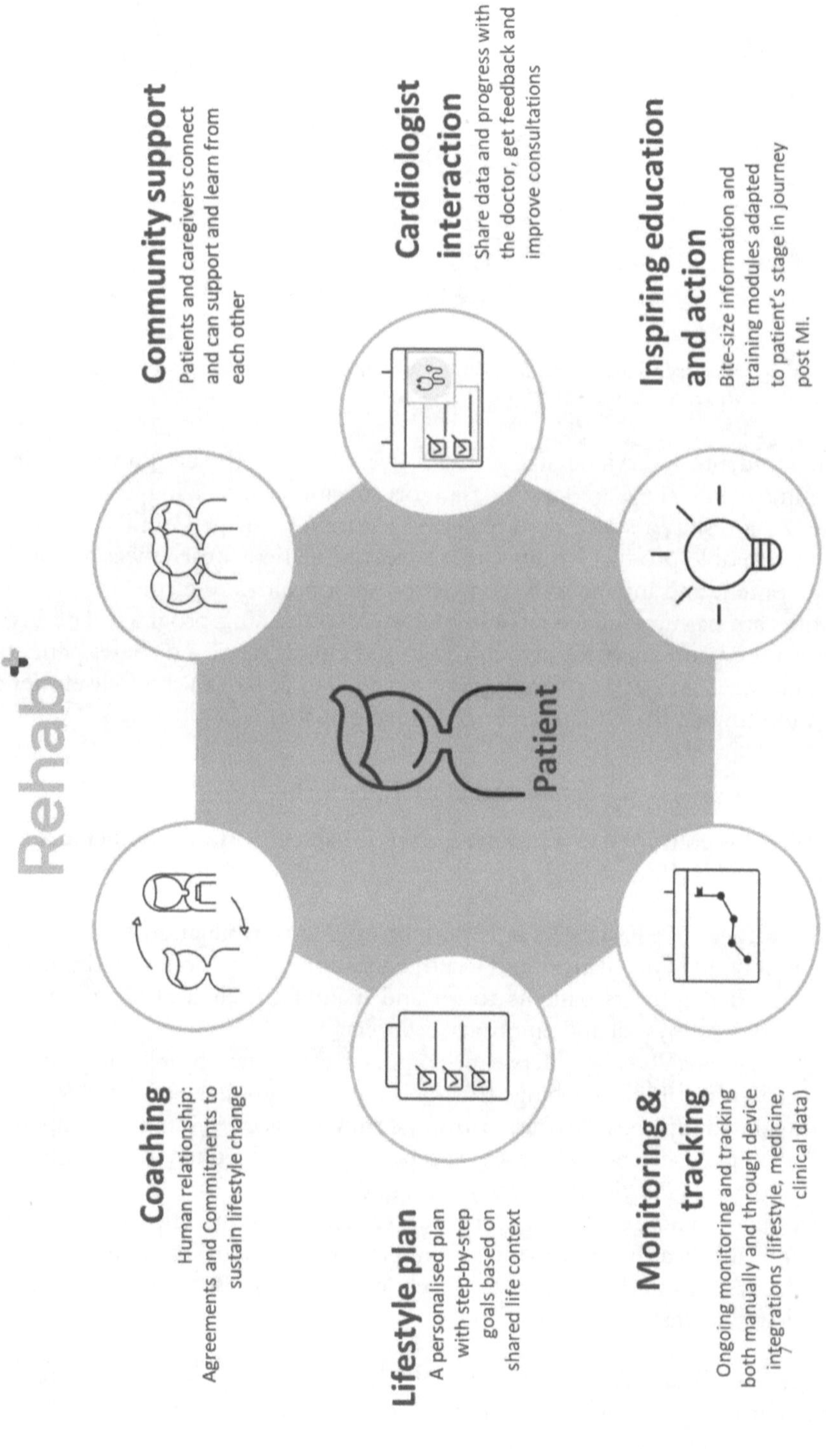

Figure 5.2 Rehab+ building elements (Image Courtesy of Amgen and EIT Health).

The coach's panel provides individual monitoring of a patient's progress, including session timelines and interaction history. Coaches can use text and video messaging for ongoing communication, offering timely feedback to keep patients engaged and motivated.

The patient interface is designed to facilitate consistent goal tracking on their physical activity, heart rate and other metrics of their choice (i.e., fruit pieces per day) while staying connected with their coaches.

A set of key features supports the collaboration of patients and coaches toward the desired behavioral change:

- **A personalized rehabilitation plan** is created collaboratively by patient and coach. It outlines achievable goals reflecting a patient's desires and capabilities. It is formalized through video or text, reinforcing commitment and revisited in subsequent scheduled coaching sessions.
- **Progress tracking** occurs in the app through historical graphs that record key lifestyle metrics, such as physical activity, nutrition and stress management. Progress visualization has been proven to enhance motivation to keep up with personal goals.
- **A content library** offers coaches educational modules or "pills" on a range of subjects to select and share to address a patient's need at a given moment. The topics were identified in collaboration with patients and rehabilitation experts, covering topics from nutrition, exercise and cardiac health education to sexual and psychosocial well-being. These contents, short and easy to read, provide actionable information that promotes autonomous lifestyle improvements and have been adapted for local use and validated with local and European guidelines for cardiovascular prevention (Figure 5.3).
- **Group interactions**: Rehab+ allows coaches to create patient groups based on similar interests, such as physical activity or adopting healthier habits. Peer support and interaction provide emotional support and motivation

Figure 5.3 Example of educational materials as shown in the Rehab+ App, Spanish version: Fish and Omega3, Cardiovascular Workout at Home, Caregiver Support, How Cholesterol Affects the Body. (Image courtesy of Amgen).

and are key elements in conventional rehabilitation (this feature will be implemented after the pilot programs).

- **Communication and human support**. Patients can ask questions and receive timely feedback from their coach without waiting for scheduled sessions, which is vital for addressing concerns and maintaining motivation when facing challenges during recovery.

All in all, Rehab+ offers a holistic and personalized solution for cardiac rehabilitation. With its robust set of features, including digital tracking, personalized plans and real-time interaction, Rehab+ aims to help users achieve lasting rehabilitation outcomes and keep their cardiovascular risk under control (Figure 5.4).

Learnings from implementation in clinical practice

Rehab+ is an educational service that combines digital and nondigital elements and is inserted in post-MI care pathways. The implementation and pilot process offered a unique learning opportunity for centers and partners to adapt the program's blueprint to the needs and resources of each hospital.

All centers maintained a common platform, library of educational materials, the service blueprint structure and common evaluation objectives. However, the adaptation required flexibility in the program, such as:

- Target populations depending on the local environment, priorities and inclusion guidelines.
- Onboarding of patients fit the specificities of each pathway.
- Each rehab team adapted the predefined interview schedule slightly to their needs. In Zuyderland, coaching was delivered by nurses and physiotherapists, the same interdisciplinary team offering conventional rehabilitation. In the Spanish hospitals, they were rehab nurses with full dedication to the digital program.

This balancing act between a common program framework and the flexibility in execution required intense alignment among partners, but eventually allowed a very consistent implementation across centers. Moreover, it has provided a solid foundation for scientific evaluation as well as a wealth of practical insight. This combination is extremely valuable for centers that wish to establish digitally delivered patient care solutions. The following paragraphs illustrate important learnings from the implementation.

Setup: Complexity of platform and data integration should not be underestimated

Implementing a digital solution that connects patients with their healthcare team in a therapeutic context demands strict quality, regulatory and safety standards, and a legal framework that reinforces the commitment of all

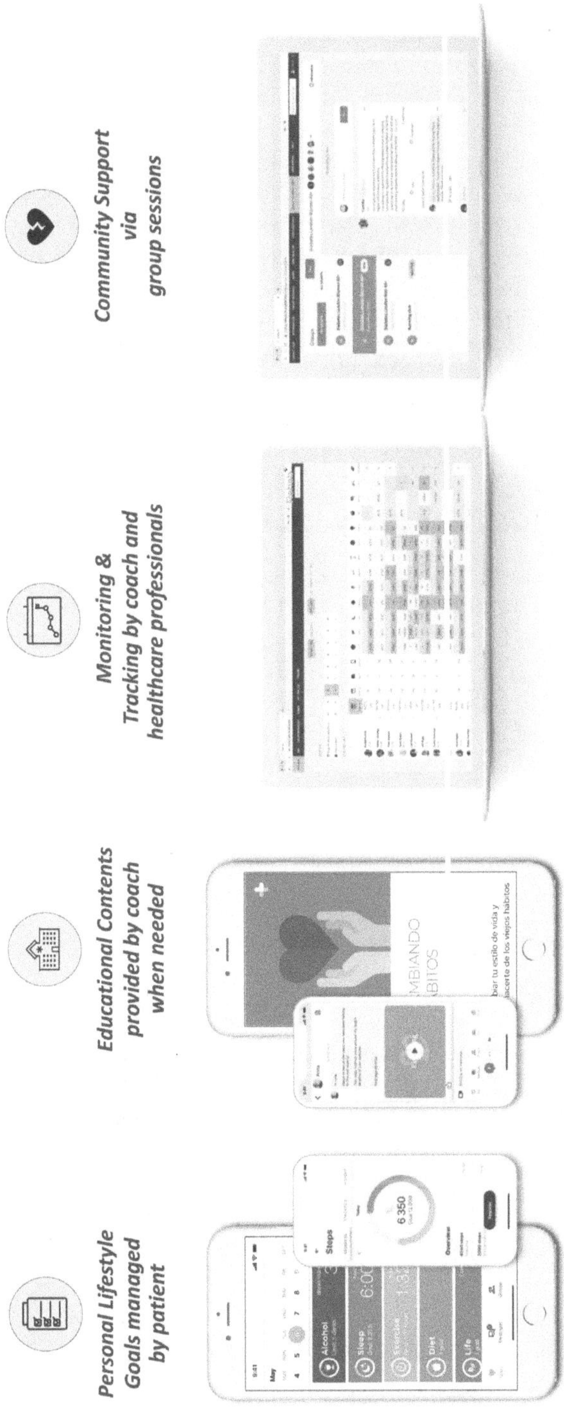

Figure 5.4 Rehab+ digital platform (Source: Live Healthcare & Amgen).

organizations involved to meet these standards. The technological foundation of Rehab+, delivered through the LIVA platform, consisted of a digital app and a coaching platform for the caregivers and, in the case of Zuyderland Hospital, a wearable device for tracking vitality and heart rate.

The Rehab+ platform was classified as a nonmedical device, which simplified the road to implementation and pilot. Aiming at simplifying the pilot setup, the platform did not integrate with electronic medical records in any of the centers. Despite these factors, the platform implementation was more complex and took longer than expected. Each center performed their own data privacy and safety evaluation (beyond compliance with common EU standards) at their own pace, and the coordination of respective data, technology and legal teams took a lot of time and effort by the investigators. The recommendation for educational programs within a therapeutic context is to understand the complexity of technology and data integration and engage with cross-functional teams and management early on from the development phase.

Zuyderland: A multidisciplinary approach fostered a culture of innovation

Zuyderland Medisch Centrum was the first hospital in the Netherlands to implement telerehabilitation, also motivated by a need for innovative treatment methods during the COVID-19 pandemic. The implementation was led by a core team including medical specialists, rehabilitation nurses, physiotherapists, platform support specialists, hospital management, IT and data experts, investigators and a healthcare consultant. The collaboration extended to patients and facilitated continuous adaptation, making the service blueprint robust and human-centered. This ongoing partnership addressed immediate challenges and fostered a culture of innovation that will help integrate new digital behavioral interventions in the future.

Patient engagement in synch with post-MI care pathway

The Rehab+ program was integrated in the care pathways following center-specific inclusion criteria. For instance, patients at very high risk were prescribed only in-person rehabilitation in Malaga, leaving the digital program for moderate- to high-risk patients. The program had to comply with the guidelines for cardiovascular rehabilitation in each center. This is the reason, for instance, why Zuyderland had to incorporate a wearable device for registering the patient's heart rate when exercising. After onboarding, each center adapted the general blueprint depending on their resources and objectives as well as their established care path for patients post MI, in line with a common service blueprint to promote sustained lifestyle improvement.

Adopting a digital program involves evolving roles and adapting workflows

With the introduction of telerehabilitation, the role of the rehab team changes substantially and requires specific training. For Rehab+, the rehabilitation professionals received training on how to master the platform and interact with patients digitally, including role-play to simulate patient interactions.

Digital coaches' new responsibilities (onboarding, coaching sessions, monitoring progress, providing motivational support and education via the platform, etc.) demanded adjustments of routines and workflows, and particular challenges for teams offering both regular rehab and telerehabilitation. The Zuyderland team worked collaboratively to address this challenge and solve specific patient issues together. A different approach was adopted in Malaga, where a rehabilitation nurse was solely dedicated to Rehab+.

Step-by-step implementation and feedback loops enabled continuous improvement

In Zuyderland, the pilot was implemented in phases. In a starting "beta" phase with 10 patients, feedback from patients and healthcare professionals led to valuable improvements. For example, the onboarding process was simplified by eliminating several unnecessary steps, and the number of mandatory coaching sessions was adjusted following patients' feedback. Young patients with high digital literacy provided specific feedback on the app, ensuring that a broader audience would accept it in the future. A second phase expanded the program to a larger patient group using Rehab+. Having incorporated lessons learned from the initial group, regular feedback loops were maintained to enable iterative improvement.

Impact evaluation

> *"I am very positive about using the app—it has made my progress more visible and understandable, which really motivates me to keep going. It's encouraging to see my own improvements laid out clearly."*
>
> (Patient in Zuyderland telerehabilitation program).

> *"This is truly something remarkable that we're building here. With the use of a device, patients are able to maintain much closer contact with their healthcare team, giving them an extra push to stay on track and fostering a supportive health environment focused on lifestyle. It's still in its early stages, but this could add real value for cardiac rehabilitation in the future."*
>
> (Healthcare Professional in Zuyderland)

The pilot implementation of Rehab+ as a telerehabilitation service at Zuyderland, Virgen de la Victoria and Vall d'Hebron hospitals presents an opportunity to evaluate how digital health programs can improve patient engagement and lifestyle. Within the consortium plan, these hospitals and CARIM from Maastricht University set up a non-randomized observational study comparing Rehab+ participants with patients in conventional or no rehabilitation programs (van Mierlo et al., 2024). Additionally, team communications and regular activity analyses enrich conclusions about the program's impact. The evaluation focuses on several levels:

- *Clinical impact*: Does Rehab+ reduce cardiovascular risk and improve the quality of life while fostering positive health habits? Rehab+ is assessed against the gold standard of in-person rehabilitation. Previous research establishes that telerehabilitation can be as effective as traditional rehab for reducing cardiovascular risks. Yet, demonstrating acceptable outcomes for Rehab+ is essential for clinical adoption beyond the pilot study. The study's primary outcome measures quality of life and examines dimensions like vitality, physical and emotional functioning, pain and mental health. Secondary measures include rehospitalization rates, physical activity changes, smoking cessation, fitness and lipid and glucose levels. Patients are evaluated at 3, 6 and 12 months after their event.
- *Patient reach and adoption*: Can telerehabilitation effectively reach more patients, especially those unable to access conventional programs? What barriers to adoption exist, and which patient cohorts benefit most from a remote approach? The trial design is unique, allowing participants to choose between center-based and telerehabilitation options (except Vall d'Hebron, which lacks in-person rehab). This design will offer precious insight into patient decision-making. The evaluation will analyze patients' attitudes toward e-health and measure engagement and effectiveness in practice. Demographic and biomedical data will help identify patient profiles that benefit most, informing future program optimization.
- *Patient experience*: What is the specific value created by a digitally delivered program, and how does it affect the participant's engagement? What are the defining factors for building participants' trust in a digital platform? What makes patients adhere to the program for one year? What are the challenges to persevere?

  As of May 2025, the study is ongoing, with data collection completed and data analysis and conclusions in progress. However, two years of experience and early data analysis offer a positive prospect for Rehab+ compared to conventional rehab. Additionally, the study has offered several preliminary learnings.

Rehab+ does improve access to vulnerable patients...

Regular rehabilitation involves intensive in-person support from a multidisciplinary team over a short period (six weeks in Malaga, three months in Zuyderland) requiring frequent hospital visits. Telerehabilitation, in turn, allows patients to engage in personalized recovery programs remotely, which fits easily in their daily routines.

Rehab+ has indeed enabled access for patients previously excluded and deprived of post-MI care: people living far from the hospital (particularly relevant in Virgen de la Victoria, with a substantial part of the target population living remotely), patients with pressing professional obligations (i.e., freelancers) or care responsibilities (this one affecting women disproportionately, according to experience of investigators and rehabilitations teams involved).

The free choice for patients between Rehab+ and the conventional program in Zuyderland is an opportunity to gain a deeper understanding of the motivations and drivers of patients to adopt telerehabilitation, beyond the previously mentioned hypothesis, and why adoption is slower than previously assumed.

... yet personal support is still needed to address the digital barrier

Lack of digital literacy limits the potential of telerehabilitation to expand access and impacts elderly patients the most. To mitigate this barrier, all centers introduced support measures beyond the digital platform to help patients use the app confidently to monitor their progress and communicate with their coach. Each patient received setup assistance and, in the Dutch case, training on using wearables. Personalized support smooths the transition to digital care: in Malaga, family members joined onboarding of elderly patients to ensure technical support for vulnerable patients, reinforcing inclusivity. Sustained engagement relied on close collaboration between patients and the care team, emphasizing the importance of personal touchpoints in digital coaching.

Generally, patients show high appreciation for the continuous support by the coach, but trust must be established early

Although still pending formal evaluation, all investigators highlight how patients appreciate coaches' support and the possibility to contact them when needed. Prof. Arnoud Van't Hof highlights the importance of establishing personal trust at the beginning via direct conversations as a prerequisite for patients to engage with the digital tool and the tracking program afterward. If patients trust their team, they will trust the tool and engage with it, so trust in digitally delivered support must be established early on.

From rehab nurse to health coach

Prof. Van't Hof describes differences in attitude and inclination to become Rehab+ coaches in rehabilitation teams. For instance, the fact that group sessions were unavailable in digital format, so highly valued in rehab teams for motivation, was a limitation. However, those early adopters who embraced the coaching function were able to present and motivate patients in a particularly efficient manner. Coaches' attitude has an influence on patients' adoption of telerehabilitation.

With Rehab+, the coach is "practically at home with the patient" (in the words of one of the coaches): there is a connection. Dr. Gómez Doblas points out that soft skills to motivate patients are crucial for health coaches, as much as their clinical rehabilitation capabilities.

Future perspectives: A reflection on Rehab+ for the transformation of healthcare education

Rehab+ as an educational program facilitates patient learning for lifestyle improvement and training of healthcare professionals into a digitally delivered coaching role. It can arguably serve as a model for future health education, with the following factors illustrating its educational and training value.

Innovative pedagogical approaches

Content "pills" are provided by the coach to serve specific needs at a given moment. This hands-on approach helps patients internalize health behaviors and understand their significance, making the learning process more meaningful. The program also fosters collaborative learning, which enables peer interactions among patients. Sharing experiences in both digital and face-to-face settings enhances collective understanding and builds a supportive community, which is crucial for motivation and commitment to lifestyle changes.

A focus on empowerment and mindset change

The program prioritizes patient empowerment by shifting from disease management to health promotion. The final objective is to help participants transition from a passive, recovery mindset to a proactive one of prevention and self-care. This pedagogical shift encourages patients to take control of their health and actively engage in their rehabilitation process, thereby enhancing their sense of agency and improving their decision-making ability.

Digitally enabled personalization

In the context of the coaching conversation and feedback from healthcare professionals, patients receive personalized educational contents that address their specific challenges and goals at the moment. This individualized approach ensures a deeper understanding and retention of health concepts.

Integration of digital health tools and hybrid approaches

The Rehab+ app and platform (including wearables) showcase technology and devices integrated into a health education program that combines digital and nondigital interactions. The digital platform serves as a case study for the application of e-health technologies and a best practice in digital coaching and remote patient management.

Interdisciplinary learning and cocreation

The involvement of diverse healthcare professionals, including cardiologists, nurses and physiotherapists, illustrates the importance of interdisciplinary collaboration in health education. This multifaceted approach enriches the learning experience for both patients and professionals, emphasizing the need for teamwork and interdisciplinarity in achieving optimal health outcomes.

Feedback and continuous improvement

Ongoing feedback mechanisms, such as patient interviews and surveys, provide valuable insights into the program's strengths and areas for improvement. This iterative process can serve as a model for integrating feedback in educational settings, ensuring that curricula remain responsive to learners' inputs.

Focus on patient education with long-term impact

The emphasis on long-term lifestyle changes, expressed by the commitment to supporting patients for a full year, underscores the program's dedication to sustaining health education beyond initial rehabilitation efforts. This approach can serve as a framework for developing educational curricula that prioritize continuous learning.

Future perspectives: Rehab+ and digital rehabilitation at scale

> *"Without a doubt, telerehabilitation solutions are the future to respond to the impossibility of offering face-to-face rehabilitation to the entire target population. Simple and intuitive tools that are easy to navigate for patients of all ages like this one (Rehab+) are necessary. A requirement is that these tools are free to access."*
> (Dr. Juan José Gómez-Doblas)

Looking ahead, the evolution of Rehab+ is likely to take the form of a hybrid care model, blending digital activity with key in-person sessions. Although the digital approach offers convenience and accessibility, patients still value face-to-face interactions, particularly at the beginning. A likely future approach could include initial in-person sessions to build trust and rapport, followed by a period of telerehabilitation, with periodic follow-ups to sustain motivation. This hybrid model must support both patients' needs and efficient healthcare delivery.

Another requisite for establishing the program is to become financially sustainable by fitting the reimbursement model. Currently in the Netherlands, insurance companies provide lower financial support for telerehabilitation compared to traditional care, partly due to an underestimation of the time invested in delivering digitally enabled care. Even for a hospital with a strategic focus on digital transformation (Zuyderland), low reimbursement makes human coaching delivered digitally less appealing. For Rehab+ or an equivalent program to be widely adopted, it's essential that reimbursement policies reflect the time and effort all healthcare professionals, particularly nurses, invest in delivering both in-person and digital care.

In the Spanish hospitals, the adoption of a specific digital platform as standard in care is a long and complex process from an administrative, financial and technology standpoint. The continuation of the program through the current platform is therefore uncertain. However, Malaga Center is currently exploring alternatives to maintain telerehabilitation given the positive results in reaching new groups of patients.

On a broader scale, the experience with Rehab+ reveals that expanding telerehabilitation programs internationally, particularly across Europe, must occur on a country-by-country, region-by-region basis, because every healthcare system tailors the program to their unique approval and reimbursement framework, environment and needs. Rehab+, having developed a robust therapeutic digital framework adaptable to different healthcare ecosystems, **highlights the importance of supporting international collaboration to create and develop digital health programs**. In this regard, EIT Health plays a key role in enabling collaborative innovation efforts to scale solutions.

There is, undoubtedly, a European trend toward the adoption of telerehabilitation programs as a new standard of care, especially in cardiac rehabilitation. Similar initiatives are emerging across the continent, signaling that digital health solutions like Rehab+ are becoming integral to modern healthcare.

Conclusions

Rehab+ represents a transformative approach to cardiac rehabilitation for patients after a heart attack, seeking to shift from an acute recovery mindset to a proactive one of self-care and prevention: training for a new life. It emphasizes long-term engagement to achieve sustainable behavioral change and the integration of digital health solutions into the secondary care pathways. Rehab+ was designed, implemented and evaluated between 2020 and 2024, enabled and supported by the EIT Health in a consortium of diverse partners in the Netherlands and Spain.

The program has demonstrated its ability to reach a broader range of patients, particularly those unable to access traditional rehabilitation due to distance, work or care obligations, although limited health literacy still requires additional support efforts. Although final analysis of data is still pending, personal and holistic support sustained over time and offered remotely has been very positively received by patients. It has also helped transform the role of the rehabilitation professional by highlighting the importance of emotional and interpersonal skills as much as clinical education.

The inclusive, human-centered approach involved patients, caregivers and healthcare professionals throughout the process. It has been instrumental in refining the program to meet real-world needs, ensuring adherence and establishing a value-based framework for its evaluation. The ongoing scientific evaluation of Rehab+ will offer a deeper understanding of the value of telerehabilitation for patients and the levers to multiply adoption.

The program's adaptability to diverse healthcare environments, as shown in the pilot studies, highlights its future potential for scaling and translating to new centers. The adoption of telerehabilitation, however, is far from automatic: it requires adaptation of roles and ways of working, a strong commitment from management and a step-by-step approach.

Rehab+ could be adapted and delivered through a different platform, applying the already refined service blueprint, features, coach training and educational contents. The translation of Rehab+ to other platforms, leveraging the experience gathered during the pilots, is a necessity as centers consolidate digital patient engagement platforms across different therapeutic areas. The ability to transfer Rehab+ to a new platform opens new perspectives for continuity, but it takes time, effort and commitment from the team and leadership.

All in all, the future permanence and further expansion of Rehab+ and other telerehabilitation programs depend on gaining a richer understanding of patients' needs, integrating flexible hybrid care models, securing a sustainable financial model and translating its application across different healthcare systems. Scientific societies and health authorities already recognize the clinical value of telerehabilitation (Frederix et al., 2019): it is a growing trend. Going forward, insurance plans and public health systems should gradually adjust their models to support digital solutions for patient engagement in cardiovascular secondary prevention at scale. In this context, Rehab+ can serve as a blueprint for modern cardiac rehabilitation, driving patient inclusion and better outcomes, helping shape the future of digital healthcare in Europe and inspiring new paths in health education.

Acknowledgments

Special thanks go to Professor Arnoud Van't Hof, head of the department of Interventional Cardiology in Maastricht University Medical Center and Zuyderland Medical Center in Heerlen (the Netherlands) and Dr. Juan Jose Gómez Doblas, Head of Clinical Cardiology of University of Hospital Virgen de la Victoria in Malaga, Spain. They provided guidance, feedback and inspiration to the creation of this piece.

We want to express our gratitude to all the organizations that formed the consortium: Liva Healthcare (Denmark), Zuyderland Hospital (Netherlands), University Hospital of Virgen de la Victoria in Malaga (Spain) and Hospital Vall d'Hebron in Barcelona (Spain), CARIM (Cardiovascular research Institute of Maastricht University) and Amgen (both its global and Spanish organization). Their determination and commitment of resources (human and financial) were instrumental in making Rehab+ a reality.

The implementation and evaluation of Rehab+ was supported by an Education grant from EIT Health in 2021 (Grant Number 210707). The initial conceptualization and design were driven and financed by Amgen with the support of The Care Lab.

References

Brandt, C. J., Clemensen, J., Nielsen, J. B., & Søndergaard, J. (2018). Drivers for successful long-term lifestyle change, the role of e-health: A qualitative interview study. *BMJ Open*, 8(3), e017466. https://doi.org/10.1136/bmjopen-2017-017466

Brouwers, R. W. M., van Exel, H. J., van Hal, J. M. C., Jorstad, H. T., de Kluiver, E. P., Kraaijenhagen, R. A., Kuijpers, P. M. J. C., van der Linde, M. R., Spee, R. F., Sunamura, M., Uszko-Lencer, N. H. M. K., Vromen, T., Wittekoek, M. E., & Kemps, H. M. C. (2020). Cardiac tele-rehabilitation as an alternative to centre-based cardiac rehabilitation. *Netherlands Heart Journal*, 28, 443–451. https://doi.org/10.1007/s12471-020-01432-y

Frederix, I., Caiani, E. G., Dendale, P., Anker, S., Bax, J., Böhm, A., Cowie, M., Crawford, J., de Groot, N., Dilaveris, P., Hansen, T., Koehler, F., Krstačić, G., Lambrinou, E., Lancellotti, P., Meier, P., Neubeck, L., Parati, G., Piotrowicz, E., ... van der Velde, E. (2019). ESC e-cardiology working group position paper: Overcoming challenges in digital health implementation in cardiovascular medicine. *European Journal of Preventive Cardiology*, 26(11), 1166–1177. https://doi.org/10.1177/2047487319832394

Komkova, A., Brandt, C. J., Pedersen, D. H., Emneus, M., & Sortsø, C. (2019). Electronic health lifestyle coaching among diabetes patients in a real-life municipality setting: Observational study. *JMIR Diabetes*, 4(1), e12140. https://doi.org/10.2196/12140

Luengo-Fernandez, R., Walli-Attaei, M., Gray, A., Torbica, A., Maggioni, A. P., Huculeci, R., ... & Leal, J. (2023). Economic burden of cardiovascular diseases in the European Union: a population-based cost study. *European Heart Journal*, *44*(45), 4752–4767. https://doi.org/10.1093/eurheartj/ehad583

Raymond, C., Cho, L., Rocco, M., & Hazen, S. L. (2014). New guidelines for reduction of blood cholesterol: Was it worth the wait? *Cleveland Clinic Journal of Medicine*, 81, 11–19. https://doi.org/10.3949/ccjm.81a.13161

Ryan, R. M., & Deci, E. L. (2000). Self-determination theory and the facilitation of intrinsic motivation, social development, and well-being. *American Psychologist*, 55(1), 68–78. https://doi.org/10.1037/0003-066X.55.1.68

Scherrenberg, M., Wilhelm, M., Hansen, D., Voller, H., Cornelissen, V., Frederix, I., Kemps, H., & Dendale, P. (2021). The future is now: A call for action for cardiac telerehabilitation in the COVID-19 pandemic from the secondary prevention and rehabilitation section of the European Association of Preventive Cardiology. *European Journal of Preventive Cardiology*, 28(5), 524–540. https://doi.org/10.1177/2047487320939671

van Mierlo, R. F. R., Houben, V. J. G., Rikken, S. A. O. F., Gomez-Doblas, J. J., Lozano-Torres, J. J., & van 't Hof, A. W. J. (2024). Cardiac (tele)rehabilitation in routine clinical practice for patients with coronary artery disease: Protocol of the REHAB+trial. *Frontiers in Cardiovascular Medicine*, 11, 1387148. https://doi.org/10.3389/fcvm.2024.1387148

Wilkins, E., Wilson, L., Wickramasinghe, K., Bhatnagar, P., Leal, J., Luengo-Fernandez, R., ... & Townsend, N. (2017). *European cardiovascular disease statistics 2017. European Heart Network*, Brussels. pp. 1–192. https://ehnheart.org/wp-content/uploads/2023/07/CVD-Statistics.pdf

6 PsyHealth worXs! The Road to Health-Promoting Working Conditions

Jessica Lang and Lisa Auweiler

Introduction: The need to learn about mental health prevention

In 2020, the massive open online course (MOOC) "PsyHealth worXs! Psychosocial Health Prevention and Work Standards" started its first instructor-paced course run on an open educational learning platform. The online training provides information and hands-on material concerning psychosocial risk assessment (PRA) in companies to support the relevant stakeholders responsible for occupational safety and health (OSH) at work in conducting the legally required preventive action. As of 2023, more than 2,800 learners from all over the world have participated in the course, mainly stemming from the *human health and social work activities* and *education* disciplines. In this chapter, we discuss the need for PRA, why and how we implemented the training content in an online format, what learners have taken home from it so far and how this training could be implemented in a curriculum and extended for a more applied learning experience.

Why is dealing with mental health at work relevant at all? Isn't a person's mental well-being often described as a private issue? Or is dealing with mental well-being – when it comes to work-related illnesses – not a caring duty of the employer? In fact, when we look at specific work characteristics and demands that are posed to individuals at work, it becomes clear that regarding OSH, as with any other physical, chemical, or biological hazards, psychosocial hazards fall under the same responsibility. When we think about the rapidly changing working conditions due to digitalization, we already know that they pose a significant challenge to mental health (Parteka et al., 2024) and innovative potential (Nöhammer & Stichlberger, 2019), particularly within small and medium-sized enterprises (SMEs) (European Agency for Safety and Health at Work., 2019; Latos et al., 2017). Especially within the healthcare sector, mental health is a serious concern, starting as early as in medical training (Braquehais & Vargas-Cáceres, 2023; Patel et al., 2021). In addition to time pressure, dealing with difficult patients is a major source of workplace stress (European Agency for Safety and Health at Work, 2019).

Because work-related challenges to mental health result from job requirements and workplace characteristics, there is the official requirement under

DOI: 10.4324/9781003568650-7

European regulations to systematically assess psychosocial risk factors at work for employees (Hünefeld, 2020). However, many SMEs, including startups, struggle to meet these legal requirements due to a lack of knowledge and skills necessary to conduct effective PRAs (European Agency for Safety and Health at Work., 2013; van den Heuvel et al., 2018). Therefore, this chapter describes the co-development process, implementation and impact of the digital MOOC PsyHealth worXs!, which is designed to empower those responsible with an easily accessible tool to focus on the pedagogical strategies employed.

What is a psychosocial risk assessment?

PRA involves the assessment of psychological and social work characteristics to systematically evaluate whether these characteristics are present in a way that is known from scientific research to function as a potential hazard to worker health and (mental) well-being. The goal of the systematic assessment is to mitigate risks that can significantly impact employees' mental health and productivity by implementing interventions for an optimized work design. According to European Council Directive 89/391/EEC Article 5.1 of 12 June 1989 on the introduction of measures to encourage improvements in the safety and health of workers at work, "the employer shall have a duty to ensure the safety and health of workers in every aspect related to work" (89/391/EEC, 1989). According to Article 6, the employer has the obligation to adapt the workplace to the individual regarding technological aspects, the organization of work, the general working conditions, social relationships and the working environment (89/391/EEC, 1989).

Current challenges for implementing PRA

Despite its importance for health prevention based on scientific knowledge and the legal backing from Europe and national OSH acts, less than 50% of companies have procedures in place to deal with psychosocial risks. The main reason for the low implementation of the important policy is a lack of related knowledge and skills (Beck & Lenhardt, 2019). With the term psychosocial risks, people often assume that the process involves subjective assessment of individual mental health instead of the objective assessment of work demands that may pose a risk to the individual. This accompanies the fear of addressing a stigmatized topic, and companies refrain from the risk assessment to avoid evoking any conflicts. Or, if one wants to discuss occupational stress, employers might say that workers are not stressed so that the assessment is not needed (European Agency for Safety and Health at Work, 2019). Aside from the many misunderstandings, responsibilities are often unclear among different stakeholders and disciplines dealing with OSH. Disciplines that consult on this topic especially report having too little influence on the procedures in place (Beck & Lenhardt, 2019).

In addition, especially SMEs find PRA implementation challenging or even lack an implementation at all. Research has shown that the primary contributing factors for this research-political-practitioner gap are limited financial and human resources and the absence of a systematic approach to OSH management (Beck & Lenhardt, 2019; Champoux & Brun, 2003; van den Heuvel et al., 2018). SMEs typically add the tasks of OSH management to one individual on top of their usual work duties and therefore often lack dedicated, specialized support from trained consulting management structures (Beck & Lenhardt, 2019; European Agency for Safety and Health at Work., 2019). Therefore, it is critical to support employers in gaining knowledge concerning their duties and responsibilities and provide easy access to the relevant information. In fact, a recent qualitative study on barriers and drivers of PRA in German micro and small-sized enterprises with owners and managers showed that these enterprises specifically benefit from easy access to information materials, external support through experts and comprehension of the contents and benefits of PRA (Pavlista et al., 2021).

A further specific barrier in the healthcare sector might be the reversed viewing angle in PRA. A typical approach found in healthcare is to heal, which is also referred to as tertiary prevention. That is, employers and employees working in healthcare are accustomed to treating ill or impaired patients with health issues after they arise. Unlike this relevant perspective, within OSH, the focus of PRA is primary prevention. That is, for those who are responsible for worker health, it is all about tackling potential psychosocial hazards before they negatively impact employee health. Training healthcare professionals and raising awareness about mental health fosters healthy workplaces from the start. Implementing preventive strategies is a didactic shift that is essential and inevitable for reducing psychosocial risks, sustaining employee well-being and ultimately bridging the gap between science, policy and practice. Considering the peculiarities of the healthcare sector and SMEs, when looking for a way to reach out to healthcare professionals and entrepreneurs, it might be to provide them with an easily accessible and flexible educational training program that considers their limited financial and personnel resources to compensate for a lack of expert knowledge.

Cocreation and implementation of PsyHealth worXs!

What exactly is PsyHealth worXs!?

PsyHealth worXs! is a free 6-week online training, hosted on an educational learning platform, that guides participants step-by-step through the PRA process. This MOOC aims to bridge the knowledge and skills gap from research to the practical implementation of PRA, especially in SMEs, as a low-threshold learning opportunity. All the information is presented in short video-based lecture sessions that learners can follow at their own pace. Each week, new content, such as instructional videos, recorded expert interviews, workplace examples, supplementary materials, quizzes and assignments, is sequentially published. The course language is English, but subtitles in nine additional languages are available. By enabling the participants to gain extensive knowledge and skills in PRA implementation and training them in identifying and reducing psychosocial risks before they pose negative health impacts on employees, the MOOC follows a primary prevention approach. Raising awareness of the latter aspect is crucial for establishing the need to start the systematic integration of PRA into workplace safety practices.

What is the target group of PsyHealth worXs!?

The MOOC is suitable for all stakeholders working in the OSH field: first, those responsible for executing OSH at work (e.g., employers, executives, managers, supervisors, HR representatives in the name of the employer); second, all disciplines that have a consultative role for those responsible (e.g., occupational health physicians, occupational safety specialists, occupational health managers); and third, for employee representatives that have a participative role within OSH. The training supports the cooperation of interdisciplinary teams and includes information about responsibilities and roles. It is useful for large companies with many employees, but also especially for SMEs with limited experience, time and resources. The content is broadly applicable for all sectors and industries, but regarding the examples within the training, one focus is on the healthcare sector and occupational health physicians as consulting stakeholders.

How did we conduct cocreation to fulfil learners' expectations?

The first development phase of the MOOC content and design was started with several cocreation activities inviting all addressed stakeholders and practitioners, most of them coming from the healthcare sector. The interdisciplinary workshops provided real-world insights from professionals in different roles and occupations actively working in the field, offering us the opportunity to provide more than only theory teaching in the MOOC. The close collaboration with practitioners was vital for understanding and assessing the actual needs, expectations and challenges that are most crucial and urgent in conducting PRA. We designed a needs assessment to identify the most challenging steps and knowledge gaps in the PRA process cycle (Figure 6.1), that is, where participants reported the strongest need for more knowledge gain. Importantly, the first step, *specification of activities and work areas,* in the risk assessment was already considered a major challenge by most participants. In addition, stakeholders were unsure about the OSH measures available to specifically change psychosocial hazards into better working conditions or how they could ensure that the selected interventions would be successful.

To gain an even deeper understanding of the knowledge gaps in the needs assessment, a qualitative approach was added. It was inspired by so-called user

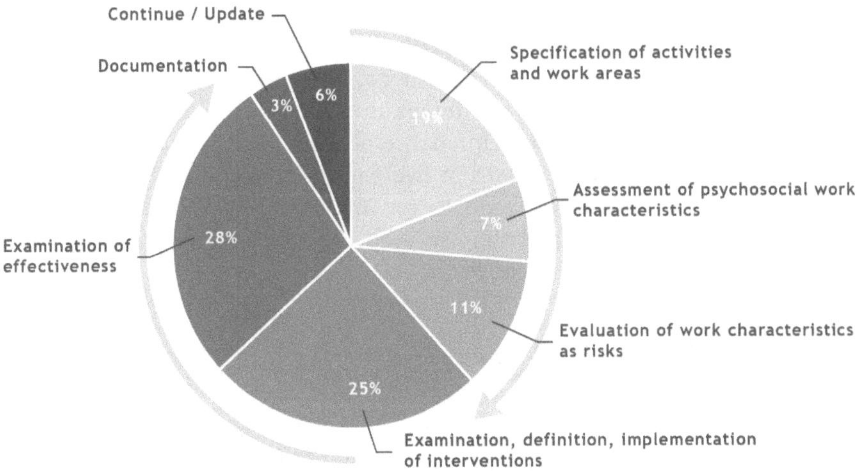

Figure 6.1 The seven steps of the Psychosocial Risk Assessment (PRA) process, showing the distribution of the most challenging steps, due to the highest knowledge deficit, from the cocreation activities with relevant stakeholders (multiple responses possible, 28 individuals participated in the survey, providing a total of 68 answers). The arrow indicates the starting point and direction of the PRA cycle.

stories as established in agile software development (Rupp, 2014). Specifically, at cocreation events, we presented story cards to participants on which they wrote each of their requirements for the MOOC, following a prescribed sentence structure, and provided a corresponding reason (aim) for the requirements. First, they had to indicate their expectations regarding the content they would most urgently require by completing the following sentence: "As a/an [INSERTION OF THEIR OCCUPATIONAL ROLE/responsible person in occupational safety and health, I expect from the MOOC's content that [USER-STORY] so that [USER-STORY]". A completed statement from a workshop participant was for example: "As a MANAGER / responsible person in occupational safety and health, I expect from the MOOC's content AN OVERVIEW OF VARIOUS INTERVENTIONS so that I CAN PREPARE FOR THE INTERVENTIONS DURING THE PLANNING STAGE" [translated from German]. Second, they had to indicate their expectations regarding the design of the learning activity: "As a learner, I expect regarding the MOOC design that [USER-STORY] so that [USER-STORY]". An example of a completed statement is "As a learner, I expect regarding the MOOC design that THERE ARE SIMPLE AND PRACTICABLE OPTIONS FOR THE PRA so that I CAN GET EVERYONE INVOLVED ON BOARD" [translated from German]. Using inductive content analysis (Mayring, 2010), two independent researchers coded the results according to the stakeholder group and summarized them by consensus. This qualitative approach guaranteed that we received well-structured feedback for developing the storyline of the course and setting highlights for more in-depth coverage of the most required topics from a learner's perspective.

In addition to the cocreation workshops, we relied on a project advisory board for ongoing evaluation and integration of continuous feedback loops in both the development and maintenance of the course. The advisory board consisted of seven stakeholders from five European countries. The advisory board provided constructive feedback for integrating realistic use cases and scenarios in the MOOC, and thus ensured the relevance of contents in an ever-changing working environment.

What about course design and pedagogical approach?

Instructional design approach

The MOOC was designed as a step-by-step guide for self-learning and skills adaptation with the goal of training professionals in independently conducting the PRA in their own work contexts. The structure of the MOOC focuses on the main principle of enabling and equipping responsible stakeholders with knowledge and skills to adapt it and reframe it for their own purposes. The learners are guided through the circular PRA process as depicted in Figure 6.1. Week by week, new information is released to deliver chunks of consecutive knowledge and to clarify the sequence of steps. The structure and content of the MOOC are summarized in Table 6.1.

Applied methods

The MOOC employs cutting-edge pedagogical methods in a blended learning design to enhance learning effectiveness and engagement (Guo et al., 2014). The different methods used to provide knowledge, skills and applicational transfer were as follows:

- *Instructional Videos*: The content of the course is presented in instructional videos by two lecturers, who categorize and explain the information using presentation slides, reporting on the key facts through listings, figures and tables with key figures. The combination of showing visual materials and simultaneously guiding through them engages multiple senses, making learning more accessible for diverse learning styles and therefore more effective. Each video lasts about 10 min and there are about three videos per week. The videos present basic knowledge that is checked with quizzes and supplementary materials (Table 6.1). All presentations are available for download on the learning platform.
- *Expert Interviews*: Several interview partners, actively working in the field of occupational health management (but in different roles, branches and company sizes), were invited to conduct semi-structured interviews for the MOOC. The prepared questions covered a broad range of key topics along

the risk assessment cycle and concerns that were raised from the initial co-creation activities. The questions were thematically sorted according to the different steps of the PRA cycle and enriched the learning material with real-world expertise, practical knowledge and varied approaches to solutions to overcome obstacles that textbooks alone cannot offer. Because the experts came from different disciplines, each learner was able to gain insight from the perspective of a neighboring discipline to broaden their horizons.

- *Workplace Examples*: By presenting examples from various job activities (classic office work, patient care, production work, elder care), learners observe how PRA can be applied in different contexts that might fit the specific work content for which they are responsible in their daily routine. Incorporating the practical application of PRA into the healthcare sector illustrated how different activities are distributed and organized in one organization, as well as how the same job requirements can occur and appear in different workplace activities. Contextual learning examples make the content highly relevant and practical by bridging theory and practice. As can be seen from the job examples, they fit well within the healthcare sector.

Practical tools and resources

In addition to the lecture and expert videos, many supplementary materials are offered to the learners for downloading each week. They provide MOOC participants with, for example, a list of more detailed country-specific legal regulations, comprehensive checklists for PRA preparation, scientifically approved assessment tools, risk evaluation and many more topics, as well as further reading recommendations and a ready-to-use intervention catalog. Equipping learners with practical tools, checklists and the necessary resources allows them to immediately apply their learnings in real-world contexts. The supplements represent a learners' toolbox that they can take as the basis for their daily work. These adaptive learning methods set the MOOC apart from traditional training programs.

Learner engagement strategies

To ensure active engagement and promote the obtained knowledge, a few mandatory *quizzes* follow each video lecture, and short peer polls are optional to answer. Two essay *assignments*, released after the first half and at the end of the MOOC, promote the transfer of knowledge into practice by offering graded feedback to learners' theoretical application of PRA in their own work contexts. The combination of methods supports the learners in reinforcing not only repetition but also practical learning from mistakes and experience.

Additionally, a *discussion forum* on the learning platform provides a unique opportunity to interact and exchange thoughts and learnings with a like-minded community of practitioners. Learners ask questions to the MOOC staff, give and learn from each other's tips, solutions to challenges, and experiences, and share stories and insights. These interactive components offer immediate feedback and encourage critical thinking about the learned information, which is essential in healthcare education where precision and accountability are key.

Finally, within each instructor-paced course run, there is one online meeting where participants can have a live exchange with the course instructors. The "Meet your instructors" meeting is advertised in the discussion forum. Learners are asked to send their more complex questions – for example, regarding the MOOC content in a peculiar job setting – in advance to the PsyHealth worXs! team, to more efficiently use the meeting time.

User experience

The user experience of the PsyHealth worXs! MOOC is designed to be accessible and customizable to meet the needs of a diverse range of learners, including those with varying professional backgrounds, varying prior experience in PRA and different levels of technical expertise. The content is applicable based on the learner's background and work environment, providing relevant insights for a wide range of roles in the healthcare sector and other industries. The interviews with professionals from diverse fields offer multiple perspectives on PRA, making the content adaptable to different contexts and promoting interdisciplinary use. With subtitles available in ten languages to support non-native speakers, the MOOC is accessible to learners worldwide based on multilingual reach and scalability opportunities. This feature ensures that language barriers are minimized, which enables participants from different countries to benefit from the content using a barrier-free approach if required. The learning platform where the MOOC is hosted was chosen for its well-proven user-friendly design, which ensures a smooth learning experience for all participants, regardless of their digital literacy. No prior experience with online learning or with conducting PRA is necessary, making the course beginner-friendly and suitable for learners at all levels. Additionally, learners have access to ongoing technical support throughout the MOOC. This ensures that any issues are quickly addressed and allows participants to focus on their learning without unnecessary interruptions.

Impact of PsyHealth worXs!

To measure the MOOC's effectiveness, the four-level model of Kirkpatrick (D. Kirkpatrick, 1996; D. L. Kirkpatrick & Kirkpatrick, 2006) and the Theory of Planned Behavior (TPB) (Ajzen, 1991; Francis et al., 2004) were used as the theoretical scientific bases of the questionnaire design. Kirkpatrick's model of training evaluation was used to assess the *reaction* and *learning* of the participants (Levels 1 and 2). This model captures insights into participants' satisfaction and engagement with the training, reflects their immediate responses, their development of competencies and their knowledge regarding conducting PRAs. Complementarily, we applied the TPB to assess indicators of behavioral changes. Specifically, we focused on one predictor for behavioral intention – perceived behavioral control – so we could explore participants' confidence in their ability to perform PRAs (Francis et al., 2004).

The design applied for MOOC evaluation consisted of a pre-post-questionnaire assessment with two cohorts of learners in 2020 and 2021 (Auweiler et al., 2022). For this chapter, we focused on a subsample of learners who are affiliated with the healthcare sector to also show the MOOC's impact in a specific field. Most of the initial sample is actively working in the healthcare sector, with 166 learners filling out the pre-questionnaire and only 33 learners responding to the post-questionnaire. A combination of quantitative and qualitative questions ensured a comprehensive understanding of participants' feedback.

Participant Feedback and Experience

- *Acceptance and Impressions*: According to Kirkpatrick's first level of evaluation, participants reported high levels of acceptance and positive impressions of the MOOC overall. The appreciative feedback accentuated the good usage and real-world application of the MOOC due to combining its comprehensive content, practical examples and the flexibility of the online format. In the open-ended questions, the learners reported the biggest strengths of the course, for example: 'To provide a theoretical framework; application examples and information about possible pitfalls and how to overcome them.', 'Structure and organization as well as the expert advice' and 'Step by Step guided approach to the cycle with experts' views'. The overall positive feedback showed that the MOOC is user-friendly, interesting and easily accessible for stakeholders in the healthcare sector (Auweiler et al., 2022).
- *Challenges Encountered*: Some participants faced challenges such as time management and the initial complexity of the material. Feedback highlighted the importance of providing clear instructions and additional supportive resources to help learners navigate these challenges. Consistent with the challenges reported in the introduction from past research, many participants described the challenge of convincing their management to implement PRA strategies.
- *Learning Experience*: Pre-post analysis of the data shows a significant increase in learning (Kirkpatrick's Level 2), particularly in the knowledge about the PRA process and the implementation of interventions. Based on widely recognized psychological research standards, effect sizes for both variables ($d = 1.047$ and $d = 1.004$) indicate substantial impact of the MOOC (Cohen, 1988).

Finally, the participants' perceived behavioral control, according to the TPB, reflects their confidence in their abilities to conduct PRA effectively, indicating that feeling more skilled and empowered will increase the assumption of new responsibilities and therefore the implementation of psychosocial risk management. The results show a notable overall improvement in participants' perceived confidence and subjective ability to handle PRA after completing the course. Participants found all steps of the PRA process and the requirements for its successful implementation easier to manage. Particularly, their perceived ability to interpret psychosocial risks and motivate employees to participate in the process showed significant enhancement. This demonstrates the course's practical impact on essential skills. According to well-established benchmarks for evaluating practical improvements, the training resulted in medium effect sizes (Cohen, 1988).

The MOOC's success is further evidenced by registration numbers exceeding 2,800 learners worldwide by 2023. The materials are already translated into nine languages, and a Serious Game is being added for practical application in a virtual hospital setting.

Integration into local curricula

With the MOOC in its current status on the learning platform, access to instructional materials is granted to every interested learners all over the world. The content provided is generalizable to primarily every European country and offers the basic knowledge for every stakeholder and job setting. Still, for a better translation of the course content in specific applied settings, we provide an outlook on how the MOOC content can be effectively integrated into specific health or healthcare curricula (e.g., elective classes in medicine, health science, or health management), or for specific target groups (e.g., either for health professionals or entrepreneurs, occupational physicians, occupational safety experts or workers' council representatives).

Table 6.1 provides the basic structure of the MOOC and provides an overview of its fixed instructional features, like videos with handouts, supplements and quizzes, but many possibilities for adapting and expanding the concept. The main tool for adaptation is the development of additional supplementary material. On this basis, adapted home assignments or quizzes provided to learners can guide them to focus on either regional specialties or peculiarities regarding stakeholder groups or branches.

With the help of the materials, one can offer workshops and seminars for practitioners on national levels to include country-specific or even regional regulations. Within the EIT Health seminar series, for example, a seminar with entrepreneurs was conducted to raise awareness about their duties as employers in startups concerning OSH. Alternatively, a specific professional development program can be implemented by accreditation of the extended course concept and materials in specific occupational associations. In Germany, for example, a professional association for safety, health and environmental protection already awards its members continuing education points for participation in the general course. Hospitals could adapt the content to their needs and require it as mandatory staff training for new hires in OSH management

Table 6.1 Basis structure of the MOOC PsyHealth worXs! and adaptable specification.

Week	*1*	*2*	*3*	*4*	*5*	*6*
Topic	*About PRA*	*Specification*	*Risk Management*	*Interventions*	*Effectiveness*	*Continuation*
Type of content						
Instructional Videos	• What and why? • Need • Legal background • Definitions • Categorization	• Process overview • Preparation • Obstacles • Specification • Best-practice strategies	• Assessment options • Assessment tools • Risk Analysis • Job examples	• Planning • Implementation • Success factors	• Evaluation of effectiveness • Best-practice examples	• Documentation • Continuation • Conclusion
Expert Interviews	N.A.	• Obstacles • Preparation • Best-practice strategies	• Assessment options • Evaluation of work characteristics	• Useful examples • Success factors	N.A.	• Conclusions and tips
Supplements	• Useful Websites (EU) • Further Readings (EU) • Legal Guidelines (EU) • Remote Work	• Checklists	• Checklists • Scientific standards with quality criteria • Instruments	• Checklists • Intervention Examples • Intervention Catalogue	• Checklist	• Checklist
Adaptation: Elaboration of specific supplements	• Specific country regulations of PRA • Regulations for specific stakeholder groups • Local support networks	• Specific for… • …Branches • …Company sizes	• Branch specific assessment tools • Specific job examples/ use cases	• Specific interventions for specific jobs	• Solutions for use cases	• Solutions for use cases • Branch-specific requirements
Slides	All slides from the content videos provided as handouts					
Quizzes	General quiz questions and assignments concerning the instructional videos					
Adaptation Assignments	Requiring home assignments for specific stakeholder groups or branches; application to a specific use case; project outline for applying the content to the learners' own job setting/responsibility; experimentally selecting an assessment tool from Week 3 and let learners conduct their own risk assessment					

to define an organizational PRA standard. A similar approach could be to train worker representatives on the topic of PRA.

In addition to further education, the materials can also be employed in a flipped classroom concept with students, to sensitize stakeholders and future leaders in the earliest educational stage as possible. Specific components, such as the assessment tools and supplementary materials, can be used for hands-on training sessions and to deepen understanding and applicability. Within the flipped classroom, additional experts and practitioners could be invited to extend the range of experts already interviewed within the MOOC. Also, in a student setting, different videos could be required over the course of more than six weeks to fill a complete semester if needed.

Some partners within the PsyHealth worXs! consortium offer the training on their own, within their general consultative services. A health insurance company provides it to leaders from companies to which they offer health insurance funds as a further education and sensitization offering. Another partner has developed branch-specific content with an organization offering certified continuing education models.

Conclusion

The PsyHealth worXs! MOOC has proven effective in enhancing the knowledge and skills necessary for PRA in SMEs, addressing a significant gap in OSH management. By providing easily accessible digital training and increasing awareness of employee mental health, the MOOC bridges the policy, research and practice gap, paving the way for healthier and more innovative workplaces. Several European countries have started translating the MOOC's digital material into certificate courses for further education. These adaptations cater to various responsible stakeholder groups and specific company settings, demonstrating the MOOC's scalability and real-world applicability. Readers interested in exploring the MOOC and its impact further are invited to visit the official website, which is also listed in the references (RWTH Aachen University, 2024). Future efforts should focus on expanding and adapting this training model to further enhance its impact and outreach.

Acknowledgment

The development of the MOOC was funded by EIT Health e.V. (co-funded by the European Union; Funding numbers: 20458, 220140 and 230137). We want to deeply thank all our European Project Partners from RWTH Aachen University in Germany, University of Luxembourg, Maastricht University, The Netherlands, Faculty of Human Kinetics, University Lisboa, Portugal, Atelierul de Idei Train-IC SRL, Rumania, University Medical Centre Ljubljana, Slovenia, DKV Servicios, S. A., Spain and KTH Royal Institute of Technology and University of Gothenburg, Sweden, for putting your effort into this great success story, as well as our advisory board team including colleagues from Belgium.

References

Ajzen, I. (1991). The theory of planned behavior. *Organizational Behavior and Human Decision Processes*, *50*(2), 179–211. https://doi.org/10.1016/0749-5978(91)90020-T

Auweiler, L., Lemmens, V., Hülsheger, U., & Lang, J. (2022). Digital training for psychosocial risk assessment as an approach to foster primary prevention for SMEs: An evaluation study. *WORK*, *72*(4), 1549–1561. https://doi.org/10.3233/WOR-211264

Beck, D., & Lenhardt, U. (2019). Consideration of psychosocial factors in workplace risk assessments: Findings from a company survey in Germany. *International Archives of Occupational and Environmental Health*, *92*(3), 435–451. https://doi.org/10.1007/s00420-019-01416-5

Braquehais, M. D., & Vargas-Cáceres, S. (2023). Psychiatric issues among health professionals. *The Medical Clinics of North America*, *107*(1), 131–142. https://doi.org/10.1016/j.mcna.2022.04.004

Champoux, D., & Brun, J. (2003). Occupational health and safety management in small size enterprises: An overview of the situation and avenues for intervention and research. *Safety Science*, *41*(4), 301–318. https://doi.org/10.1016/S0925-7535(02)00043-7

Cohen, J. (1988). *Statistical power analysis for the behavioral sciences* (2nd ed.). Erlbaum. https://doi.org/10.4324/9780203771587

Council Directive of 12 June 1989 on the introduction of measures to encourage improvements in the safety and health of workers at work, June 29, 1989.

European Agency for Safety and Health at Work. (2013). *Annual report 2012: Summary*. Publications office. https://doi.org/10.2802/52513

European Agency for Safety and Health at Work. (2019). *Third European Survey of Enterprises on new and emerging risks (ESENER 3): First findings*. http://osha.europa.eu

Francis, J., Eccles, M. P., Johnston, M., Walker, A. E., Grimshaw, J. M., Foy, R., Kaner, E. F. S., Smith, L., & Bonetti, D. (2004). *Constructing questionnaires based on the theory of planned behaviour: A manual for health services researchers*. Centre for Health Services Research.

Guo, P. J., Kim, J., & Rubin, R. (2014). How video production affects student engagement: An empirical study of MOOC videos. *Proceedings of the First ACM Conference on Learning at Scale Conference*, 41–50.

Hünefeld, L. (2020). *Öffentlicher Dienst: hohe Arbeitsintensität, starke Belastung*. Bundesanstalt für Arbeitsschutz und Arbeitsmedizin.

Kirkpatrick, D. (1996). Great ideas revisited: Revisiting Kirkpatrick's four-level model. *Training & Development*, 50(1), 54–57.

Kirkpatrick, D. L., & Kirkpatrick, J. D. (2006). *Evaluating training programs: The four levels* (3rd ed.). Berrett-Koehler. https://ebookcentral.proquest.com/lib/subhh/detail.action?docID=335391

Latos, B. A., Harlacher, M., Przybysz, P. M., & Mutze-Niewohner, S. (2017). *Transformation of working environments through digitalization: Exploration and systematization of complexity drivers*. https://publications.rwth-aachen.de/record/711251 https://doi.org/10.1109/IEEM.2017.8290059

Mayring, P. (2010). *Qualitative Inhaltsanalyse: Grundlagen und Techniken* (11. Neuausgabe). *Beltz Pädagogik*.

Nöhammer, E., & Stichlberger, S. (2019). Digitalization, innovative work behavior and extended availability. *Journal of Business Economics*, *89*(8–9), 1191–1214. https://doi.org/10.1007/s11573-019-00953-2

Parteka, A., Wolszczak-Derlacz, J., & Nikulin, D. (2024). How digital technology affects working conditions in globally fragmented production chains: Evidence from

Europe. *Technological Forecasting and Social Change*, *198*, 122998. https://doi.org/10.1016/j.techfore.2023.122998

Patel, M., Swift, S., & Digesu, A. (2021). Mental health among clinicians: What do we know and what can we do? *International Urogynecology Journal*, *32*(5), 1055–1059. https://doi.org/10.1007/s00192-021-04805-y

Pavlista, V., Angerer, P., & Diebig, M. (2021). Barriers and drivers of psychosocial risk assessments in German micro and small-sized enterprises: A qualitative study with owners and managers. *BMC Public Health*, *21*(1), 1376. https://doi.org/10.1186/s12889-021-11416-1

Rupp, C. (2014). *Requirements-engineering und -management: Aus der Praxis von klassisch bis agil* (6., aktualisierte und erw. Aufl.). Hanser.

RWTH Aachen University. (2024). *RWTHx: PsyHealth worXs! Psychosocial Health Prevention and Work standards.* edX. https://www.edx.org/learn/workplace-wellness/rwth-aachen-university-psyhealth-worxs-psychosocial-health-prevention-and-work-standards

van den Heuvel, S., Bakhuys Roozeboom, M., Eekhout, I., & Venema, A. (2018). *Management of psychosocial risks in European workplaces: Evidence from the second European survey of enterprises on new emerging risks (ESENER-2)*. European Agency for Safety and Health at Work. https://doi.org/10.2802/5030

7 EUPATI's Journey toward Enhancing Patient Engagement through Education

Maria Dutarte

Introduction: The premise of patient involvement

Patients possess unique information and experience of living with a health condition, which often is a lifelong journey affecting their daily lives. Patient insights are unique in nature because only someone who has experienced being a patient knows how the symptoms affect different aspects of life, how the use of different treatment options impacts the course of the disease and what unmet needs still exist. These insights are also shared by caregivers, patient representatives and patient organizations, strengthening the patient voice and raising awareness around this unique experience and knowledge.

Because patients are directly affected by the outcomes of research and development (R&D) of medicines and other health technologies, patient insights provide valuable input in the different stages of the development of these solutions.

Patient involvement, also referred to as patient engagement, is the active contribution of patients in the development of medicines and health technologies, and in healthcare. Patients engage in different ways in these processes as active and equal partners with all other involved stakeholders – researchers (from academia and industry), regulators, health technology assessment (HTA) bodies and healthcare providers – creating patient-oriented treatments and healthcare systems, aiming at improved health outcomes (Geissler et al., 2017).

In meaningful patient involvement, patients' unique perspective is valued as specialist knowledge and complementary to the work of other experts. It is about working as equal stakeholders and partners in R&D and cocreating solutions together.

The promise of patient involvement

Involving patients in the R&D processes benefits all stakeholders. Understanding what matters most for patients and shaping the research questions and design based on this information ensures that research priorities and methods are relevant from the outset to the community it serves (Hunter et al., 2018).

DOI: 10.4324/9781003568650-8

Incorporating patient feedback in the design of clinical trials improves recruitment and retention and results in therapies and health interventions that are better tailored to patients' needs. Information on patient preferences and patient observations of how a certain treatment performs in real-life settings can also shine light on the long-term benefits, safety and effectiveness. In this way, more useful evidence is created for clinical and health policy decision-making (EMA 2024; FDA, 2024).

Through the involvement of patient communities, an increased awareness of and advocacy for different conditions and associated research can be created. Through collaboration, trust is also built between the different stakeholders (Vat et al., 2020).

Overall, meaningful patient engagement leads to better allocation of resources and trust, and it increases transparency and accountability for all stakeholders involved. Patient involvement, as a genuine cross-stakeholder activity, also fosters a special type of learning. Patients learn about R&D processes, while researchers learn about the patients' views and insights.

The prerequisite of patient involvement

There are several prerequisites to meaningful patient involvement, and education and capacity building are inarguably two of the most important. Throughout its work, the European Patients' Academy on Therapeutic Innovation (EUPATI, 2025) has testified that the patient voice benefits from enhanced knowledge about the lifecycle of medicines and other health technologies and about the role patients can have in these processes.

The core idea of EUPATI is based on the belief that education and training are empowering and powerful tools for change. A patient, equipped with their personal and lived experience with a condition, becomes an expert patient by acquiring understanding of the different stages of health innovation – medicines research, regulatory affairs, HTA, health systems in general and the development of digital health, medical devices and so on. This knowledge base provides patients with easier access to the other stakeholders and facilitates collaboration (Egher & Zvonareva, 2024). The need for other stakeholders to understand the views of patients and their role in research is also recognized and can be addressed by information, training and collaboration.

Building a campus for patient involvement

Prior to EUPATI, a gap was identified in accessible information and training available for patients about medicine development and their involvement therein. There was also an overall lack of guidance and understanding of meaningful patient involvement and its implementation among the different stakeholders (industry, academia, regulatory and HTA).

EUPATI was originally launched as a multistakeholder public–private partnership project by the European Commission's Innovative Medicines Initiative

(IMI) in 2012 to address this need and to establish a platform, a place – or rather a campus – for learning, training and sharing information (Innovative Health Initiative, 2024). After the IMI-project period, EUPATI was hosted by the European Patients' Forum (EPF), and has been, since 2020, an independent nonprofit foundation based in the Netherlands supported by more than 50 partner organizations representing different stakeholder groups (EUPATI, 2025).

The mission of EUPATI focuses on leveraging education as a helpful tool for all involved stakeholders. First, educational programs and materials are an instrument for all patient communities, independent of the disease area or condition, to enable and enhance their involvement in health innovation and research. Second, guidance and training other stakeholders raises awareness and increases their preparedness for meaningfully involving patients at the different stages of developing medicines and other health technologies.

EUPATI's view of education is based on the principles of accessibility, innovativeness and inclusiveness. Learning outcomes focus on the specific knowledge, skills and competencies required from patients and the other stakeholders to effectively engage and partner with each other. EUPATI has established a robust training content production, review and delivery process based on co-creation, involving all stakeholders. This approach ensures accuracy, neutrality and accessibility of all the material. Through education and information, EUPATI promotes a vision of positive change in the global health innovation ecosystem where patients and all other stakeholders collaborate, cocreate and innovate together.

Inside the EUPATI campus

The main "buildings" of the EUPATI campus are as follows: the library, which is the Online Toolbox on Medicines R&D and Patient Engagement; the classroom, which is the Patient Expert Training Program; the online Open Classroom, which is a center for cross-stakeholder learning; the Learning Lab; and the career and collaboration center, which is called EUPATIConnect. These activities are also replicated across 24 countries via the EUPATI national platforms.

First, the EUPATI library has many avid readers. The multilingual open access Online Toolbox reached 8 million users around the world as of 2025. This lay-language resource library is searchable by keyword and by category, and has thousands of content items available in 14 languages (e.g., articles, downloadable presentations, webinars, fact sheets, infographics and glossary entries) about nonclinical and clinical research, regulatory affairs, HTA, digital health and medical devices. It also contains helpful resources and guidance on patient involvement. The Toolbox contributes to overall health literacy and understanding of the patient role in medicine R&D. It is today established as the key reference for patients and members of the wider health-interested public who are searching for easily accessible and reliable materials on these topics. The content is also used for training among patient organizations and communities.

Second, EUPATI has a large classroom, a place dedicated to patients and patient representatives and their learning about the medicine R&D processes. The EUPATI Patient Expert Training Program has been running since 2015 and was transferred to an open access, flexible and on-demand online platform, the EUPATI Open Classroom, within the framework of the EIT Health-supported EUPATI Reload project (2020–2021) (EIT Health, 2024). This expert-level program, mixing e-learning with live-streaming/in-person trainings, provides generic (non-disease-specific) knowledge about the different steps in the medicine R&D process and patients' involvement therein. The program covers six online modules (containing 28 courses) available on the Open Classroom, two live-streaming/in-person training events, and takes about 12–14 months to complete. The e-learning content is presented as short lessons including images, infographics, videos, real-world examples and case studies. Assessments are problem-based, multiple-choice questions and are used to determine the competency of the established learning outcomes for each course. The Open Classroom content meets accessibility criteria to ensure, for example, that learners with visual impairment can fully participate in the learning process. The platform is also adapted for different devices such as desktops, tablets and mobile phones. The live-streaming/in-person training events provide the learners with opportunities to put their learnings into practice through interactive exercises, lectures and discussions conducted in collaboration with EUPATI's multistakeholder expert faculty. The content of the Patient Expert Training Program and the Open Classroom is constantly updated, and new modules are added as adequate (e.g., during the EUPATI Reload project, content on medical devices and digital health were added).

Graduates of the program are awarded the title "EUPATI Fellow" and are equipped with knowledge and practical tools to collaborate with different stakeholders (e.g., industry, academia, regulators and HTA bodies). Since the launch of the program, 415 patient experts have graduated, and currently more than 130 trainees are enrolled every year. The online platform also allows self-paced learning, and more than 282,000 learners are currently accessing it, browsing through the materials, and completing the modules and courses of their choice.

The third building of the EUPATI campus is the Learning Lab, a center for cross-stakeholder learning. This training portfolio of online and in-person workshops is addressed to representatives of academia and industry looking to upskill in the area of patient engagement. Although patient education is at the heart of EUPATI's mission, the Learning Lab focuses on the other core aspect of EUPATI's mission, fostering a shared understanding among all other stakeholders of the value and effective implementation of patient involvement. Through its multistakeholder content development process, EUPATI has developed a syllabus for the Learning Lab based on the key methods and best practices of patient involvement. It provides individual professionals, organizations or research project consortia with the essential tools to involve patients in the different phases of setting research priorities, design, planning, clinical trial operations, regulatory and HTA processes. The Learning Lab has trained more than 1,100 individuals to date from more than 115 organizations worldwide, and the training workshops are codeveloped and co-delivered by EUPATI Fellows and other patient representatives together with nonclinical and clinical research, regulatory and HTA experts.

The latest addition to the EUPATI campus structure is a career and collaboration center, EUPATIConnect. It is an online matchmaking platform bringing together EUPATI Fellows (patient experts) and researchers from academia and industry for mutually beneficial engagement opportunities. EUPATI Fellows can create a profile on the platform indicating their availability to participate in various projects, while researchers submit their requests to find patient partners for their projects related to the medicine R&D process (e.g., protocol review, focus groups, speaking opportunities, patient advisory boards, etc.). The EUPATI Secretariat, assisted by the EUPATIConnect matching capabilities, connects the parties. EUPATI Fellows can therefore find opportunities to put their learnings from the EUPATI Patient Expert Training into practice, and researchers can implement in practice the guidance accessed through the Learning Lab.

The EUPATI campus has expanded around Europe and beyond. EUPATI has established national platforms in 24 countries, mostly in Europe but also in Japan, and several new platforms are being established. These independent entities reflect the multistakeholder structure and mission of the EUPATI Foundation. The national platforms vary in size and the types of activities they organize at the national level in their own languages (e.g., webinars, workshops, awareness campaigns, national adaptations of the EUPATI Patient Expert Training Program, etc.).

Driving change for patient involvement through education

EUPATI's impact has been significant. The Toolbox is being accessed across the world and the number of users continues to grow exponentially every year. New translations are being constantly added, widening the reach of the materials in different languages. While the impact of the use of these materials by, e.g., patient organizations, has not been systematically measured, there is some evidence of the benefits of these materials to the knowledge building of patient communities and health literacy in general.

The interest in the EUPATI Patient Expert Training Program and the Open Classroom is growing rapidly, and the number of individuals interested in joining the full program (including the live-streaming/in-person events) significantly outnumbers the currently available seats. Repeated longer-term surveys of the EUPATI Fellows have shown that these individuals are engaged in patient organizations, often in leadership positions, and collaborative activities with industry, academia, regulators and HTA bodies to a significantly higher degree after the program than before joining the EUPATI training. Fellows have reported that the program has provided them with a better grasp of R&D-specific language, boosted their communication skills and resulted in partnering in concrete projects with the other stakeholders. Many Fellows have taken on a mediator role between other patients and the R&D stakeholders and can "speak the language" of both communities. The program has also enhanced the development of an international network among the Fellows, creating synergies and strong links between different patient communities.

The impact of stakeholder training and matchmaking via EUPATIConnect is yet to be documented, but there is already some evidence of how this type of education and collaborative activity contributes to making patient involvement the new norm in medicine R&D. EUPATI's core belief in education and training is a powerful tool for positive change and a strong and sustainable foundation for its activities. It brings together different stakeholders, not only in Europe but also worldwide because the model inspires the establishment of similar spaces for learning in different countries. The EUPATI campus is today a well-established place for learning, equipping all stakeholders for collaboration, cocreation and innovation, creating positive societal impact.

The future of patient involvement

In addition to EUPATI, numerous initiatives by patients and patient organizations, policies implemented by regulators (e.g., the European Medicines Agency (EMA, 2024) and the US Food and Drug Administration (FDA, 2024)) and multistakeholder projects supported by the European Commission and the pharmaceutical industry (e.g., IMI-PARADIGM and IMI-PREFER) have contributed to rethinking the role of patients in R&D (PARADIGM, 2024; PREFER, 2024). There is a growing understanding of the importance of systematically incorporating the patient voice among researchers, academia, the pharmaceutical industry, regulatory agencies and HTA bodies. Today, patient involvement is moving beyond proof of concept and early adoption toward large-scale implementation and measurement of the long-term impact.

This development is happening against the backdrop of fast-paced technological advancements in digital health and artificial intelligence (AI). Although new technologies hold great potential for innovation and use of, for example, real-world data (RWD) and real-world evidence (RWE) in medicine R&D, they also present additional challenges in ensuring that patients are involved at every stage of developing these solutions (Faulkner et al., 2023). Education and training have key roles to play in enhancing, on the one hand, patients' understanding about these developments, and, on the other hand, increasing the know-how among manufacturers about how to bring patients onboard as co-designers of these solutions.

For EUPATI, these developments translate into a need for increasing efforts concerning information, education and collaboration for patients and all other stakeholders, and constantly expanding the contents of the materials and training into new areas of R&D.

The EUPATI campus develops and adjusts to the changing environment of the health ecosystem while remaining committed to its foundational belief that education serves as a catalyst for positive change, enhancing patient involvement and cross-sectional learning and benefiting all stakeholders.

Conclusion

EUPATI's journey toward enhancing patient engagement through education is unique. It demonstrates the roles that education and training can play in bringing about change, enabling cross-stakeholder collaboration and creating opportunities for engagement through acquired knowledge, skills and capabilities. Creating true equity in multistakeholder processes such as medicine R&D first requires recognition of the gaps, challenges and obstacles and systematically addressing them through tailored information and training offerings. EUPATI's model serves as an inspirational example for other sectors aiming to involve citizens and civil society actors, using education as a tool to find a common language for meaningful dialogue.

Acknowledgments

EUPATI is, by nature, a collaborative initiative, and this chapter is a synthesis of the work of hundreds of individuals who have contributed in different ways. I would like to thank the Innovative Medicines Initiative (IMI) and the European Patients' Forum (EPF) for their support throughout the years leading up to EUPATI's independence as a nonprofit and my predecessors Jan Geissler and Matthew May whose leadership was instrumental during those earlier stages. David Haerry and Wolf See also provided key input for the establishment of the foundation and EIT Health has supported the development of the Open Classroom. EUPATI has benefited from strong governance and support from, for example, Nicola Bedlington, Matthias Gottwald, Anders Olauson and Kay Warner. I would especially like to thank Matthias Gottwald for his help in writing this chapter and to acknowledge the support of the EUPATI partners, national platforms and the EUPATI Secretariat Team.

References

Egher, C., & Zvonareva, O. (2024). Knowledge-based representation: Patient engagement in drug development. *Health Expectations*, *27*(1), e13912. https://doi.org/10.1111/hex.13912

EIT Health. https://eithealth.eu/. Last accessed: December 2024.

EMA, European Medicines Agency (2024). *Patients and consumers*. Available at: https://www.ema.europa.eu/en/partners-networks/patients-consumers. Last accessed: December 2024.

European Patients' Academy on Therapeutic Innovation (2025). https://eupati.eu/. Last accessed: April 2025.

Faulkner, S. D., Somers, F., Boudes, M., Nafria, B., & Robinson, P. (2023). Using patient perspectives to inform better clinical trial design and conduct: Current trends and future directions. *Pharmaceutical Medicine*, *37*(2), 129–138. https://doi.org/10.1007/s40290-022-00458-4

FDA (2024). *US food & drug administration. CDER patient-focused drug development.* Available at: https://www.fda.gov/drugs/development-approval-process-drugs/cder-patient-focused-drug-development. Last accessed: December 2024.

Geissler, J., Ryll, B., di Priolo, S. L., & Uhlenhopp, M. (2017). Improving patient involvement in medicines research and development: A practical roadmap. *Therapeutic Innovation & Regulatory Science*, *51*(5), 612–619. https://doi.org/10.1177/2168479017706405

Hunter, A., Facey, K., Thomas, V., Haerry, D., Warner, K., Klingmann, I., & See, W. (2018). EUPATI guidance for patient involvement in medicines research and development: Health technology assessment. *Frontiers in Medicine*, *5*, 231. https://doi.org/10.3389/fmed.2018.00231

Innovative Health Initiative (2024). https://www.ihi.europa.eu/projects-results/project-factsheets/eupati. Last accessed: December 2024.

PARADIGM (2024). *Patients active in research and dialogues for an improved generation of medicines.* https://imi-paradigm.eu/. Last accessed: December 2024.

PREFER (2024). *Patient preferences in benefit risk assessments during the drug life cycle.* https://www.imi-prefer.eu/w/ip. Last accessed: December 2024.

Vat, L. E., Finlay, T., Jan Schuitmaker-Warnaar, T., Fahy, N., Robinson, P., Boudes, M., Diaz, A., Ferrer, E., Hivert, V., Purman, G., Kürzinger, M. L., Kroes, R. A., Hey, C., & Broerse, J. E. W. (2020). Evaluating the "return on patient engagement initiatives" in medicines research and development: A literature review. *Health Expect*, *23*(1), 5–18. https://doi.org/10.1111/hex.12951

8 Generative AI in International Higher Education

Challenges, Applications and Future Directions

Rainer Busch, Malte Busch, Christian May and Eva Nefen

Introduction

"AI is the first technology in history that can make decisions and ideas independently. All previous human inventions have strengthened humans, because no matter how powerful an instrument was, the decision about its use remained in our hands. Knives and bombs do not decide for themselves who to kill. They are stupid tools because they lack the intelligence needed to process information and make decisions independently. AI, on the other hand, is able to process information without human intervention, thus making humans redundant in the decision-making process. "AI is not a tool, AI is an actor" (Harari, 2024, p. 23).

Generative artificial intelligence (GenAI) is becoming increasingly important in the modern business world and is changing the way companies make strategic decisions, drive innovation and develop new business areas. In this context, it is essential for Master of Business Administration (MBA) programs to prepare future leaders for the use of this technology. The Ludwigshafen University of Business and Society, for example, offers consecutive, part-time and dual MBA programs (in collaboration with companies and other organizations) in various formats, including on-site, hybrid and distance-learning options. In general, MBA programs provide a broad, interdisciplinary education that spans the entire spectrum of societal and organizational contexts. Increasingly, these programs are not solely designed for specialists and executives in the business sector, but also target professionals from other fields. For example, senior physicians, self-employed doctors and other healthcare professionals have successfully completed their MBA programs.

The ability to understand and use GenAI strategically will become a key success factor in management. Because GenAI offers a wide range of applications in the areas of decision-making, process automation and innovation support, one can ask how this technology can be meaningfully integrated into the education of future leaders. **If higher-education programs do not incorporate GenAI into their curricula, there is a risk that graduates will be inadequately prepared for a business environment in which the strategic use of AI is crucial to building and maintaining a competitive advantage,**

DOI: 10.4324/9781003568650-9

as well as for tackling societal challenges that are becoming increasingly salient in the context of their professional activities.

We will shed light on the relevance and potential use of GenAI in MBA education and develop practical recommendations. MBA programs must evolve to provide students with traditional management skills and equip them with the skills and technological understanding required to handle AI and particularly GenAI. The focus is, for example, on how GenAI can influence strategic decision-making and innovation management and how MBA programs must respond to train future-oriented leaders. We performed an intensive literature analysis highlighting MBA education, AI, GenAI, strategic management and entrepreneurship. Particularly, we focused on the perspectives of AI and GenAI to understand its basic concepts and functioning. We analyzed how AI and GenAI can be used in management processes to achieve efficiency gains and improve decision-making. We also examined the MBA graduates' skills needed to fully exploit the potential of GenAI.

The concept and development of AI

A systematic presentation of AI from its basic definitions and levels of hierarchy to the various levels of analysis and the underlying technology is provided. Key challenges related to the use of AI are discussed, particularly ethical, legal and societal aspects. The more MBA students develop a thorough understanding of AI definitions, hierarchy, levels of analysis, functionality and challenges, the better prepared they are to strategically exploit the opportunities and risks of AI in the business world (Figure 8.1).

AI definitions

To contextualize, operationalize and classify AI strategically, definitions are essential. McCarthy et al. (1955) coined the term "artificial intelligence" for machines mimicking human perception and decision-making, such as facial recognition systems analyzing biometric data. McLuhan (1962) and Bozkurt et al. (2023) highlight how AI extends human capabilities, for example, translation tools that improve communication and accelerate information processing. Bawack et al. (2019) define AI as algorithms performing tasks requiring human intelligence, such as text generation and complex data analysis. These include image recognition and speech processing, where AI surpasses human speed and accuracy (Gursoy et al., 2019).

Zweig (2023) identifies a key AI challenge: "black box" models, which lack transparency due to proprietary technologies and complexity. Xu et al. (2019) emphasize two explainable AI research areas: transparency design, which reveals model operations, and post hoc explanations, which clarifies specific outputs.

Updated AI definitions (Kelly et al., 2023) and comprehensive AI timelines documenting technological breakthroughs (Bowen & Watson, 2024; Floudas, 2024) provide valuable context.

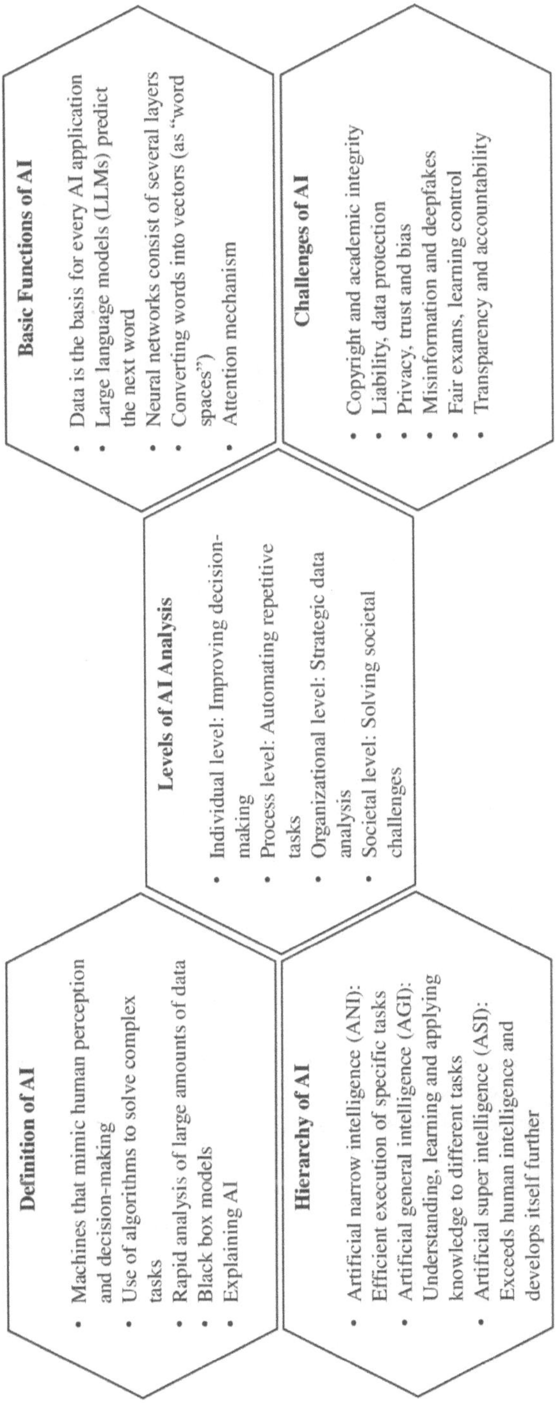

Figure 8.1 Basic concepts of AI.

AI hierarchy

Kelly et al. (2023) classify AI into three categories: artificial narrow intelligence (ANI), artificial general intelligence (AGI) and artificial super intelligence (ASI), reflecting AI's progression from task-specific systems to potentially superhuman intelligence. ANI refers to systems designed for specific tasks, such as voice assistants (e.g., Siri, Alexa) or recommendation algorithms (e.g., Netflix, Spotify). These systems are efficient but limited in scope. AGI represents more advanced AI capable of learning and applying knowledge across various tasks. Zhang et al. (2023) suggest OpenAI's GPT-4 could be a step toward AGI, highlighting advancements in GenAI. Achieving AGI requires replicating human cognition and significant computing power (Latif et al., 2023).

ASI, at the top of the hierarchy, is a hypothetical stage where AI surpasses human intelligence in all areas. It could simulate emotions and handle highly complex tasks. Although ASI remains speculative, it points to a future where AI exceeds human cognitive abilities (Bawack et al., 2019; Kelly et al., 2023).

Level of AI analysis

AI's impact spans individuals, processes, organizations, interorganizational dynamics and society (Bawack et al., 2019). At the individual level, AI enhances capabilities like personalized health monitoring and real-time translation. In processes, AI automates tasks and performs analyses, improving efficiency and reducing errors, as seen in AI-driven quality control and logistics optimization.

Organizationally, AI supports strategic decisions by analyzing trends and customer behavior to enable tailored strategies. At the interorganizational level, AI promotes collaboration, such as BASF's use of AI to engage partners in innovation networks. Societally, AI addresses global challenges like climate change, with organizations like Google using AI for climate modeling and predictions. AI-powered educational platforms, such as Khan Academy, personalize learning, increasing accessibility and effectiveness worldwide.

Basic functionality of AI

AI relies on data as its foundation, with big data essential for training models like large language models (LLMs) such as GPT. LLMs use the transformer architecture to process and generate text, with attention mechanisms enhancing prediction relevance (Lee & Trott, 2023; Yao et al., 2024).

Neural networks, composed of input, hidden and output layers, recognize patterns in data. For example, AI-driven credit-scoring systems analyze income, credit history and debt levels to predict creditworthiness, with hidden layers identifying complex patterns for accurate risk assessment (Tschöpe et al., 2021).

Challenges of AI

AI poses challenges, particularly regarding ethics, data privacy and accountability. GenAI raises concerns about authorship and academic integrity because

AI-generated content often resembles human work, leading to plagiarism and attribution issues (Al-kfairy, 2024). Educational institutions must implement detection tools and establish clear usage guidelines. Regulatory challenges include copyright laws, privacy concerns and bias in large datasets, necessitating measures like anonymization, encryption and bias audits.

AI also facilitates misinformation and deepfakes, which can sway public opinion. Solutions include AI-based detection systems and media literacy programs. In education, AI may reduce critical thinking and authentic learning (Ratten & Jones, 2023). Addressing this issue requires updated integrity guidelines, responsible AI training and retraining programs to mitigate labor market disruptions while promoting transparency.

GenAI and selected management challenges

GenAI can be integrated into various management and innovation processes, bringing strategic implications for managers and companies. The typologies of GenAI, its role in corporate governance, entrepreneurship and innovation management are discussed. The more MBA students understand the importance and dimensions of a GenAI mindset – especially the continuous incorporation of cobots (collaboration between humans and AI) into decision-making processes while keeping humans in the loop – the more successfully they will be able to use GenAI as a strategic partner to drive innovation and business success (Figure 8.2).

GenAI definitions

GenAI can be defined as a field of technology that is based on deep learning models to generate new content such as images, music or text. This content is generated in response to diverse and complex **prompts** (e.g., language, instructions, questions) and is created from scratch, not just classified or processed (Gimpel et al., 2023). According to Strobel et al. (2024), GenAI is also regarded as a **disruptive technology** with the potential to transform industries, from those pertaining to productivity (e.g., ChatGPT-4) to those concerning creativity (e.g., DALL-E). This renders GenAI a **game-changer** for reforming management and education (Lim et al., 2023).

GenAI typology

Based on the key characteristics of "degree of creativity" (enhancement vs. innovation) and "degree of modification" (preservation vs. creation), Strobel et al. (2024) present a **typology of GenAI**:

- *Generators* (Type I – high creativity and high modification) offer the possibility of creating novel and innovative content based on a few user inputs (e.g., text-to-image generators such as Midjourney or text-to-video generators such as Synthesia).

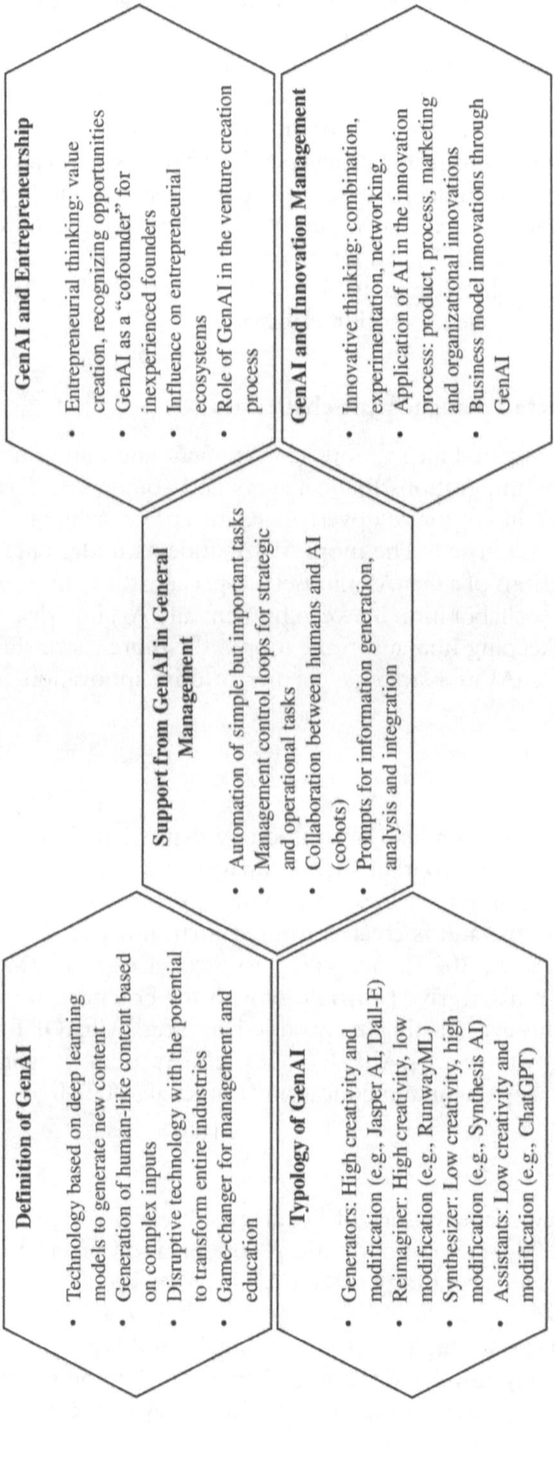

Figure 8.2 Key concepts of GenAI in the context of selected management challenges.

- *Reimaginers* (Type II – high creativity and low modification) aim to reimagine data (e.g., image-to-image reimagination by RunwayML).
- *Synthesizers* (Type III – low creativity and high modification) are applications that closely follow the original input but produce novel but realistic data (e.g., synthetic image data through Synthesis AI).
- *Assistants* (Type IV – low creativity and low modification) support the user within an application area (e.g., software development, law accounting) with domain-specific expertise or skills (e.g., CoPilot, ChatGPT, Perplexity).

This typology of GenAI offers a valuable framework for enhancing comprehension of the diverse potential applications and for identifying the optimal tools for specific tasks.

GenAI support in general management

Table 8.1 summarizes the **management tasks**. This classic model of controlling and optimizing management processes may be significantly supported using AI (Berndt et al., 2016).

Mollick (2024) criticizes the lack of strategic focus on AI's potential and emphasizes the ability of LLMs to automate tasks and enhance learning, enabling leaders to address complex challenges. The dual role of LLMs highlights opportunities for GenAI to optimize processes and drive innovation. Organizations are leveraging off-the-shelf and customized models based on industry-specific needs (McKinsey, 2024).

AI–human collaboration in management presents both challenges and opportunities. GPT-4 has improved efficiency in "inside-the-frontier" tasks like brainstorming but may not suit "out-of-the-frontier" tasks such as strategic

Table 8.1 Overview of management tasks

Task	*Example*
1. Situation analysis	PESTEL, Five Forces, analysis of the relevant markets
2. Corporate and marketing objectives	Corporate mission statement, basic international orientation, international positioning, target markets, stakeholders, target groups/market segments, corporate culture, key performance indicators (KPIs)
3. Corporate strategies	Preference vs. cost leadership, cross-border timing of international market entry, country-specific timing of international market entry, standardization vs. differentiation, offensive vs. defensive competitive strategy
4. Budgeting	Budget size and distribution
5. Instruments	Product, communication, distribution, price
6. Organization	Centralization/decentralization, standardization vs. differentiation of structure and processes, employee training, international coordination, intercultural teams
7. Controlling	Target-actual comparison of country-specific sales, profits, market shares, reporting; marketing audit (control of the marketing planning system, planning premises

distribution recommendations (Dell'Acqua et al., 2023). Sowa et al. (2021) predict AI's future lies in human–AI collaboration, not full automation, with virtual assistants handling administrative tasks.

Maggioncalda (2024a) outlines categories for AI prompts to foster creativity and innovation, such as "Generate" for developing new markets, "Summarize" for condensing information, and "Evaluate" for assessing business models. Experts create explicit, systematic prompts, while nonexperts rely on opportunistic methods (Zamfirescu-Pereira et al., 2023). Acar (2024) argues that as AI becomes more intuitive, prompt engineering will become less relevant.

Maggioncalda (2024b) suggests five rules for responsible AI use: reflect on results for coherence, confirm facts and sources, debate critically, filter diverse options and integrate relevant information into actionable strategies. These practices help students and decision-makers use AI responsibly in decision-making and strategy development.

GenAI and entrepreneurship

Entrepreneurship involves generating value in uncertain contexts, identifying opportunities and making decisions with limited information (Daspit et al., 2023). AI is transforming startups by optimizing processes like programming, marketing, product development and recruitment. Tools such as ChatGPT and GitHub Copilot enable faster scaling compared to traditional methods. For inexperienced founders, AI simplifies complex tasks, like understanding legal documents, reducing costs and building confidence ("think of GenAI as your cofounder"). By cutting costs for services like accounting and market research, AI helps startups allocate resources strategically (Ember, 2024).

AI impacts entrepreneurial ecosystems in three ways (Fossen et al., 2024). First, it restructures building blocks by redefining roles and creating new resources, such as automated methods in innovation management. Second, it increases productivity and fosters new business opportunities by enabling faster, more precise product development. Third, it improves processes and collaboration within ecosystems, automating knowledge exchange and reducing reliance on geographic location. For example, AI accelerates coordination between research and development (R&D), suppliers and market analysts.

Entrepreneurs balance AI algorithms (formal rationality) with personal interactions (substantive rationality) to shape innovation strategies (Roundy, 2022). AI excels in market data analysis, whereas direct interactions provide deeper customer insights, essential for disruptive innovations. Jia and Stan (2021) describe a virtuous growth cycle where companies achieve continuous growth through AI-driven strategies.

GenAI and innovation management

In today's competitive environment, an innovative mindset is crucial for success. Key traits include combining ideas, questioning assumptions, observing trends, networking and experimenting (Dyer et al., 2011). For example, integrating blockchain into logistics optimizes supply chains, whereas observing customer behavior reveals insights. Experimentation, such as prototyping, helps organizations enhance innovation and market position.

MBA programs can foster innovation by integrating cross-disciplinary concepts and encouraging experimentation through case studies and practice-based projects; for example, integrating data-driven approaches from IT into strategic management or applying agile methods in healthcare to optimize processes and improve patient care. An innovative approach in the MBA curriculum could also provide the space for experimentation and prototyping. Case studies, simulations and practice-oriented projects enable students to test innovative approaches. In healthcare, for example, MBA students could develop prototypes for new care models or carry out test projects for the implementation of digital technologies in hospital management.

Companies adopt varying AI innovation approaches (Füller et al., 2022). Occasional innovators, like small physiotherapy practices, use AI sparingly for tasks like scheduling. AI practitioners, such as hospitals, implement AI to improve efficiency in diagnostics and patient records, blending traditional and new technologies. AI frontrunners, like pharmaceutical firms, extensively leverage AI for drug development and clinical trials, investing heavily in internal and external capabilities.

GenAI levels the playing field for innovators by combining factual knowledge with creativity, enabling rapid development of value-generating offerings (Kanbach et al., 2024). Although GenAI is transformative, it primarily enhances established innovation types – product, process, marketing and organizational innovation (Mariani & Dwivedi, 2024). Moderna exemplifies this: GenAI aids product innovation in mRNA medicines and process innovation through automated clinical data analysis, accelerating decision-making and improving efficiency in vaccine development (Moderna x OpenAI, 2024).

Integration of AI in higher education

AI is increasingly recognized as pivotal in management and education, influencing core competencies and future capabilities in a globally interconnected world. Its integration into management education enables novel pathways, cultivates critical thinking and models economic performance. AI also transforms learning methodologies, offering personalized experiences and engaging with various levels of Bloom's taxonomy. Although its transformative power presents opportunities, it also raises challenges, such as maintaining academic integrity and addressing ethical concerns. For instance, MBA students exposed to AI applications develop a stronger AI mindset, reflected in enhanced analytical thinking, creative problem-solving and entrepreneurial competence (Figure 8.3).

AI in the context of management competencies

The World Economic Forum's *Future of Jobs Report 2023* emphasizes the importance of analytical and creative thinking, alongside resilience, flexibility,

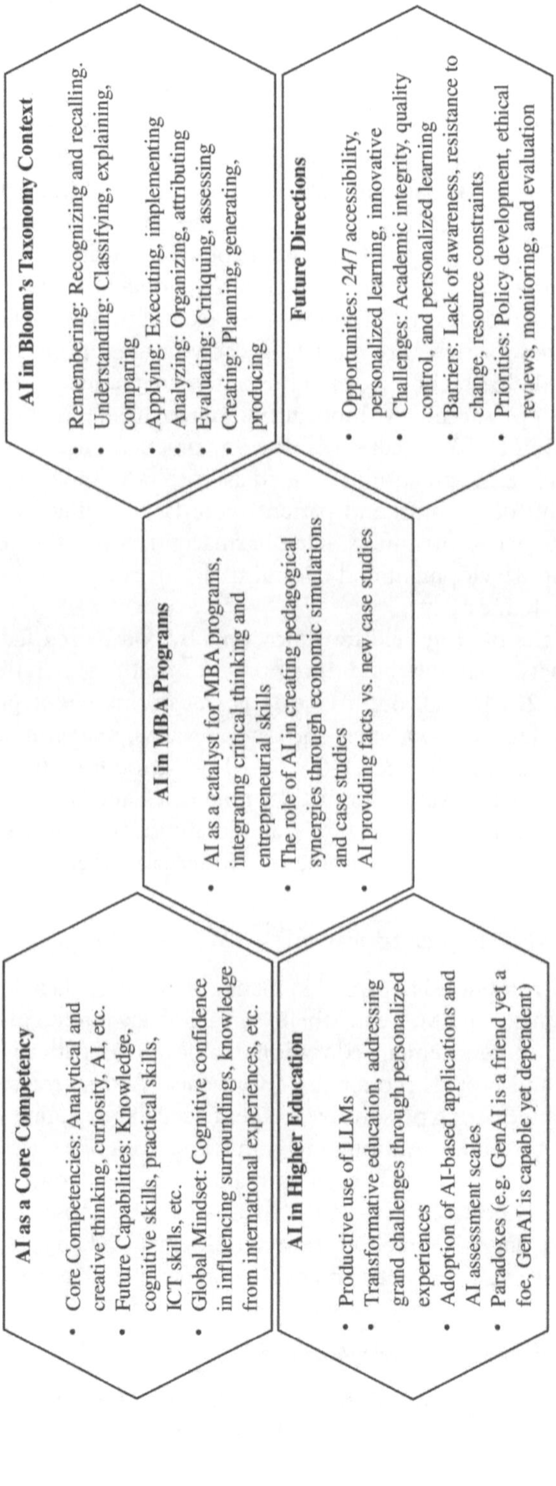

Figure 8.3 The integration of AI into higher education.

motivation and empathy, for adapting to dynamic environments and collaboration (Di Battista et al., 2023). The rise of team-based work highlights the value of interpersonal skills, while proficiency in AI, big data and digital literacy is increasingly vital due to digitalization's influence.

"Future skills" such as problem-solving, critical thinking, creativity and ethical responsibility are essential for navigating complexity. Business simulations promote these skills by engaging participants in real-world scenarios, enhancing decision-making and problem-solving. AI can also identify and address individual knowledge gaps (Sheikh et al., 2023).

A global mindset is vital in today's business world, enabling understanding of cultural differences and global interrelations. Felício et al. (2015) identify cognition, knowledge and behavior as key components. Cognitive skills involve interdisciplinary collaboration and adaptability, whereas knowledge is derived from international experience and foreign language proficiency. Behavior reflects openness to internationalization. For MBA students, developing a global mindset is crucial for leadership roles. AI tools, like GenAI, can aid this process by offering interactive learning environments, addressing knowledge gaps and enhancing cognitive, knowledge-based and behavioral skills through simulations like business negotiations.

AI in higher education

According to the German Association of University Teachers (Hochschullehrerbund, 2023), LLMs like GPT-4 can produce content indistinguishable from human-generated work and are being used productively in universities. However, public discourse often assumes misuse by students, hindering constructive debates on managing these technologies. An objective discussion is essential given the expected societal impact. Nguyen et al. (2023) stress the need for collaboration among students, educators, developers and policymakers as key stakeholders in AI adoption.

Lim et al. (2023) propose transformative education to fundamentally reshape learning processes, enabling learners to critically examine norms and address global challenges like climate change. Methods like project-based learning emphasize teamwork and critical thinking over memorization. Desired outcomes include developing critical thinking and problem-solving skills to address complex issues and integrating science, politics and ethics into educational programs.

Lim et al. (2023) also identify paradoxes of GenAI, such as being both a *friend* and an *enemy*, and *accessible* but *restrictive* (Scherpereel, 2024). Zawacki-Richter et al. (2019) categorize AI in higher education into four areas: Profiling & Prediction for optimizing programs and predicting dropout rates, Intelligent Tutoring Systems for personalized learning support, Assessment & Evaluation for automating grading and teaching feedback and Adaptive Systems & Personalization for tailored academic assistance (Figure 8.4).

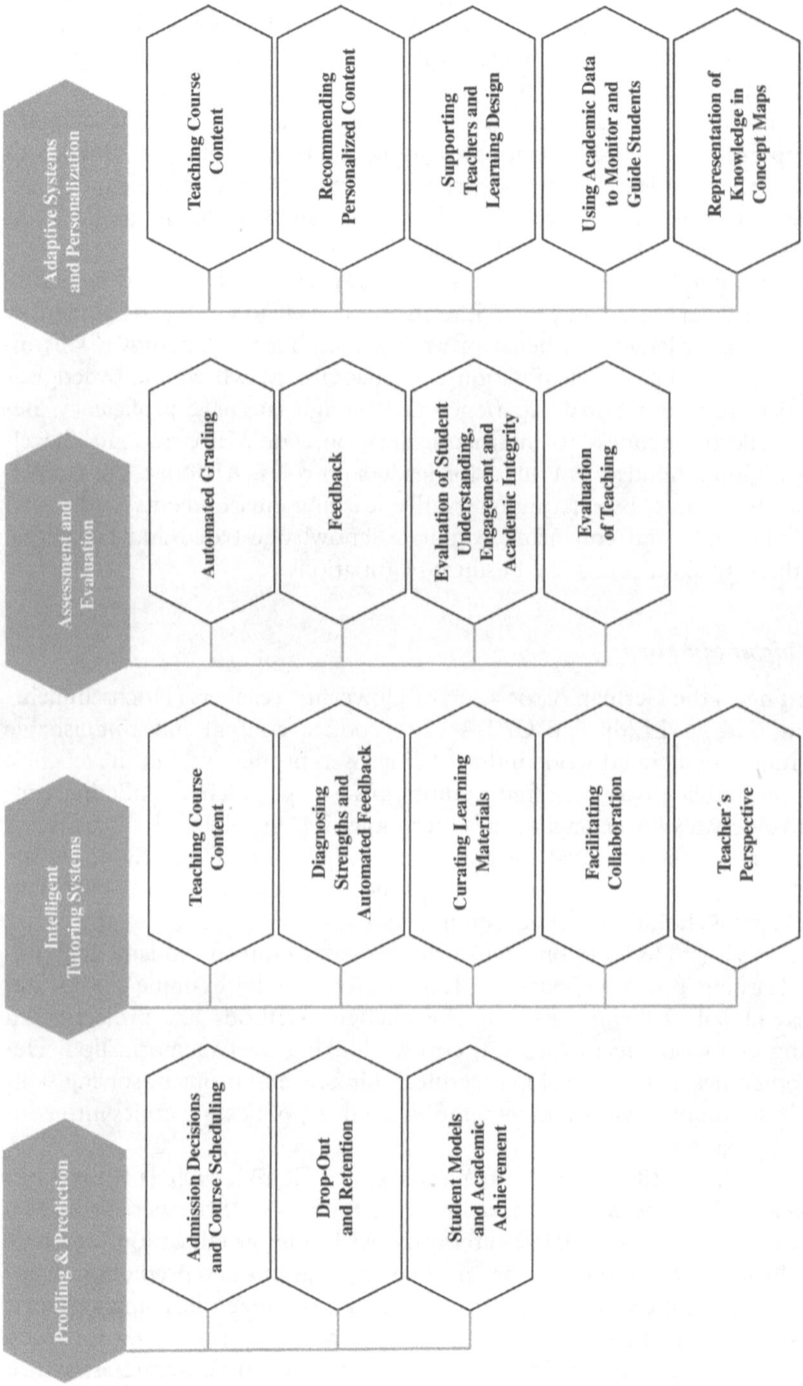

Figure 8.4 The integration of AI into higher education (Bond et al., 2024, on the basis of Zawacki-Richter et al., 2019).

Perkins et al. (2024) introduce the AI Assessment Scale (AIAS) to guide ethical AI use in education. The five-level model ranges from no AI use (Level 1) to full integration without labeling (Level 5). Intermediate levels allow AI for ideation but not final content, while Level 4 requires critical evaluation of AI outputs. This framework balances creativity and integrity in academic contexts.

AI in MBA programs

Online MBA programs are often viewed critically regarding quality (Graduate Management Admission Council, 2022). Barsky (2023) suggests GenAI could significantly enhance them through personalized learning, simulations, data analysis and improved teaching tools. In 2022, MBA exam papers from South African business schools were tested with ChatGPT and passed 12 of 15 modules. Although it provided factual answers successfully, it struggled with applying knowledge to new case examples (Calitz & Cullen, 2023).

Similarly, Somià and Vecchiarini (2024) found that ChatGPT improved students' entrepreneurial skills, particularly in valuing ideas. GenAI also helps educators foster critical thinking and innovation while reducing administrative burdens (Herold et al., 2024). However, uncertainty remains about integrating AI into business education, driven by the gap between employer demands and curriculum changes (Sollosy & McInerney, 2022).

AI in the context of Bloom's taxonomy

Bloom's taxonomy is a framework for structuring learning objectives that progresses through six cognitive stages: remembering, understanding, applying, analyzing, evaluating and creating (Krathwohl, 2002). It guides learning from simple tasks like knowledge recall to complex skills like critical problem-solving. The updated Bloom's taxonomy (Oregon State University Ecampus, 2024) highlights how GenAI as a "cobot" (Sowa et al., 2021) supports learning. GenAI excels at lower levels, such as remembering and understanding, by accessing and retrieving information quickly (Thanh et al., 2023). It helps recall details, explain concepts and provide examples, relieving learners of rote memorization and aiding comprehension.

At higher levels, like evaluating and creating, GenAI performs moderately. It can suggest evaluation criteria and analyze pros and cons but lacks the ethical reflection and judgment required for strategic decisions. Critical thinking, identified by the World Economic Forum as a future management skill, remains a human strength (Di Battista et al., 2023).

Experience-based learning (Salinas-Navarro et al., 2024) complements GenAI by fostering deep understanding through practical and reflective activities. This approach reinforces that humans are central at the higher cognitive levels of Bloom's taxonomy.

Future directions

The integration of ChatGPT into higher education offers opportunities but also presents challenges requiring structured reflection (Michel-Villarreal et al., 2023; Rasul et al., 2023; Zhang & Aslan, 2021). Higher-education institutions (HEIs), as central actors, are well-positioned to evaluate and guide the responsible use of ChatGPT while addressing uncertainties that evoke both optimism and concern. National and international stakeholders, including students, educators and policymakers, share responsibility for supporting these efforts.

HEIs can lead in exploring ChatGPT's potential, such as 24/7 availability and personalized learning, while critically assessing its capabilities (Gatrell et al., 2024). They play key roles in addressing academic integrity risks, quality control and subject matter expertise, using their international networks to develop ethical guidelines for AI use in education.

Collaboration with ministries, accreditation bodies and international organizations is essential for managing uncertainties and setting standards for AI use. HEIs can act as innovation drivers and regulators, shaping global debates on ChatGPT and other AI technologies through their leadership in teaching and research.

ChatGPT has the potential to enhance learning by providing personalized opportunities, immediate feedback and accessible tools for students, including those with disabilities. However, its integration should complement rather than replace lecturers and foster critical thinking and problem-solving (Dwivedi et al., 2023). Empirical studies are needed to evaluate its effectiveness and acceptance. Regarding scientific writing, for example, human creativity remains essential, even if ChatGPT acts as a coauthor. HEIs must continue discussing the use of ChatGPT to ensure responsible use and to maximize its positive impact on education and research.

AI can also address unresolved problems by generating new insights beyond human knowledge. For instance, Fraunhofer IAIS (2024) uses AI to analyze medical images, uncovering patterns and diagnoses that are challenging for professionals, which demonstrates its potential for groundbreaking discoveries and innovation. Escotet (2023) underscores AI's role in tackling unknown future challenges, emphasizing its ability to extend human knowledge.

Conclusions

We have examined the characteristics and implications of GenAI in higher education, focusing on its potentials, challenges and future developments. A literature review and case studies informed a typology categorizing GenAI applications by their innovation level and capacity to modify content, helping institutions and students make informed decisions about their use.

GenAI offers transformative potential, enhancing efficiency through personalized learning pathways, innovative teaching methods and administrative automation. For instance, it enables tailored learning and automated feedback during exams. However, challenges like plagiarism and distinguishing human from AI-generated work highlight the need for clear ethical standards to maintain academic integrity.

The findings suggest that GenAI could reshape education by personalizing learning and optimizing administrative tasks. Educators may adopt roles as moderators, guiding learning processes rather than just transmitting knowledge. However, safeguarding academic integrity remains crucial.

Institutions must strategically decide how to integrate GenAI, such as allowing AI-generated content in exams or evolving plagiarism checks. Students must consider when to use GenAI for tasks like data analysis and when traditional methods are better for deeper understanding. Both teachers and students must remain accountable for the reliability of their work, ensuring ethical use of AI while leveraging its benefits.

References

Acar, O. A. (2024). AI prompt engineering isn't the future. *Harvard Business Review*. https://hbr.org/2023/06/ai-prompt-engineering-isnt-the-future

Al-kfairy, M., Mustafa, D., Kshetri, N., Insiew, M., & Alfandi, O. (2024). Ethical challenges and solutions of generative AI: An interdisciplinary perspective. *Informatics, 11*(58), 1–29.

Barsky, N. (2023). MBA Programs Need Generative AI For A Massive Reboot. https://www.forbes.com/sites/noahbarsky/2023/03/20/microsoft-ai-move-is-exactly-what-mba-students-need-employers-want-and-slumping-b-schools-dread/?sh=25b95a6721ad.

Bawack, R. E., Wamba, S. F., & Carillo, K. D.. (2019). Artificial intelligence in practice: Implications for IS research. *AMCIS 2019 Proceedings*. 2. pp. 1-10.https://aisel.aisnet.org/amcis2019/ai_semantic_for_intelligent_info_systems/ai_semantic_for_intelligent_info_systems/2

Berndt, R., Fantapié Altobelli, C., & Sander, M. (2016). *Internationales marketing-management* (5th ed.). Springer Gabler.

Bond, M., Khosravi, H., De Laat, M., Bergdahl, N., Negrea, V., Oxley, E., Pham, P., Chong, S. W., & Siemens, G. (2024). A meta systematic review of artificial intelligence in higher education: A call for increased ethics, collabora-tion, and rigour. *International Journal of Educational Technology in Higher Education, 21*(1), 44.

Bowen, J. A., & Watson, C. E. (2024). *Teaching with AI: A practical guide to a new era of human learning*. Johns Hopkins University Press.

Bozkurt, A., Junhong, X., Lambert, S., Pazurek, A., Crompton, H., Koseoglu, S., Farrow, R., Bond, M., Nerantzi, C., Honeychurch, S., Bali, M., Dron, J., Mir, K., Stewart, B., Costello, E., Mason, J., Stracke, C. M., & Romero-Hall, E. (2023). Speculative futures on ChatGPT and generative artificial intelligence (AI): A collective reflection from the educational landscape. *Asian Journal of Distance Education, 18*(1), 53–130. Article 1. https://doi.org/10.5281/zenodo.7636568.

Calitz, A. P., & Cullen, M. (2023). *ChatGPT - the new MBA student in your class* (pp. 24–27). International Business Conference (IBC 2023).

Daspit, J. J., Fox, C. J., & Findley, S. K. (2023). Entrepreneurial mindset: An integrated definition, a review of current insights, and directions for future research. *Journal of Small Business Management, 61*(1), 12–44.

Dell'Acqua, F., Lifshitz-Assaf, H., Kellogg, K. C., Krayer, L., Lakhani, K. R., Krayer, L., Mollick, E., & Rajendran, S. (2023) *Navigating the jagged technological frontier: Field experimental evidence of the effects of AI on knowledge worker productivity and quality.* Harvard Business School. pp. 1–56.

Di Battista, A., Grayling, S., Hasselaar, E., Leopold, T., Li, R., Rayner, M., & Zahidi, S. (2023). *Future of jobs report 2023.* In *World Economic Forum, Geneva, Switzerland.* https://www. weforum. org/reports/the-future-of-jobs-report-2023

Dwivedi, Y. K., Kshetri, N., Hughes, L., Slade, E. L., Jeyaraj, A., Kar, A. K., Baabdullah A. M., Koohang, A., Raghavan, V., Ahuja M., Albanna, H., Albashrawi M. A., Al-Busaidi A. S., Balakrishnan J., Barlette Y., Basu S., Bose I., Brooks L., Buhalis D., … Wright, R. (2023). "So what if ChatGPT wrote it?" Multidisciplinary perspectives on opportunities, challenges and implications of generative conversational AI for research, practice and policy. *International Journal of Information Management*, 71, 1–63.

Dyer, J., Gregersen, H., & Christensen, C. M. (2011). *The innovator's DNA: Mastering the five skills of disruptive innovators.* Harvard Business Review Press.

Ember, S. (2024). A.I. is helping to launch new businesses. The New York Times. https://www.nytimes.com/2024/08/18/business/economy/ai-business-startups.html.

Escotet, M. Á. (2023). The optimistic future of artificial intelligence in higher education. *Prospects*, *54*, 531–540. https://doi.org/10.1007/s11125-023-09642-z

Felício, J. A., Caldeirinha, V. R., & Ribeiro-Navarrete, B. (2015). Corporate and individual global mind-set and internationalization of European SMEs. *Journal of Business Research*, *68*(4), 797–802.

Floudas, D. A. (2024). *Proposed taxonomy for the evolutionary stages of artificial intelligence: Towards a Periodisation of the Machine Intellect Era.* University of Cambridge. pp.1–4. https://www.researchgate.net/profile/DemetriusFloudas/publication/381293765_A_Proposed_Taxonomy_for_the_Evolutionary_Stages_of_Artificial_Intelligence_Towards_a_Periodisation_of_the_Machine_Intellect_Era/links/66664a88a54c5f0b945c527f/A-Proposed-Taxonomy

Fossen, F. M., McLemore, T., & Sorgner, A. (2024). Artificial intelligence and entrepreneurship, *Foundations and Trends® in Entrepreneurship*, *20*(8), 781–904. https://www.iza.org/publications/dp/17055/artificial-intelligence-and-entrepreneurship.

Fraunhofer IAIS. (2024). Medizinische Bildverarbeitung: KI-Potenziale in der Gesundheitsbranche. Fraunhofer-Institut für Intelligente Analyse- und Informationssysteme IAIS. https://www.iais.fraunhofer.de/de/geschaeftsfelder/healthcare-analytics/medizinische_bildverarbeitung.html.

Füller, J., Hutter, K., Wahl, J., Bilgram, V., & Tekic, Z. (2022). How AI revolutionizes innovation management – Perceptions and implementation preferences of AI-based innovators. *Technological Forecasting & Social Change*, *178*, 1–22.

Gatrell, C., Muzio, D., Post, C., & Wickert, C. (2024). Here, there and everywhere: On the responsible use of artificial intelligence (AI) in management research and the peer-review process. *Journal of Management Studies*, *61*(3), 739–751.

Gimpel, G., Hall, K., Decker, S., Eymann, T., & Lämmermann, L., Maedche, A., Röglinger, M., Ruiner, C., Schoch, M., Schoop, M., Urbach, N., & Vandirk, S. (2023). *Unlocking the power of generative AI models and systems such as GPT-4 and ChatGPT for higher education: A guide for students and lecturers, hohenheim discussion papers in business*, Economics and Social Sciences, pp. 1–57.

Graduate Management Admission Council (2022). *GMAC prospective student survey.* Summary Report.

Gursoy, D., Chi, O. H., Lu, L., & Nunkoo, R. (2019). Consumers acceptance of artificially intelligent (AI) device use in service delivery. *International Journal of Information Management*, *49*, 157–169. https://www.sciencedirect.com/science/article/abs/pii/S0268401219301690.

Harari, Y. N. (2024). *Nexus: Eine kurze Geschichte der Informationsnetzwerke von der Steinzeit bis zur künstlichen Intelligenz.* Penguin.

Herold, D., Murphy, G., & Buck, C. (2024). *Preparing the next generation: Integrating generative AI in entrepreneurship education for graduate capability development* (Working paper). Queensland University of Technology.

Hochschullehrerbund (2023). Positionspapier: Wissensschaftsbasierte Lehre und generative KI-Systeme. https://www.hlb.de/fileadmin/hlb-global/downloads/Positionen/2023-06-12_hlb-Positionspapier_Wissenschaftsbasierte_Lehre_und_generative_KI-Systeme.pdf.

Jia, P., & Stan, C. (2021). Artificial intelligence factory, data risk, and VCs' mediation: The case of ByteDance, an AI-powered startup. *Journal of Risk and Financial Management, 14*(5), 1–19.

Kanbach, D. K., Heiduk, L., Blueher, G., Schreiter, M., & Lahmann, A. (2024). The GenAI is out of the bottle: Generative artificial intelligence from a business model innovation perspective. *Review of Managerial Science, 18*(4), 1189–1220.

Kelly, S., Kaye, S.-A., & Oviedo-Trespalacios, O. (2023). What factors contribute to the acceptance of artificial intelligence? A systematic review. *Telematics and Informatics, 77*, 1–33.

Krathwohl, D. R. (2002). A revision of Bloom's taxonomy: An overview. *Theory into Practice, 41*(4), 212–218. https://doi.org/10.1207/s15430421tip4104_2

Latif, E., Mai, G., Nyaaba, M., Wu, X., Liu, N., Lu, G., Li, S., Liu, T., & Zhai, X. (2023). Artificial general intelligence (AGI) for education. AI4STEM Education Center, University of Georgia, pp. 1–34.

Lee, T. B., & Trott, S. (2023). Large language models, explained with a minimum of math and jargon. *Understanding AI, 27*, https://www.understandingai.org/p/large-language-models-explained-with

Lim, W. M., Gunasekara, A., Pallant, J. L., & Pechenkina, E. (2023). Generative AI and the future of education: Ragnarök or reformation? A paradoxical perspective from management educators. *The International Journal of Management Education, 21*, 1–13.

Maggioncalda, J. (2024a) GenAI as your "thought partner". https://www.coursera.org/learn/gen-ai-for-university-leaders/lecture/PIf8Y/using-genai-as-your-thought-partner-part-1.

Maggioncalda, J. (2024b). Your role as critical thinker at GenAI. https://www.coursera.org/learn/gen-ai-for-university-leaders/lecture/ibGUL/your-role-as-a-critical-thinker-with-genai.

Mariani, M., & Dwivedi, Y. K. (2024). Generative artificial intelligence in innovation management: A preview of future research developments. *Journal of Business Research, 175*, 1–21.

McCarthy, J., Minsky, M. L., Rochester, N., & Shannon, C. E. (2006). a proposal for the dartmouth summer research project on artificial intelligence, August 31, 1955. *AI Magazine, 27*(4), 12. https://doi.org/10.1609/aimag.v27i4.1904

McKinsey (2024). *The state of AI in early 2024: Gen AI adoption spikes and starts to generate value*. McKinsey & Company.

McLuhan, M. (1962). *Understanding media: The extensions of man*. McGraw-Hill.

Michel-Villarreal, R., Vilalta-Perdomo, E., Salinas-Navarro, D. E., Thierry-Aguilera, R., & Gerardou, F. S. (2023). Challenges and opportunities of generative AI for higher education as explained by ChatGPT. *Education Sciences, 13*(856), 1–18.

Moderna x OpenAI. (2024, April 25). Moderna's AI revolution: Transforming healthcare with OpenAI collaboration. https://healthmanagement.org/c/it/News/modernas-ai-revolution-transforming-healthcare-with-openai-collaboration.

Mollick, E. (2024). Confronting impossible futures. https://www.oneuse-fulthing.org/p/confronting-impossible-futures.

Nguyen, A., Ngo, H. N., Hong, Y., Dang, B., & Nguyen, B.-P. T. (2023). Ethical principles for artificial intelligence in education. *Education and Information Technologies, 28*, 4221–4241. https://doi.org/10.1007/s10639-022-11316-w.

Oregon State University Ecampus. (2024). Bloom's taxonomy revisited [infographic]. Oregon State University. https://ecampus.oregonstate.edu/faculty/artificial-intelligence-tools/blooms-taxonomy-revisited-v2-2024.pdf.

Perkins, M., Furze, L., Roe, J., & MacVaugh, J. (2024). The AI assessment scale (AIAS): A framework for ethical integration of generative AI in educational assessment. *Journal of University Teaching & Learning Practice*, *21*(6), 1–18.

Rasul, T., Nair, S., Kalendra, D., Robin, M., Santini, F. O., Ladeira, W. J., Sun, M., Day, I., Rather, R. A., & Heathcote, L. (2023). The role of ChatGPT in higher education: Benefits, challenges, and future research directions. *Journal of Applied Learning & Teaching*, *6*(1), 1–16.

Ratten, V., & Jones, P. (2023). Generative artificial intelligence (ChatGPT): Implications for management educators. *The International Journal of Management Education*, *21*, 1–7.

Roundy, P. T. (2022). Artificial intelligence and entrepreneurial ecosystems: Understanding the implications of algorithmic decision-making for startup communities. *Journal of Ethics in Entrepreneurship and Technology*, *2*(1), 23–38.

Salinas-Navarro, D. E., Vilalta-Perdomo, E., Michel-Villarreal, R., & Montesinos, L. (2024). Using generative artificial intelligence tools to explain and enhance experiential learning for authentic assessment. *Education Sciences*, *14*, 83–24. https://www.mdpi.com/2227-7102/14/1/83.

Scherpereel, C. M. (2024). The AI paradox: Unpacking the potential and perils in business education. *Developments in Business Simulation and Experiential Learning, Proceedings*, *51*, 33–45.

Sheikh, R. A., Abdalkrim, G. M., & Shehawy, Y. M. (2023). Assessing the impact of business simulation as a teaching method for developing 21st century future skills. *Journal of International Education in Business*, *16*(3), 351–370.

Sollosy, M., & McInerney, M. (2022). Artificial intelligence and business education: What should be taught. *The International Journal of Management Education*, *20*(3), 1–7.

Somià, T., & Vecchiarini, M. (2024). Navigating the new frontier: The impact of artificial intelligence on students' entrepreneurial competencies. *International Journal of Entrepreneurial Behavior & Research*, *30*(11), 236–260.

Sowa, K., Przegalinska, A., & Ciechanowski, L. (2021). Cobots in knowledge work: Human–AI collaboration in managerial professions. *Journal of Business Research*, *125*(C), 135–142.

Strobel, G., Banh, L., Möller, F., & Schoormann, T. (2024). *Exploring generative artificial intelligence: A taxonomy and types*. Proceedings of the 57th Hawaii International Conference on System Sciences. University of Hawaii at Manoa.

Thanh, B. N., Vo, D. T. H., Nhat, M. N., Pham, T. T. T., Trung, H. T., & Xuan, S. H. (2023). Race with the machines: Assessing the capability of generative AI in solving authentic assessments. *Australasian Journal of Educational Technology*, *39*(5), 59–81.

Tschöpe, C., Mühle, M., Ju, Y. C., Kraljevski, I., & Wolff, M. (2021). Künstliche Intelligenz in der ZfP – Welchen Beitrag kann KI in der ZfP leisten? *DGZfP-Jahrestagung 2021* (pp. 1–5).. https://jt2021.dgzfp.de/portals/jt2021/bb176/inhalt/19.pdf

Xu, F., Uszkoreit, H., Du, Y., Fan, W., Zhao, D., & Zhu, J. (2019). Explainable AI: A brief survey on history, research areas, approaches and challenges. In J. Tang, M. Y. Kan, S. Li, & H. Zan (Eds.), *Natural language processing and Chinese computing* (pp. 563–574). Springer.

Yao, Y., Duan, J., Xu, K., Cai, Y., Sun, Z., & Zhang, Y. (2024). A survey on large language model (LLM) security and privacy: The good, the bad, and the ugly. *High-Confidence Computing*, *4*, 1–21.

Zamfirescu-Pereira, J. D., Wong, R., Hartmann, B., & Yang, Q. (2023). Why Johnny can't prompt: How non-AI experts try (and fail) to design LLM prompts. Proceedings of the 2023 CHI Conference on Human Factors in Computing Systems (CHI '23), Hamburg, Germany. ACM.

Zawacki-Richter, O., Marín, V. I., Bond, M., & Gouverneur, F. (2019). Systematic review of research on artificial intelligence applications in higher education – Where are the educators? *International Journal of Educational Technology in Higher Education*, *16*(39), 1–27.

Zhang, C., Zhang, C., Li, C., Qiao, Y., Zheng, S., Dam, S. K., Zhang, M., Kim, J. U., Kim, S. T., Choi, J., Park, G. M., Bae, S. H., Lee, L. H., Hui, P., Kweon, I. S., & Hong, C. S. (2023). One small step for generative AI, one giant leap for AGI: A complete survey on ChatGPT in AIGC era. *arXiv*, *2304*, 06488. https://doi.org/10.48550/arXiv.2304.06488

Zhang, K., & Aslan, A. B. (2021). AI technologies for education: Recent research & future directions. *Computers and Education: Artificial Intelligence*, *2*, 1–11.

Zweig, K. (2023). *Die KI war's!: Von absurd bis tödlich: Die Tücken der künstlichen Intelligenz*. Heyne Verlag.

9 How a Digital Mindset Behavior Analysis Tool Can Help Healthcare Students Develop an Entrepreneurial Mindset

Paul Coyle

Introduction

This chapter begins by considering the strategic challenges in healthcare arising from the increasing needs of aging populations and the corresponding difficulty of maintaining financially sustainable healthcare systems. Several questions are considered: What knowledge and skills might future healthcare professionals need to rise to these challenges? What are the current skills gaps that are preventing the strategic healthcare challenges from being addressed? What are the implications for educating future healthcare professionals and developing current staff?

The chapter then considers definitions of the entrepreneurial mindset. There is a diverse range of source material about entrepreneurs available in print (e.g., books, newspapers and academic journals) and in electronic media (e.g., blogs, videos and social media). The authors of these sources are experienced entrepreneurs, small business owners, academic researchers, journalists and bloggers. The existence of consensus among the diverse range of authors about a standard definition of the entrepreneurial mindset is examined.

If we accept that healthcare professionals should have an entrepreneurial mindset, and we can agree on a definition of the entrepreneurial mindset, then we must ask how current and future healthcare professionals should be helped to understand, develop and make use of this mindset. The chapter considers pedagogical questions related to the development of the mindset. What evidence exists about how best to teach the entrepreneurial mindset? Where in the world are the educators who have experience helping students learn about the value and practice of the entrepreneurial mindset? Are educators required to take particular approaches to curriculum, teaching and extracurricular activities?

If the entrepreneurial mindset will be of benefit throughout the career of a healthcare professional, students need to embrace the idea of lifelong learning. Many healthcare courses incorporate reflective practice techniques. Therefore, the chapter next seeks to understand what reflective practice is and then to establish the potential benefits and limitations of this approach to learning. What is the evidence in the academic literature? How does reflective practice

DOI: 10.4324/9781003568650-10

align with the entrepreneurial mindset? Can students develop and strengthen their entrepreneurial mindset using reflective practice?

Finally, the chapter integrates the key themes of strategic challenges in healthcare, the definition of the entrepreneurial mindset, healthcare pedagogy and the role of reflective practice. It describes a digital Mindset Behavior Analysis tool that has been designed to introduce the concept of the entrepreneurial mindset to healthcare students and to stimulate their reflective practice. Based on feedback from students and educators, the conclusion is drawn that the digital Mindset Behavior Analysis tool has been proven to help healthcare students develop an entrepreneurial mindset.

Why do healthcare students need an entrepreneurial mindset?

An overview of the Future of Health Systems in all 38 Organisation for Economic Co-operation and Development (OECD) countries notes that population aging and tight healthcare budgets are putting pressure on healthcare systems: "Growth in health spending … could lead to a potential high of 11.8% of GDP being dedicated to health spending by 2040" (OECD, 2024). The strategic challenge will be to maintain sustainable healthcare systems while delivering the best possible health outcomes. More investment will be needed to exploit technological advances. One way to control costs might be to empower patients to actively manage their health and well-being through preventative measures.

A report of skills needs in the European health sector is based on responses to a survey of 472 Venture Capital fund managers in 27 European Union (EU) countries. This report identifies the five most important soft skills in the biotech, medtech and digital health sectors, highlighting "entrepreneurial skills: the ability to take risks in creating something new" (WorkInHealth Foundation, 2024, p. 21). A main conclusion is that "these (soft) skills combined with an entrepreneurial mindset are essential … in the European health ecosystem … for driving innovation … and are also the main skills missing" (WorkInHealth Foundation, 2024, p. 80). Therefore, healthcare students are likely to need an entrepreneurial mindset.

A review of healthcare entrepreneurship current trends and future directions notes that "the healthcare sector presents unparalleled opportunities for entrepreneurial innovation, promising substantial improvements in efficiency, patient outcomes and overall system resilience …. Moreover, as healthcare continues to evolve in response to technological advancements and changing patient demographics, there is a pressing need for entrepreneurs to contribute to this transformation, ensuring that the healthcare system remains adaptive and sustainable." (Lim et al., 2024, p. 3). Therefore, entrepreneurs can help identify new opportunities (e.g., in biotechnology and gene therapy) and more user-centric approaches using digital healthcare technologies.

"An entrepreneurial employee is someone who … takes collaborative action despite inherent uncertainty and risk, trying to create something new envisioned to be of significant value for others" (Lackéus et al., 2020, p. 9). When an employee adopts these behaviors, they are often said to be an "intrapreneur". Both entrepreneurs and intrapreneurs are equally considered to have an entrepreneurial mindset. This mindset is relevant to the adoption of new technologies and to innovation in service design and work practices. If healthcare professionals are going to be able to develop this mindset, these behaviors and work practices, then they will need training and support.

It might be possible to address the strategic challenges in healthcare through a combination of entrepreneurship and intrapreneurship. Both will require an entrepreneurial mindset. There is a need to educate healthcare students so that, when they qualify, they can use such entrepreneurial behaviors. There is also a need to develop current healthcare professionals so that they can adopt entrepreneurial behaviors in their existing jobs. However, a review of the entrepreneurial mindset in healthcare observed that healthcare professionals are unlikely to think of themselves as "entrepreneurial" (Gillin & Hazelton, 2021, p. 2). Therefore, it is important to give examples that convince healthcare professionals that the mindset is both relevant and of practical use in healthcare settings.

What is the entrepreneurial mindset?

A literature review by Daspit et al. of 61 publications about the entrepreneurial mindset concluded that "little consensus exists on what an entrepreneurial mindset (EM) is, how it is developed, or its precise outcomes" (Daspit et al., 2021, p. 13). Nevertheless, Daspit notes that "most researchers agree that value can be created by individuals with an EM" (Daspit et al., 2021, p. 13) and that "engaging in self-exploration and reflection support the development of an individual's EM" (Daspit et al., 2021, p. 21).

The definition of the entrepreneurial mindset that was chosen for the Mindset Behavior Analysis tool is the one created by the Entrepreneurial Mindset Network (© 2024). This definition is based on seven entrepreneurial behaviors and uses a mnemonic in which one entrepreneurial behavior is allocated to each letter of the word "mindset" (see Figure 9.1).

This definition was chosen because the use of the mnemonic aids understanding, and summarizes the complex concept of the entrepreneurial mindset into seven easily recognizable behaviors. The mnemonic definition has been translated into 16 languages and can be downloaded from the website of the Entrepreneurial Mindset Network (https://entrepreneurial-mindset.network).

Figure 9.1 Definition of the entrepreneurial mindset.

Early work to create this mnemonic definition identified behaviors that entrepreneurs consider important for launching a new business. The definition was subsequently sense-checked during ten workshops on the entrepreneurial mindset in 2015 and 2016, involving 227 participants from 29 countries (Coyle, 2017, p. 9). Later, a content analysis was undertaken of 76 dimensions (e.g., innovation and risk-taking) identified in a literature review of the entrepreneurial mindset (Commarmond, 2017). Dimensions were grouped together so they could be allocated to the mindset mnemonic. The terminology chosen to describe the behaviors is deliberately entrepreneurial and avoids the use of generic business terms.

How can we teach the entrepreneurial mindset?

Mawson et al. (2023) define the entrepreneurial mindset concept in higher education as "a set of learnable cognitive and emotional competences conducive to developing and enacting behaviors to support value creation activity ... [and] seek to start a critical and scholarly conversation on the practicalities of operationalizing the EM concept within HE [higher-education] teaching" (Mawson et al., 2023, p. 3). The emphasis on behaviors aligns with the mnemonic definition of the entrepreneurial mindset.

Daspit et al. found that "most pedagogical studies focused on an EM are conducted in European countries", "the United States accounts for the most studies beyond Europe" and "other contexts, like Africa and the Middle East, are represented in the pedagogical EM literature but to a lesser degree" (Daspit et al., 2021, p. 35). Therefore, teaching the entrepreneurial mindset is internationally significant.

"Scaling higher-education innovation using the entrepreneurial mindset" (SHINE) is an ongoing project involving 40 higher-education professionals in 28 countries from Africa, Asia, the Americas and Europe (Coyle, 2024). To date, the project has organized 18 webinars concerning pedagogy and the entrepreneurial mindset. Topics have included "entrepreneurial mindset for all academic disciplines" and "educating students about entrepreneurship". A summary of each webinar documents the contributions of speakers and participants, their experiences and recommendations. All the summaries are available on the SHINE Project website (https://shine-project.eu). Educators are encouraged to use these resources to reflect on and improve their own educational practice.

SHINE has created a series of recommendations for educators about actions that they can take in relation to developing the curriculum, teaching and extracurricular activities, to engage more students from a diverse range of backgrounds and subject disciplines (Coyle, 2024, pp. 238–240). Table 9.1 summarizes these recommendations.

McLuskie et al. (2024) undertook the first comprehensive literature review of entrepreneurship self-assessment tools (ESATs) used in entrepreneurship education. The conclusion states, "educators use ESATs both for predicting entrepreneurial potential and fostering self-reflection among learners.

Table 9.1 SHINE Project recommendations for the curriculum, teaching and extracurricular activities

Area	*Recommendations*
Curriculum	Increase the number of learners who understand the concept and application of the entrepreneurial mindset by including a suitable learning outcome in the curriculum of every academic discipline.
Teaching	Engage more learners through a pedagogy based on learning by doing, using practical projects that address real-world problems.
Extracurricular activities	Engage more learners by offering regular opportunities for them to interact with industry speakers, employers from the local ecosystem and alumni who can act as role models.

However, there is significant variation in what these tools measure and how they are applied, reflecting different understandings of entrepreneurship" (McLuskie et al., 2024, p. 9). Therefore, this chapter seeks to clarify the definition of the entrepreneurial mindset used and how the digital Mindset Behavior Analysis tool can be used by educators to foster self-reflection among learners.

What is the role of reflective practice in developing the entrepreneurial mindset?

Schön defined the role of reflective practitioner as dealing with "situations of uncertainty, instability, uniqueness, and value conflict" (Schön, 1992, p. 49). A practitioner cannot do this successfully "by applying standard theories or techniques" (Schön, 1992, p. 129). "Even when he makes conscious use of research-based theories and techniques, he is dependent on tacit recognitions, judgments, and skillful performances" (Schön, 1992, p. 50). Schön argues that a practitioner may gain a better understanding of their own "professional judgement" (Schön, 1992, p. 4) through a process in which "he reflects on the phenomena before him, and on the prior understandings which have been implicit in his behavior" (Schön, 1992, p. 68).

Schön states that the primary goal of a practitioner is "designing a desirable future and inventing ways of bringing it about" (Schön, 1992, p. 16). He argues that a process of reflection can lead not only to greater self-understanding of practice but insights into the process of creativity as "the practitioner allows himself to experience surprise, puzzlement, or confusion in a situation which he finds uncertain or unique" (Schön, 1992, p. 68). Reflection is not just a process of thinking, but crucially, it also involves taking action "which serves to generate both a new understanding … and a change in the situation" (Schön, 1992, p. 68).

A successful process of reflective practice is not intuitive. It is difficult to gain an understanding of one's own tacit knowledge, and the tolerance for ambiguity or uncertainty varies among individuals. Questioning one's own behaviors may bring greater understanding but may simultaneously be seen by others as showcasing weaknesses. New insights may call into question the behavior of colleagues, and this could lead to conflict within an organization. Practitioners may, therefore, need to be guided through the process of reflective practice and assisted in managing their emotions when faced with frustration and stress.

The first umbrella review (Fragkos, 2016) to address reflection in healthcare education examined studies from the medicine, nursing and allied health professions (physiotherapists, occupational therapists, pharmacists, therapists, social workers and psychologists). The educational levels of participants ranged from undergraduate to continuing professional development. Theoretical models were found to originate from the epistemology of practice as envisaged by Schön. The study concluded that "many reflective techniques used in healthcare education have been associated with deep learning, understanding, attitudes, beliefs and satisfaction, and reflection appears to be positively associated with various learning outcomes" (Fragkos, 2016, p. 13). Therefore, there could be value in the Mindset Behavior Analysis tool stimulating reflective practice by healthcare students.

There is a strong overlap between Schön's reflective practitioner and the notions of entrepreneurs and intrapreneurs. All three can be said to be designing a desirable future, inventing ways of bringing it about and dealing with situations of uncertainty. Both reflective practice and the entrepreneurial mindset are more than just thinking because they require action to be taken with the aim of changing the situation and generating new understanding. Guidance is needed to help practitioners engage in reflective practice and adopt more entrepreneurial behaviors. The next section explores how this can be achieved using a digital Mindset Behavior Analysis tool.

Can a digital tool help healthcare students develop an entrepreneurial mindset?

The Mindset Behavior Analysis tool aims to address the skills gap in healthcare by giving educators a digital tool that they can incorporate into their teaching of healthcare students. The tool has been designed to introduce healthcare students to the concept and application of the entrepreneurial mindset. The tool uses a series of questions that stimulate a process of reflective practice about the entrepreneurial mindset. By using the tool, a student is encouraged to reflect on their entrepreneurial behaviors and to make a commitment to taking action in the future to improve those behaviors.

The tool was developed by the SHINE Project, which is promoting the use of the entrepreneurial mindset in higher-education teaching, research and organizational change. SHINE has been gathering data through a series of webinars. Speakers from higher education have been invited to respond to open-ended questions designed to stimulate reflections on their teaching practice. This approach of using open-ended questions was also used to develop the Mindset Behavior Analysis tool, prompting a student to self-reflect and requiring that they make a commitment to action.

A Google form was created for the Mindset Behavior Analysis tool. Users are required to enter their email address so that a copy of all the information that they enter can be sent to them immediately after they complete the tool. A student is prompted to answer a series of questions that are designed to introduce the concept of the entrepreneurial mindset and also stimulate their reflection. As a student answers the questions about their entrepreneurial behaviors, they can see their progress at the bottom of the screen.

Care has been taken to ensure that the Mindset Behavior Analysis tool complies with the European Union's General Data Protection Regulation (GDPR). The tool requires consent from a student for them to submit their email address, which is used only for the purpose of sending a private copy of all the information that they have entered into the tool. The tool states, "Press the [Submit] button if you agree to have a copy of your completed Mindset Behaviors Analysis immediately emailed to you."

Students are also made aware of why their data is being collected and what use will be made of the data in the future. The tool states, "Data from all completed Google Forms is downloaded from Google into a spreadsheet maintained by the Entrepreneurial Mindset Network. Your email address is not downloaded, and your Google form is deleted. In effect, therefore, no data is stored that could identify you. Data which has been irreversibly anonymized in this way may be processed during the conduct and dissemination of research." Once data is truly anonymous and individuals are no longer identifiable, the data does not fall within the scope of the GDPR. This offers the legitimate opportunity to process the data to obtain statistical information and further insights that will be of value to healthcare educators.

A student is presented with a separate page for each of the seven entrepreneurial behaviors in the entrepreneurial mindset mnemonic. Each page has an explanation of the benefit to entrepreneurs of that particular behavior and a corresponding description of the value a student could gain by adopting the same entrepreneurial behavior. As students complete each of the seven sections, they are introduced to the concept and application of the entrepreneurial mindset. After each of the seven behaviors has been introduced, the student sees a page with a summary of all seven behaviors and a link to enable them to download a description of the entrepreneurial mindset in one of 16 languages.

Each of the seven sections in the Mindset Behavior Analysis tool also includes two questions designed to stimulate reflective practice and action planning by the student. For example, in relation to the first entrepreneurial behavior M, Meet real needs, the first question is: "How often in your studies do you consider how to meet real needs? Aways, often, sometimes, rarely or never?" The second question asks, "Could you try to meet real needs more often? What action should you take?" The questions are designed to create an active and personalized learning experience that is tailored to the understanding, skills and context of each learner.

How have Mindset Behavior Analysis tools been used by students and educators?

The SHINE Project has developed a range of Mindset Behavior Analysis tools. At the time of this writing, people from 33 countries have used these digital tools in Africa, Asia, Australasia, Europe and South America. In the preceding sections, this chapter described the Mindset Behavior Analysis tool for higher-education students. This tool has been designed to be useful to students of any academic discipline, and it has been used by healthcare students in 13 European countries.

Educators have used the Mindset Behavior Analysis tool for groups of higher-education students in seminars and workshops. A session with students typically includes the following exercises: First, an educator asks students to work by themselves to complete all the questions in the digital tool. Second, each student receives an immediate copy of their results by email. Next, students can be invited to discuss their results in small groups. Finally, the small groups can report back to the whole group. This framework allows an educator to present additional information, suggest questions for discussion, interact with each small group and explore how the actions created by the students will progress after the session.

Educators could use the tool to support deeper learning. Educators have the option to request that the SHINE Project provide an analysis of all the responses from a student group and share it with students. This would allow each student to benchmark their responses against their peers and to benefit from the group's cocreated list of actions for improvement. Educators have a further option to use the tool with students at two times, for example, at the beginning and end of a course. An analysis of these two data sets could provide much-needed evidence of the development of entrepreneurial behaviors over time, evidence that an educator could use in assessment, quality assurance and marketing.

A workshop example is one that took place during a healthcare startup competition, hosted at the TBS Education campus in Barcelona in 2023. Facilitators observed that the level of engagement with the tool by individual students was very high in the following ways: During the time when students were completing the tool, the room was silent. All the students completed all the questions and offered nearly 300 suggestions for intended action. Similarly, there was a high level of engagement in the small group and whole group discussions. Every student appeared to be engaged in a way that was meaningful to them as an individual, and therefore, the structure of the workshop ensured an active learning experience.

Immediately before a student submits their responses to the Mindset Behavior Analysis tool, they are asked to rate the tool. First, they are asked, "How would you rate the way in which this tool introduced you to the concept of the entrepreneurial mindset and the seven essential entrepreneurial behaviors? Very good, good, acceptable, poor, very poor." At the time of writing, the feedback from students for this question has been: very good 37% + good 52% = 89%/100%. The second question is, "How would you rate the way in which this tool helped you to make an initial consideration of actions that will help you to use entrepreneurial behaviors more often?" At the time of writing, the feedback from students for this question has been: very good 30% + good 50% = 80%/100%. This data will be used to help continuously improve this Mindset Behavior Analysis tool for higher-education students.

When educators think about educating students about the entrepreneurial mindset, they consider what students will gain in terms of knowledge, skills and competencies. Educators ask the simple question, "What do we want the students to be like?" However, insufficient attention has been given to the associated question, "If we want the students to be like this, what do the educators need to be like?" Although educators are designing learning experiences in which the aim is for students to develop an entrepreneurial mindset, educators themselves rarely consider the strengths or weaknesses of their own entrepreneurial mindset.

The SHINE Project also created a Mindset Behavior Analysis tool for educators. A proposal for a professional development workshop using this tool was peer-reviewed and selected for delivery at the 3E2024 conference in Amsterdam in May 2024 (Coyle & Lamas, 2024). The workshop attracted 19 participants from eight countries in Australasia and Europe. The tool allows exploration of three key questions: 1. Do educators have entrepreneurial mindsets, and do they apply the mindset in their teaching, research and societal engagement? 2. Can educators role model the behaviors associated with the entrepreneurial mindset to their students? 3. By understanding their own entrepreneurial mindset, will educators be better able to deliver successful student outcomes?

Conclusions and recommendations

The chapter began by considering the strategic challenges in healthcare arising from the increasing needs of aging populations and the corresponding difficulty of maintaining financially sustainable healthcare systems. An analysis of skills needs in the European health sector identified the need for entrepreneurial skills and an entrepreneurial mindset. Therefore, there is a need to educate healthcare students so that, when they qualify, they can use entrepreneurial behaviors. There is also a need to develop current healthcare professionals so that they can adopt entrepreneurial behaviors in their current jobs. The digital Mindset Behavior Analysis tool is designed to help address this skills gap.

Next, the chapter noted that there is no consensus on a standard definition of the entrepreneurial mindset, but there is agreement that having an entrepreneurial mindset is valuable for entrepreneurs and employees in healthcare. The advantages of the mnemonic definition of the entrepreneurial mindset created by the Entrepreneurial Mindset Network were noted. A mnemonic makes the entrepreneurial mindset easy to understand and quick to remember. This particular definition has the virtue of being based on seven essential behaviors, chosen through an analysis of the way entrepreneurs think and act, and written using entrepreneurial terminology. The mnemonic definition was, therefore, chosen as the one to be used in the digital Mindset Behavior Analysis tool.

The SHINE Project is an ongoing collaboration involving forty higher-education professionals in twenty-eight countries exploring pedagogy and the entrepreneurial mindset. One of its key recommendations is that learners should be engaged through a pedagogy that is based on learning by doing, using practical projects that address real-world problems. Therefore, the digital Mindset Behavior Analysis tool attempts to provide an active and personalized learning experience in which a learner is helped to understand how the entrepreneurial mindset is of practical relevance to their own professional context, their individual goals, knowledge and skills.

Reflective practice is an established pedagogy in healthcare education. There is a strong overlap between the concepts of the reflective practitioner, entrepreneurs and intrapreneurs. All three are engaged in imagining a desirable future, inventing ways of bringing it about and dealing with situations of uncertainty. Therefore, reflective practice is embedded into the digital Mindset Behavior Analysis tool. The aim is to help learners generate new understanding by requiring them to identify actions that they can take, in a manner comparable to the actions taken by an entrepreneur, to bring about change in their behaviors and in the discharge of their professional responsibilities.

The digital Mindset Behavior Analysis tool offers a contemporary pedagogy for the education of healthcare students that enables them to quickly understand the concept of the entrepreneurial mindset and appreciate how it can benefit their studies and future career plans. It encourages self-reflection and a choice of actions that can put the entrepreneurial mindset into practice. By using the tool with students at the beginning and end of a course, educators can generate evidence of the development of entrepreneurial behaviors over time. Based on very positive feedback from students and educators, the conclusion is that a digital Mindset Behavior Analysis tool has been proven to help healthcare students develop an entrepreneurial mindset.

References

Commarmond, I. (2017). *In pursuit of a better understanding of and measure for entrepreneurial mindset.* The Allan Gray Orbis Foundation.

Coyle, P. (2017, February 7-10). *The entrepreneurial mindset in higher education* [Conference presentation]. Australian Centre for Entrepreneurship (ACE) Research Exchange Conference, Deakin University, Melbourne, Australia. https://www.academia.edu/77941850/The_Entrepreneurial_Mindset_in_Higher_Education

Coyle, P. (2024). Scaling higher education innovation using the entrepreneurial mindset. In R. J. Crammond, & D. Hyams-Ssekasi (Eds.), *Entrepreneurship education and internationalisation* (pp. 230–245). Routledge. https://doi.org/10.4324/9781003378570-15

Coyle, P., & Lamas, M.. (2024, May 15). *Entrepreneurial mindset for entrepreneurship educators* [Conference presentation]. 3E Conference 2024, Entrepreneurship Education: A play ground for impact, Amsterdam University of Applied Sciences, Amsterdam, the Netherlands. https://www.academia.edu/121590236/Workshop_Title_Entrepreneurial_Mindset_for_Entrepreneurship_Educators

Daspit, J. J., Fox, C. J., & Findley, S. K. (2021). Entrepreneurial mindset: An integrated definition, a review of current insights, and directions for future research. *Journal of Small Business Management*, *61*(1), 12–44. https://doi.org/10.1080/00472778.2021.1907583

Fragkos, K. C. (2016). Reflective practice in healthcare education: An umbrella review. *Education Sciences*, *6*(3), 27. https://doi.org/10.3390/educsci6030027

Gillin, L. M., & Hazelton, L. M. (2021). Bringing an entrepreneurial mindset to health-care: A new tool for better outcomes. *Journal of Business Strategy*, *42*(4), 278–287. https://doi.org/10.1108/JBS-03-2020-0049

Lackéus, M., Lundqvist, M., Williams Middleton, K., & Inden, J. (2020). *The entrepreneurial employee in the public and private sector – What, why, how*. European Commission: Joint Research Centre. https://data.europa.eu/doi/10.2760/460123

Lim, W. M., Ciasullo, M. V., Escobar, O., & Kumar, S. (2024). Healthcare entrepreneurship: Current trends and future directions. *International Journal of Entrepreneurial Behavior & Research*, *30*(8), 2130–2157. https://doi.org/10.1108/IJEBR-02-2023-0197

Mawson, S., Casulli, L., & Simmons, E. L. (2023). A competence development approach for entrepreneurial mindset in entrepreneurship education. *Entrepreneurship Education and Pedagogy*, *6*(3), 481–501. https://doi.org/10.1177/25151274221143146

McLuskie, P., Rogers-Draycott, M., Mave, M., Djebali, Z., Aluthgama-Baduge, C., Unger, V. L., & Todt, G. (2024, September 2-6). *Self-assessment tools in entrepreneurship education* [Conference presentation]. British Academy of Management Conference, Nottingham Trent University.

OECD. (2024). *Fiscal sustainability of health systems: How to finance more resilient health systems when money is tight?* https://doi.org/10.1787/880f3195-en

Schön, D. A. (1992). *The reflective practitioner: How professionals think in action* (1st ed.). Routledge. https://doi.org/10.4324/9781315237473

WorkInHealth Foundation. (2024) *Addressing skills needs in the European health sector*. European Investment Fund. https://www.eif.org/files/records/eithealth-skills-european-health-sector.pdf

10 Connecting Academia with the Economy

Fostering Spin-offs by Implementing an Entrepreneurship Funnel into University Structures

Marc Kley, Constanze Duhme and Marita Mehlstäubl

Framework and culture for transfer activities at universities

The two core and classical missions of universities have been (and for many higher-education institutions [HEIs], still are) research and teaching. Basic research produces great innovations, yet it is predominantly concerned with gaining new knowledge without direct reference to application. Its main task is to provide new technical solutions bearing problem-solving potential. Applied research, on the other hand, is concerned with gaining new knowledge with the aim of application. Applied research therefore utilizes the problem-solving potential primarily to generate a technical solution to a specific application problem (Horsch, 2003).

Since the 1990s, however, additional transfer tasks and fields of activity have been added to universities, which are bundled under the heading "third mission" (Schönenberger & Steiner-Kaiser, 2023). This mission depends consistently on, and synergistically develops with, the core competencies of research and teaching and refers to areas of continuing education, knowledge and technology transfer, as well as social commitment (Hochschulrektorenkonferenz, 2017). The third mission might have the potential "to take on a mission of equal importance to research and teaching" (Schönenberger & Steiner-Kaiser, 2023). At the same time, the third mission focuses on innovation and entrepreneurship, and constitutes, thus, "transfer activities", which are closely interwoven with the research and teaching missions.

Transfer activities from a university can take place in various formats, for example, science communication, social commitment, cooperative publications and continuing education. Other forms of transfer, however, such as collaborations, academic patents and business startups from universities, might be considered more impactful because they can trigger an active transfer of knowledge and technology from a university (Backs & Buermann, 2023).

In general, the management of technology transfer organizations should not be based solely on monetary targets but should consider the economic and social effects of transfer holistically. Even if startups do not generate license income,

DOI: 10.4324/9781003568650-11

social value is created, which is given too little consideration presently (EFI – Commission of Experts for Research and Innovation, 2019). Moreover, some universities have fundamental reservations regarding the commercialization of science (Schönenberger & Steiner-Kaiser, 2023) or suffer from a lack of understanding of how entrepreneurial ideas within the university become a commercial reality and serve market needs (Belitski & Sikorski, 2024); (unfortunately) many researchers share that same shortage. However, as Fini et al. (2022) state, a shift toward exploration of research findings will enhance the impact of the entrepreneurial scientists' subsequent research. Concepts and models from other bodies of knowledge are combined in novel ways through exploitation. Commercial work by academics can drive fundamental advances in science; entrepreneurship thus leads to more impactful research, mediated by exploration. Moreover, entrepreneurship will shift scientists' attention away from intradisciplinary research questions and toward new bodies of knowledge relevant for downstream technology development. This will propel scientists in exploration, which means they will work on topics new to them (Fini et al., 2022). Entrepreneurial behavior can also be fostered by the supportive roles of teaching and research. As "an effective blend of educational programs and innovative knowledge-creation scenarios they can lead to significant benefits for both potential entrepreneurs and the university". The challenge for HEIs, however, lies in balancing their traditional roles in teaching and research with the newer demands of commercialization and technology transfer (Belitski & Sikorski, 2024).

Universities that recognize exploitation of know-how as its third objective, in addition to traditional tasks of research and education, can be called "entrepreneurial universities" or "third-generation universities". Those who see commercialization of know-how as part of their license to operate are obligated to generate value from knowledge created. Second-generation universities, instead, might already have incubators or other facilities to support "technostarters", yet they see commercialization as a private matter for their academics, maybe through a spin-off. Third-generation universities have the potential to become "the cradle of new entrepreneurial activity". Therefore, education should not only pursue the creation of scientists and scientifically trained professionals but also entrepreneurs (Wissema, 2009). If universities and research institutions view the knowledge generated there as a value that needs to be leveraged in the best interests of society, they will develop the necessary strategies and structures (Wutscher et al., 2024). Depending on whether a university sees its role as one of transfer as a second or third mission, its support structures are set up and equipped with resources accordingly.

Spin-offs as the outcome of transfer activities

Startups from the sciences play an important role in the transfer of knowledge and technology into practice (so-called spin-offs). They are more innovative in all development phases than other startups (EFI - Commission of Experts for Research and Innovation, 2019). Spin-offs benefit a wide range of stakeholders: universities (reputation gain and positioning), the founders (rapid, transparent procedures), the research location (additional spin-offs) and, ideally and holistically, the society (providing new solutions to problems, contributing to achieve the Sustainable Development Goals [SDGs]). Furthermore, spin-offs are also an important part of regional innovation systems.

To increase the number of high-quality spin-offs, universities and research institutions must strengthen their roles and functions in the innovation system. By acting like an "innovation broker" that transfers knowledge and technology permanently and intensively, research institutions can help accelerate and intensify innovation processes relating to social, ecological and economic problems (Wutscher et al., 2024). Yet research institutions should be aware that an entrepreneurial journey begins with the creation and development of business ideas, where students and researchers identify opportunities through various means such as observing macro-trends, recognizing problems needing solutions, or identifying market gaps. This phase can therefore be considered crucial because it sets the foundation for future entrepreneurial endeavors (Belitski & Sikorski, 2024). In any case, the priorities and focus of the spin-off strategy of HEIs should follow the respective institution's research strategy (Wutscher et al., 2024).

Gateway as a successful story of a Startup Center

The name Gateway came into existence in 2015 when the University of Cologne (UoC) for the first time opened an incubator. What seemed to be some kind of experiment in the beginning, quickly turned into a success story, laying the groundwork for a fruitful application to a call issued by the Ministry of Economics of the state of North Rhine-Westphalia (MWIKE) in 2018. The ministry aimed at fostering "Excellence Start-up Centers", which provide the best possible framework for university spin-offs. The UoC was one of the six universities that won that prestigious title in 2019 through Gateway. Since then, more than 100 companies have been established, among them Fimo Health (https://www.fimohealth.com/) and the research-based life science startups Prosion (https://www.prosion.eu/) and Detechgene (https://www.detechgene.de/).

The UoC is one of the oldest and largest comprehensive universities in Germany and Europe, with 45,000 students and 5,000 researchers in six faculties. Gateway is organizationally a central operating unit within the UoC. By detaching Gateway from the administration and turning it into a separate unit, the rectorate could comply with a central demand by MWIKE that asked for greater visibility and independence of the Excellence Start-up Centers. Gateway is now an established brand for the promotion of entrepreneurship at Cologne's universities. In addition to UoC, four other universities – the University of Applied Sciences Cologne (TH Köln), the German Sport University Cologne, Cologne Business School and the Rhenish University of Applied Sciences Cologne – use the label "Gateway" for their start-up services. The major aim of bundling cooperation under one brand is to bring together students and researchers from different disciplines and to coordinate the range of qualifications and extracurricular startup training courses all along the Gateway Funnel. Also, the visibility of Gateway as a central contact point for startup consultation strongly increased after joining forces in one brand.

From innovation to spin-off: The Gateway Funnel

The Gateway Funnel ranges from raising awareness via education and enablement of ongoing entrepreneurs until their empowerment to spin off a company. It was introduced when Gateway became an Excellence Start-up Center and covers the major milestones at the beginning of an entrepreneurial journey (Figure 10.1).

Raising awareness

A successful spin-off process begins long before the respective company is founded, but its effects extend far beyond this milestone. It starts with raising awareness of spin-offs at universities and research institutions. Ideas, technologies and research results that are potentially exciting for entrepreneurial exploitation are identified in the **sensitization phase**. At universities, this identification is usually carried out by cooperation between the Technology Transfer Office (TTO) and dedicated staff like technology brokers or ambassadors at the faculties (Wutscher et al., 2024). At the UoC, the so-called transfer scouts at all six UoC faculties contribute to this goal.

Innovation Day as a best practice example in sensitization

At a comprehensive university with a broad range of disciplines, innovation has various facets. To make these tangible and connect innovators with

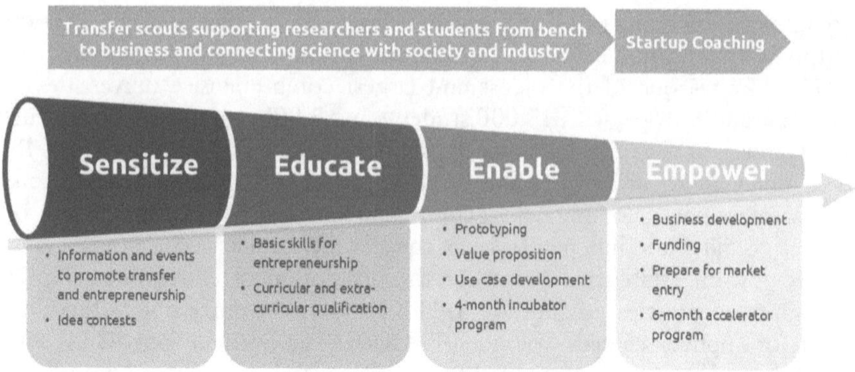

Figure 10.1 Innovation funnel at gateway fostering entrepreneurship activities for students and researchers.

each other, Gateway initiated the first **Innovation Day** at UoC (https://gateway-unikoeln.de/innovation-day-2023). The Innovation Day shows role models of spin-off and transfer projects relevant to researchers of all faculties. By giving hands-on workshops for researchers (e.g., on effectuation or research canvas) and showing structural best practices (e.g., on how transfer and teaching can be combined such that it gives inspiration and practical experiences to bachelor, master and PhD students through open innovation formats), distinct and practical ways of implementing transfer in the university's first and second missions were made tangible. Finally, a strategic panel discussion on the role and potential of transfer at UoC and its positioning as a second or third mission university aimed at opening the discussion for steering members of the university. Awarding **Gateway ambassadors** of each faculty for the first time gave a boost to enforced connections between transfer enthusiasts from academia and Gateway. Past merits were awarded, and the support that academic members of the faculty contributed to the integration of transfer scouts and Gateway services within the faculties was recognized. Innovation Day will evolve further, with the goal of closing the gap between research needs and startup support and by establishing a systematic, attractive format for researchers to regularly identify interesting transfer projects. The transfer scouts are important in creating a strong Gateway connection and network within the university, ensuring constant knowledge exchange, integration of research and teaching expertise in Gateway services and vice versa, integrating Gateway services into the teaching and research formats of the university. Innovation Day shows the results of this work on the university level. On the faculty level, the key is to connect faculty events with Gateway support.

Education and enablement

When Gateway became an Excellence Start-up Center, the UoC established startup-oriented professorships in four of its faculties to sensitize students to innovation, entrepreneurship and digitalization. However, **there is no specific program to address PhD students, postdocs or chair holders at the UoC**. In addition to contemplating the potential application of research findings in dialogue with the scientists, scouts contribute extracurricular and curricular qualifications to these target groups at all faculties. They provide access to entrepreneurial thinking via boot camps, hackathons and summer schools, as well as tailor-made plug-in modules (e.g., pitch events, ideation workshops, role-model nights, transfer grant writing workshops, or innovation labs) in existing PhD graduate school programs, retreats and science days. More examples will be illustrated ahead regarding the Medical Faculty of the UoC.

Transfer scouts are the arms into research of the university that find, encourage and guide researchers to transfer their results, eventually to build a spin-off. They are sparring partners at eye level who truly understand the research and have an overview of knowledge trends, networking partners, funding and financing opportunities and develop a milestone plan from bench to market with the scientists. Accompanying researchers, the scouts initiate special content and support various needs, such as regulation issues and implementation paths, and address topic-specific networks with industry corporations, associations and deep-tech investors.

The UoC and TH Köln have been working together in the field of startup coaching since the year 2000. Building on that relationship and sharing similar experiences regarding the difficulty in addressing scientists with entrepreneurial issues, the two HEIs decided to implement transfer scouts at the same time. The UoC employed six scouts and TH Köln two scouts, all financed with the help of the Gateway Excellence Start-up Center. Scouts can support potential entrepreneurs and transfer-affine scientists in clarifying the technical and economic feasibility of innovation. Therefore, methodological competence (e.g., design thinking) and knowledge of tools for defining technology readiness levels (TRLs) and market readiness levels (MRLs), expertise to gauge the current intellectual property status of a finding and how to initiate progress are important instruments scouts employ to educate researchers for entrepreneurship (Wissema, 2009). All scouts bring different backgrounds to the table and therefore share their competencies and coordinate their activities across faculties.

In some research areas, however, such as the arts and humanities, social and cultural sciences are currently underrepresented in the spin-off ecosystem. Awareness-raising activities for entrepreneurship are often still in their infancy in these research areas. However, these specialist areas are critical for solving urgent social and ecological problems, not least because they typically involve business models with a major (social or ecological) impact (Wutscher et al., 2024). Therefore, identifying the potential and giving distinct routes to its practical application is an important task of transfer scouts.

At the faculty or department level, scouts help initiate programs that enable researchers to develop "an instinct for spotting commercialization options for their research" (Wissema, 2009). This means the scouts benefit from being part of an organization that offers all the instruments that serve as a funnel from ideation to market entry (including incubation and acceleration).

A lack of genuinely motivated scientists to engage in spin-out activity, however, would limit the potential success of all technology transfer measures that aim to increase spin-out activity (Schultz, 2021). The relevance of relationship building also shows that transfer activities cannot be increased immediately. It is often necessary to get to know each other and build trust, followed by the presentation and repeated reporting of funding opportunities and events (Kriedel & Dibke, 2023). This trust building is crucial because researchers then dare to discuss early ideas and can be encouraged to validate the application potential of their research and entrepreneurial endeavors and incorporate the transfer of knowledge into their research planning.

Creation of scouts

Gateway had been successful for some time in addressing students and graduates from the UoC who planned to start their own business when the idea to initiate transfer scouts came up. Gateway's support in the past mainly focused on business model coaching and offering workspace, which was in high demand with students. Shortly after Gateway's start in 2015, the 35 workplaces offered by the UoC were continuously and completely utilized. Furthermore, increasing numbers of students from other universities asked for Gateway's support in the following years.

Despite good access to scientists, however, raising their interest in entrepreneurial activity remained a challenge. One of the many reasons for this is that in the German academic system, transfer activities such as intellectual property (IP) creation, building a spin-off, or generating societal impact are not incentivized by the system. Thus, in most HEIs, it does not play a role in academic appointments, career credits, or internal resource allocations. Moreover, transfer activities are not part of the academic education, incentive system, or considered relevant for scientists' career track records. Yet, academics who establish their own science- or technology-based firm, who take the initiative and are willing to take the responsibility and risk, help strengthen the competitive position of a university (Wissema, 2009).

Profile of a scout

The scouts at the UoC and TH Köln have widespread expertise and success in acquiring public transfer funds. They involve a diverse industry network as well as an innovation and research network. Furthermore, they have many years of proven qualifications and practical experience in the application of innovation methods and the design and implementation of innovation workshops, including trend analyses. Strong conceptual skills, analytical and strategic thinking, methodological competence and relevant experience in applying for larger third-party-funded projects are also required.

As Schultz (2021) illustrates, experience gathered at the University of Potsdam indicates that technology scouts need to be competent in their assigned technological area and need to have at least a basic understanding of business activities such as opportunity recognition or business planning and understanding of financing instruments (such as public and private funding). This means that scouts must demonstrate entrepreneurial orientation either by having worked in a business development division of an existing company or by having participated in an entrepreneurial team (Schultz, 2021). In addition to highly qualified and motivated scouts, the dominant success factor for their work is the ability to build personal relationships with entrepreneurial-minded scientists: "Technology scouts need to understand the motivational factors of scientists to offer some form of adequate technology transfer solution beyond a spin-out" (Schultz, 2021). This aligns strongly with the experience gained at the UoC over the last 4 years: innovation know-how, skills and technical understanding of research are important requirements for credibility, but soft skills such as communication, networking and relationship-building competencies are key for motivating and empowering researchers.

Scouts engage in various activities to identify technologies with spin-off potential, initiate interdisciplinary cooperation and increase the number of technology- and knowledge-intensive startups as well as the overall attention for startup activities. To researchers, scouts serve as first-contact persons and "consultants" for technology transfer activities.

Deep dive medical faculty

First-hand experience gathered at the **Medical Faculty of the UoC** shows the necessity to improve conditions, structures and a mindset for transfer. In an internal audit, the Faculty of Medicine and the University Hospital were found to have insufficient utilization of research results and too few transfer projects based on excellent research. This was anchored in a so-called Third Mission Strategy as an important third pillar in addition to research and teaching; however, the everyday implementation of transfer is pending.

To overcome existing limitations, incentives for transfer must be created. Special exemption programs for work in transfer projects with continued payment, analogous to the established clinician-scientist programs; university or faculty-internal scholarships, awards and prizes for excellent transfer projects; simple and cost-neutral access to infrastructure for transfer and startup projects; and suitable transfer and startup funding options would be advantageous here. It would also be desirable to integrate the topic of transfer more strongly into the curriculum to facilitate access for young scientists. To support the development of transfer-friendly structures and mindsets in the faculty, the visibility of transfer projects in the form of success stories at internal and external events, conferences, workshops, retreats and in communication via newsletters, websites, and so on, would also have to be increased.

Another hurdle on the way to successful research transfer is the previously complicated and time-consuming clarification of the IP question, which is usually non-transparent for the scientists. Structures and processes on the way from an invention disclosure to the patent application as well as in the transfer of the IP for exploitation purposes must have a simpler and more transparent structure, and the responsibilities and decision-makers must be clearly defined.

Thanks to the manifold activities implemented by the scout at the medical faculty over the last 4 years, significant achievements supporting the development of transfer-friendly structures and decision-making processes within the medical faculty have been achieved. Moreover, a transfer department was recently set up, and a transfer advisory board was established as a decision-making body.

Best practice GO-Bio initial grant

Through project planning in the form of tailor-made information events with the project sponsor and intensive application support (e.g., through workshops and support in writing and submitting the application), eight Go-Bio initial (BMBF grant, from the German Federal Ministry of Education and Research) applications from the Medical Faculty and ten from the Faculty of Natural Sciences have been submitted for the first time in the past 2 years; seven have so far been supported in the exploratory phase and three made it to the feasibility stage.

Scouts at both faculties have identified promising transfer projects with the potential for an application in the faculty and achieved high visibility for a funding program with good chances of success for early transfer projects.

Best practice innovation lab

This recurring event for young scientists and physicians from the UoC and the University Hospital with an interest in the topics of research transfer and start-ups has the motto "From Research to Application" and consists of a workshop and a networking part with experts from the regional ecosystem.

Researchers often underestimate the innovative potential and the transferability of their academic research. In an interactive workshop, they receive some hands-on advice and learn how the scout's expertise and network contribute to successfully bringing research into application. This targeted approach to young scientists is designed to help them continue working on their ideas and develop them in the direction of transfer. The networking part of the innovation lab teaches young scientists how role models and ecosystem partners can help on the journey to turn research into application.

Best practice Pitch4Med

Pitch4MED is a pitch competition for transfer projects in the idea stage of Startup4MED, the startup support of the University Medical Center Düsseldorf, together with the startup support of the Faculty of Medicine of the University of Bonn and the Gateway Excellence Start-up Center of the UoC. This competition aims to determine which innovative ideas can help shape medicine in the future.

In 8-min pitches, medical startup projects from the three locations present their fresh startup ideas from the fields of digital health, drug development, diagnostics and medical technology to a top-class jury of venture capitalists (VCs), business angels and stakeholders, and collect important feedback on their way to becoming a successful startup. In contrast to other pitch formats, startup projects are deliberately given the opportunity to pitch at a relatively early stage.

Due to an uncomplicated application process and the focus on early-stage ideas, it is possible to reach transfer projects that have not yet been scouted before. Additionally, high visibility in the faculties is achieved by greetings from the deans, vice deans and the vice rector for transfer. The top-class jury also offers a high level of attraction for the regional startup ecosystem for efficient networking.

Key learnings

Looking back at 4 years of transfer scouting at UoC, a broad range of experiences occurred, including sensitization and ideation events, structural demands and challenges of matrix positions between Gateway and the faculties, institutional framework conditions (pro-rectorate, transfer strategies, decentralized structures versus a top-down approach, incentives from the university as well as the higher education system in Germany) and third-party fundings. These intensive empirical experiences over all faculties of a comprehensive university give valuable insights into the pitfalls and necessary conditions German universities face when it comes to transferring knowledge and technology under the current conditions. These experiences will be merged in a white paper by Gateway designed for political stakeholders as well as sharing learnings and experiences with other universities that are aiming to set up scouting structures.

Prerequisites for successful transfer activities at HEIs can be summarized as follows:

- Structural money for third mission activities is needed to have a stable basic budget, minimize the significant strategic and budget-related efforts of the respective service structures and respectively free resources for more outcome-related work. This could be achieved by introducing mandatory minimum basic funding for transfer at universities, budget agreements between the university and federal state, or by adding additional steady funding for transfer activities by the federal state directly.
- Incentives for transfer activities are crucial for researchers to get involved in transfer activities and locate their time and effort (e.g., as a criterion for scientific careers, professorial appointment procedures and as a criterion for performance-oriented allocation of funds).
- Practical, proactive and strategic project supporters and facilitators with a high level of expertise are key to empowering and enabling researchers to transfer their projects (e.g., transfer scouts).
- Financial support for scientists to finance and validate innovations, as well as venture capital for early-stage projects, are essential to gain momentum for the projects.
- Innovation events (i.e., for idea development) that are directly linked and strategically implemented to curricular programs (e.g., doctoral programs, graduate schools or large-scale projects) are recommended to join forces and minimize the otherwise huge recruiting effort.
- Modern and attractive infrastructure such as labs (also for up-scaling), makerspaces or co-working facilities are necessary basic requirements to bring ideas into practice.

Empowerment

At the empowerment stage, scouts step back. After successfully feeding the spin-off funnel, they hand over responsibilities to Gateway's startup coaches. Once a business model has to be substantiated, Gateway's incubation and acceleration programs become involved.

It must be considered that no universally valid definitions of "incubator" and "accelerator" exist. The framework conditions and definitions of the individual stakeholders (e.g., universities, private sector initiatives, industry, industry associations, co-working spaces and technology centers) are too varied for this. According to the *Kreditanstalt für Wiederaufbau* (2024), an **incubator** is all about creating optimal conditions for the development of business ideas. It is therefore often referred to as an "incubator" for developing new ideas in a protected environment, aiming at projects that are at the very beginning of a startup phase and require professional support in developing a business idea. The tasks of an incubator also include training participants to become successful founders and supporting the formation of teams. The primary goal of **accelerators** is to support founders or startups with an existing business idea as a kind of "growth accelerator" to get ideas and business models ready for the market as quickly as possible. The accelerator is therefore typically akin to a boot camp, in which various startups work intensively on the further development of their business model in a creative and inspiring working environment and mutually stimulate each other in the process (Kreditanstalt für Wiederaufbau, 2024).

What incubators and accelerators have in common is the provision of resources (e.g., workspaces and infrastructure), the offer of professional support (usually through mentoring programs and coaching from experts), the existence of close relationships between founders and sponsors and, in many cases, the provision of initial or startup financing or a founder's salary for the duration of the program (especially in the case of accelerators) (Kley & Lindner, 2023). Furthermore, with some programs, founders must give up shares in their startup in return for participating in such a program. The latter two features of financial compensation are not the norm for incubators and accelerators in the university environment. Instead, they usually provide support in acquiring public funding (often involving technology or transfer scouts), such as the Exist Business Start-up Grant (https://exist.de/en/programm/exist-gruendungsstipendium/), Exist Transfer of Research (https://exist.de/en/programm/exist-forschungstransfer/), GO-Bio (https://www.go-bio.de/gobio/en/home/home_node.html) or VIP+ (https://www.validierungsfoerderung.de/).

At universities, projects that are still in the development phase and deal with the problem-solution fit are candidates for an incubator. Accelerators at universities are aimed at projects that are at least concerned with product-market fit. If incubators and accelerators were placed on a timeline in relation to startups, incubators would become relevant for founders before accelerators (Kley & Lindner, 2023). Gateway's incubator and accelerator both offer a curriculum of founders' talks, workshops and seminars on basic (legal framework, project management, among others) and advanced topics (human resource management, investment readiness, etc.). Teams of each cohort also receive education tailored to answer specific questions for their startups and their industry, often with the help of mentors from alumni companies or corporations. Education along the funnel, therefore, becomes more practice-oriented the further developed the startups are.

International collaboration best practices

Terkko Health Hub and Tartu Biotechnology Park provide two blueprints for successfully establishing an ecosystem for university spin-offs. Gateway collaborates with both partners already and is looking for further expanding joint activities.

Terkko Health Hub

The Terkko Health Hub, the biggest health hub in Finland, is a startup community, a coworking space and an event venue focusing on health and life science entrepreneurship. The hub is in the heart of Helsinki's medical campus and thus at the junction of the HUS University Hospital, the Faculty of Medicine at the University of Helsinki and HiLIFE, the Helsinki Institute of Life Science. Terkko Health Hub provides various services, events and programs for community members in collaboration with local and global partners. Its mission is to promote a new form of collaboration between entrepreneurship, research and healthcare to make their startups grow and flourish. Terkko Health Hub houses startups, researchers and corporations, as well as the entrepreneurship society of the University of Helsinki, Helsinki Think Company, which aims to help people bring their academic skills into action. Moreover, two recurring programs are taking place at Terkko: the pre-incubator program HealthX, and Health Incubator Helsinki, a unique 3-year-long incubator program for research-driven teams and startups working in the field of health and life sciences. The program is a joint project of the City of Helsinki and the University of Helsinki. It aims to transform health innovation, research findings and skills into commercial products and international businesses. Ecosystem partners also located at Terkko are Biodesign Finland, which aims to improve medical care by providing a novel entrepreneurial program to selected interdisciplinary teams and by creating new businesses, and SPARK Finland. SPARK Finland offers a program that is designed to increase the maturity of academic and clinical discoveries toward practical and value-creating solutions in the health tech and life science space. The program also supports career development by educating scientists, students and healthcare professionals on drug and health tech development and building an understanding of business aspects related to the discoveries. Terkko considers itself an active and positive change agent on campus, collaborating with the goal of bolstering and developing the innovation landscape going forward (Terkko Health Hub, 2024).

Tartu Biotechnology Park

The aim of Tartu Biotechnology Park (TBP) is to create a favorable and developing environment for the promotion of biotechnological entrepreneurship in Estonia. TBP provides physical infrastructure as well as business development and consultancy services to companies and research and development (R&D) institutions in the fields of biotechnology, medicine and veterinary medicine. It supports companies in finding cooperation partners and is active in establishing new companies. To achieve its aims and to provide better services, TBP engages in active cooperation with Estonian and foreign biotechnology companies, R&D institutions, foundations for the development of entrepreneurship and biotechnology, and other organizations, including state agencies and local authorities. Major projects, backed by European Union (EU) funding, focus on biotechnology, healthcare and food technology. (Tartu Biotechnology Park, 2024).

Business incubation is one of the main activity fields of Tartu Biotechnology Park. By offering high-quality infrastructure services as well as business development and consultancy services, it aims to create a favorable environment for startup enterprises to boost their growth and competitiveness. Since September 2005, TBP has operated the BioMed incubator for biotechnology, medical and veterinary businesses. The BioMed incubator is also open to companies outside of Tartu. The business does not have to be in Tartu Biotechnology Park; this is called virtual incubation (Tartu Biotechnology Park, 2024).

Conclusions and outlook

Currently, Gateway covers the spin-off life cycle from the first idea to market entry. The next step will be to offer support for growing startups that look for further Gateway support while scaling their business – so-called scale-ups. To this end, Gateway needs to extend its existing funnel (Figure 10.1). Although services from ideation up to incubation will largely remain unchanged, services like the accelerator will become essential to attract scale-ups and to close the gap to ecosystem partners already offering support to companies at the growth stage. This means new services will supplement the Gateway funnel. The first modules – "sensitization", "education" and "enablement" (including the transfer scouts) – will remain within the existing structure. Services to support already existing startups, however, will be implemented by a new company that Gateway launched in early 2025.

Gateway's current service portfolio is industry-agnostic. However, in the future, Gateway will establish specialized hubs, one of which will address startups from the fields of **well-being, health** and **life science**. This industry focus will build on the experiences and knowledge gained through the activities implemented in the fields of enablement and empowerment. The hub will also contribute to a stronger startup ecosystem for industries such as health and well-being. To this end, Terkko Health Hub, Tartu Biotechnology Park and others will serve as valuable blueprints. Gateway therefore looks to further cooperation.

Currently, the UoC together with the other Gateway Hochschulen and the RWTH Aachen, as well as other partners such as the Start2 Group, are developing a concept to attract national and international scale-ups. So far, the support offered through the Gateway funnel ends when startups leave the accelerator, that is, when they enter the market, usually having acquired a minor pre-seed investment. In the future, focus will also be on seed and early Series A companies that start to scale their business and go international, and the service portfolio will be extended accordingly. At the same time, the concept of the hub, which is supposed to be internationally recognized, targets startups from within and outside Europe to open the doors of the German market to them.

References

Backs, S., & Buermann, H. (2023). Wer, wie, was – wieso, weshalb, warum? Gründungsökosysteme und die Rolle einer Hochschule. In V. Breithecker, & S. Hanny-Busch (Eds.), *Handbuch Hochschul-StartUps* (pp. 41–50). Erich Schmidt Verlag.

Belitski, M., & Sikorski, J. (2024). Three steps for universities to become entrepreneurial: a case study of entrepreneurial process and dynamic capabilities. *The Journal of Technology Transfer*, *49*, 2035–2055. https://doi.org/10.1007/s10961-024-10099-1

EFI – Commission of Experts for Research and Innovation (Ed.) (2019). Report on research, innovation and technological performance in Germany 2019. Berlin. https://hdl.handle.net/10419/204778

Fini, R., Perkmann, M., & Ross, J. M. (2022). Attention to exploration: The effect of academic entrepreneurship on the production of scientific knowledge. *Organization Science*, *33*(2), 688–715.

Hochschulrektorenkonferenz (2017). *Transfer und Kooperation als Aufgaben der Hochschulen. Entschließung der 23. Mitgliederversammlung der HRK am 14.* November 2017 in Potsdam. https://www.hrk.de/fileadmin/redaktion/hrk/02-Dokumente/02-01-Beschluesse/Entschliessung_Transfer_und_Kooperation_14112017.pdf..

Horsch, J. (2003). *Innovations- und Projektmanagement. Von der strategischen Konzeption bis zur operativen Umsetzung*. Gabler.

Kley, M., & Lindner, F. (2023). Die START-UP Innovationslabore als Blaupause für Hochschul-Acceleratoren. In V. Breithecker, & S. Hanny-Busch (Eds.), *Handbuch Hochschul-StartUps* (pp. 117–128). Erich Schmidt Verlag.

Kreditanstalt für Wiederaufbau (2024) https://gruenderplattform.de/finanzierung-und-foerderung/finanzierung-finden/finanzierungsmoeglichkeiten/accelerator

Kriedel, R., & Dibke, S. (2023). Aufbau eines öffentlichen Transferfunnels von öffentlichen bis hin zu privatwirtschaftlichen Strukturen? In V. Breithecker, & S. Hanny-Busch (Eds.), *Handbuch Hochschul-StartUps* (pp. 79–102). Erich Schmidt Verlag.

Schönenberger, H., & Steiner-Kaiser, J. (2023). Wie gelingt es, eine starke Forschungs-Universität zu einer unternehmerischen Hochschule zu entwickeln? In V. Breithecker, & S. Hanny-Busch (Eds.), *Handbuch hochschul-StartUps* (pp. 69–78). Erich Schmidt Verlag.

Schultz, C. (2021). Does technology scouting impact spin-out generation? An action research study in the context of an entrepreneurial university. In D. Mietzner, & C. Schultz (Eds.), *FGF studies in small business and entrepreneurship. New perspectives in technology transfer. Theories, concepts and practices in an age of complexity* (pp. 107–128). Springer Nature.

Tartu BIOTEHNOLOOGIA PARK (2024). https://biopark.ee

Terkko Health Hub (2024). *Annual report* 2023. https://terkko.fi/wp-content/uploads/2024/05/Terkko-annual-report-2023-1.1.pdf

Wissema, J. G. (2009). *Towards the third generation university. Managing the university in transition*. Edward Elgar Publishing.

Wutscher, W., Gumpenberger, E., & Berger, M. (2024). *Akademische Spin-offs Ausgründungsrahmen für österreichische Hochschulen und Forschungseinrichtungen*. New Venture Scouting.

11 Blessings and Challenges of Social Media Marketing Strategies in Higher Education Health Program Recruitment

Jeff Wilkesmann

Introduction

To guarantee successful degree programs, potential participants must be informed of their existence. The past COVID-19 pandemic situation affected recruitment efficiency. Health educational programs are also market-dependent, and a resilient international business model must be present to counteract fluctuations. Although some criteria to assess the success of the program are the number of graduates trained in innovation and entrepreneurship, as well as the investment attracted by startups or the number of startups created by students enrolled, an important factor to be highlighted is also the program's deployment across social media. Failing to deliver in any of these indicators represents a major risk, leading to underperformance and ultimately jeopardizing the program's lifespan.

International funding organizations have identified social media as a potential promotion system and use it with enhancements to influence marketing with social media promotion (Sajid, 2016). Social media marketing (SMM) includes all marketing measures on social media, such as Facebook, Instagram and TikTok. These platforms offer an additional opportunity to interact with their target group and draw attention to themselves. Social media plays a key role in health education programs by providing a platform for raising awareness, modifying health behavior and promoting health education (Ghahramani et al., 2022). Social media has certain advantages over other marketing strategies. Costs related to social media are usually low, and it serves as a high-impact tool.

Which platform is the best suited? This will depend heavily on its offering and target group. TikTok might work better with a younger audience, whereas Facebook may meet better the demands of a more mature audience. The best-known social media channels are Facebook, YouTube, XING, Instagram, TikTok and X (formerly Twitter). Not only are these platforms ideal for health promotion, education and advocacy efforts, but they also allow fast sharing of relevant information to wide and diverse populations. It is therefore advisable for teaching and administrative staff in the health education area to integrate social media into their outreach initiatives. There is a growing demand for instant communication and concise information, and therefore an active and

DOI: 10.4324/9781003568650-12

strong presence in social media channels can only help funding organizations and higher-education institutions (HEIs) to maximize their reach and impact when promoting educational programs (Eastern Washington University, 2022; Gatewood et al., 2020).

The application of marketing techniques to social problems, like health education, is called social marketing. Here, people are encouraged or motivated to adopt specific courses of action or behavior that are generally accepted as beneficial (Birkinshaw & World Health Organization, 1989). Evaluating the performance of social media campaigns to promote health or education behaviors towards a sustainable outcome is a complex process. The methodologies used in existing studies usually target immediate behavior or social media engagement rather than the importance of the research topic per se (Ruangkanjanases et al., 2022). This chapter offers insights on the implications of social media for student recruitment strategies, based on some selected HEIs in Germany.

During the COVID-19 pandemic, several sectors, including education, adopted or enhanced their social media strategies for different purposes, including awareness, advertising and sharing information. This chapter assesses the influence of social media on participants of selected M.Sc. programs, and furthermore intends to extrapolate the significance of social media platforms for marketing purposes in the wider health education ecosystem. The potential of social media in the promotion of a specific higher-education health-related Master's program is analyzed, and the impact of social media on the program is assessed.

Social media and HEI overview

Social media

Social media has a broad and resilient definition, which is subjected to constant changes. In general, it refers to digital media or platforms that enable users to connect with one another on the internet, allowing information exchange, creating and sharing (new) media content (ideas, messages, images, etc.) individually or collectively, privately or publicly, or even in real time (Ventola, 2014). Table 11.1 provides an overview of the six main types of social media, employing two criteria, (a) self-presentation (desire to control the impressions other people form of them), and (b) social presence (acoustic, visual and physical contact that can be achieved). However, other authors (Gu & Wang, 2012) have classified the social media scope across five categories (namely, blog, microblog, social networking site, location-based service and theme community). Currently, these social media types are being used in more than one way by marketers and planners to promote their ideas of interest (Dwivedi et al., 2015).

The importance of social media depends directly upon a high number of users. The internet, social media mobile apps, and many other digital communication technologies, currently encompass billions of users (Dias Proença,

Table 11.1 Classification of social media (adapted from Kaplan & Haenlein, 2010; Ventola, 2014)

Level of social Presence	*Level of self-presentation*	
	High	*Low*
High	Virtual social worlds	Virtual Game Worlds (Second Life)
Medium	Social network sites (Facebook, MySpace, Google Plus, Twitter, Instagram) Professional networking (LinkedIn);	Content communities/Media sharing (YouTube, TikTok)
Low	Content Production Blogs (Tumbler) Microblogs (X, formerly Twitter)	Collaborative projects (Wikipedia)

2021). In addition to individuals, companies are also present on social media. Furthermore, leading social networks are generally available in multiple languages, enabling users to connect with others, eliminating any kind of geographical, political, or economic limitations. Given the large number of daily users, brands may rapidly gain high recognition in a cost-effective way.

Digital marketing and social media marketing

Digital marketing encompasses the use of technology to help improve customer understanding, which is achieved by meeting customer needs (Chaffey & Ellis-Chadwick, 2019). Digital marketing's biggest advantage is the possibility to appropriately reach the target audience using social media and search engines (Durmaz & Efendioglu, 2016). An important aspect of digital marketing is web analytics, which helps in collecting, measuring, understanding, analyzing, planning, reporting and predicting web activity for business purposes (Bala & Verma, 2018).

SMM is a type of digital marketing that uses social media platforms and websites to promote a specific product or a service. As defined by Dwivedi et al. (2015, p. 291), SMM is "a dialogue often triggered by consumers/audiences, or a business/product/service that travels in a circle amongst the stated parties to set in motion revealing communications on some promotional information, or to learn from one another's use experiences, eventually benefitting either or all of the involved parties". Thus, the use of SMM allows organizations to engage in opportune and direct end-consumer contact at (relatively) low cost and at higher levels of efficiency compared to more traditional communication tools (Alalwan et al., 2017).

Social media has steadily developed from a single marketing tool to a marketing intelligence source. Organizations can now monitor, analyze and predict user behaviors. Consequently, achieving competitive advantage and superior performance requires that marketers use and leverage social media strategically (Lamberton & Stephen, 2016). It has been pointed out that there are four general types of SMM objectives (Dias Proença, 2021; Li et al., 2021):

- to promote and sell (e.g., B2C),
- to connect and collaborate (e.g., business-with-customers),
- to listen and learn (e.g., business-from-customers) and
- to empower and engage (e.g., business-for-customers).

Social media marketing in higher education

Social media marketing in education encompasses, for example, the implementation of social media platforms with the goals of promoting and marketing educational institutions and programs to candidates, active and former students, as well as other stakeholders. Table 11.2 summarizes some uses and advantages of implementing SMM for educational purposes. Some risks and drawbacks are also explained.

HEIs use social networks mainly as a strategic tool for positioning themselves. It has been reported that HEIs in Europe and the United States give more importance to research topics than teaching activities or social commitment. The main platforms used are generally X (formerly Twitter), Facebook and LinkedIn, displaying both functional and institutional content (Capriotti et al., 2023). Compared to Europe, U.S. universities established before 2011, have a significant advantage in leveraging social media as integral components of their marketing strategies; of the 456 U.S. institutions involved in a study, all used some form of social media, with Facebook being the most prevalent platform (98%), followed by Twitter (84%) (Orgilés-Amorós et al., 2024). Yet, advertising only on one social networking site is insufficient, and it is important to invest time in monitoring users' responses and interacting with individual users to fully benefit from SMM (Palmer, 2012).

An extensive adoption of X (formerly Twitter) as a communication tool by HEIs has been detected; however, there is also strong evidence that X fails when it comes to branding and marketing purposes, chiefly because of a lack of strategic approach in social media (Orgilés-Amorós et al., 2024). The importance of SMM in HEIs can be better understood when matriculation is assessed as a variable. Among the motivating factors when students select a specific HEI for their (Master's) studies, well-established HEIs, with high reputations and strong brand images, located in major metropolitan areas attract the majority of (international) students, making recruitment challenging for lesser-known HEIs in less populated areas (Scott, 2020). The integration of SMM into the technological resources of HEIs is broadly considered positive (Aldahdouh et al., 2020) and the major benefits can be listed as:

- establishing new, maintaining existing and widening connections;
- facilitating collaboration and communication;

Table 11.2 Advantages and disadvantages of the different roles of social media marketing (SMM) implemented for educational purposes

Advantages	*Role of social media*
Higher learning opportunities	Educators share announcements and can hold live lectures (and record them for future use).
Interconnectivity among stakeholders	Connections across various audiences are fostered. HEI can communicate quickly and directly with students, faculty, staff and alumni.
Brand identity is built	HEI can attract more students, increase endowments, promote events or initiatives and improve alumni relations.
Broadcast updates and alerts via posts	Lecturers can meet participants where they are by incorporating social media platforms (e.g., Facebook or X). Students may join a Facebook Group to view posts about course updates, homework, or tests.
Education marketing	A larger audience can be approached beyond geographical borders.
Disadvantages	
Danger related to information quality	Given the reproduction of information, different sources, referring theoretically to the same content, may provide different (or not updated) information.
Damage to institutional image	Posting of unprofessional content can reflect unfavorably on the HEI's image, trajectory or credibility.
Breaches of privacy and ethics	Internal information (from courses, learning material, etc.) may leak into the public realm, leading to licensing issues, intellectual property (IP) damage, or deeper legal issues.
International legal frameworks	Sometimes legal frameworks may vary from country to country. It remains unclear how the process of opening course content to the public sphere is expected to influence academic freedom, privacy laws and intellectual property rights.

Adapted from Kaplan & Haenlein (2010); Shabur & Siddiki (2024); Ventola (2014.)

- self-development; and
- increasing one's own work visibility through dissemination (Manca & Ranieri, 2017).

The impact of SMM on brand preference was studied by focusing on the mediation influence of brand recognizability and the moderator influence of brand signature in HEIs in Germany. It was found that HEI's SMM had a significant effect on both brand recognizability and students' brand preference (Arici & Arici, 2021). A comparative analysis of international students in Germany and the United Kingdom (UK) was published, analyzing the factors involved when selecting a country for higher education (Abbas et al., 2021).

Identifying the gap

Social media measurements can be theoretically performed easily through the built-in social media tools, analytics and metrics. Nonetheless, there is no direct relationship between the number of likes or views on a specific platform and the number of participants actually registered in the program (Freeman et al., 2015). Previous research conducted on the use of social media by HEIs has focused on limited time periods and on specific platforms (Capriotti et al., 2023). Case studies corresponding to specific European geographies like Spain or the Netherlands have been reported (Orgilés-Amorós et al., 2024; Constantinides & Zinck Stagno, 2011) as well as other regions (Scott, 2020; Shabur & Siddiki, 2024). Nonetheless, limited information has been published for (Master's) programs in the health sector in Germany. Considering the significant influence of social media on the economic impact for HEIs, it is mandatory to conduct studies that explore the use of SMM in Germany. Such studies would allow us to gain insights into the marketing efforts undertaken by a given HEI to effectively adapt to new technologies and innovations, fortifying their brand awareness and image over time.

The number of studies on SMM and its effectiveness in education is not as plentiful as in other fields, and the suitability of social media as tools for higher-education marketing remains a field open to further exploration. This chapter contributes to bridging this gap by analyzing selected Master's programs and providing further discussion of common successes and lessons learned when it comes to the application of SMM for recruitment.

German HEI cases

The M.Sc. program in Health and Medical Data Analytics (HMDA) from the University of Erlangen-Nuremberg, Germany, joins four other top-notch European universities (FAU, Técnico Superior Lisboa, Université Grenoble Alpes and Universidad Politécnica de Madrid), in offering robust training in entrepreneurship combined with innovative education in healthcare data analytics. A unique and transdisciplinary academic profile is created by obligatory international student mobility and cross-organizational internships. Graduates are foreseen to be entrepreneurs and information scientists with sophisticated skills in data analytics for health applications. Furthermore, the predominant education in innovation and entrepreneurship empowers them with a well-advanced understanding of how to take advantage of exploiting their knowledge from a business perspective (Friedrich-Alexander-Universität Erlangen-Nürnberg, 2024). The program's recruitment was contrasted with the MBA International Business Management at the *Hochschule für Wirtschaft und Gesellschaft Ludwigshafen* and the Master's program in Biotechnology at the *Technische Hochschule Mannheim*.

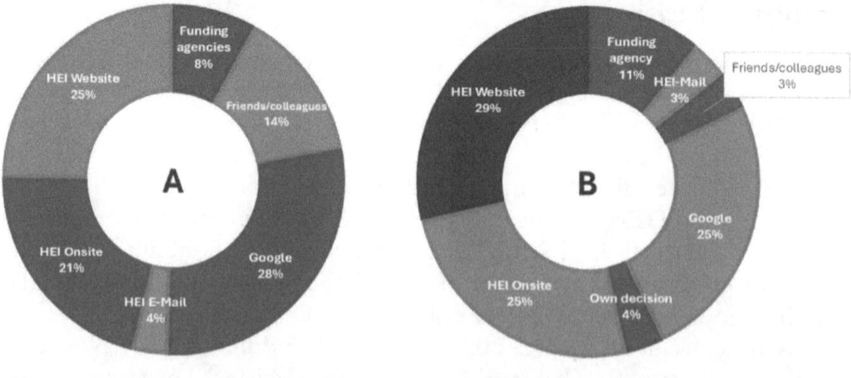

Figure 11.1 Survey results for the following questions: (A) Where did you first hear about your Master's program? (B) Which information source influenced your decision to register for your Master's program?

SMM influence on Master's program selection

The potential impact of SMM on Master's program participants was surveyed. Figure 11.1 shows the answers obtained the first time the participant heard about the program in which they participated, and which source influenced the participant's decision. It is clear that Internet search tools like Google and the HEI's own website had the highest scores, and combined for up to 50%. Nonetheless, on-site information activities remained important (25%) for getting to know the program and deciding to register.

It was also determined that 89% of the population sampled had an active social media account. Contrary to previous reports, where Facebook and X are among the favorite social media channels that influence students' selection for a Master's program, in this case LinkedIn had the highest votes (36%). Interestingly, 32% of the survey participants stated that their decision was not influenced by any social media. However, when all social media choices were combined (including Google+, Facebook, YouTube, MyGuide), they totaled 68%, leading to the idea that social media indeed played a major role in selecting a study program among the population surveyed.

According to the experts interviewed, marketing and program awareness are two key activities of a main project plan. "Marketing actions and time commitment highly depend on the academic year", because programs were promoted when registration was open. Although promotion included social media measures, one limitation was the impossibility of having one's own social media channel (e.g., LinkedIn, Instagram, X, etc.). An advantage was the use of central marketing channels (from involved HEIs) to showcase program successes, achievements and important updates. Time commitment for these activities is difficult to assign. Some of the main social media channels used were LinkedIn, Instagram and X (which were the central marketing social media channels).

Table 11.3 Recommendations provided by the participants to enhance the robustness of their Master's program in the different social media

Participants' recommendations
"Ensure that your program curriculum stays current with the latest industry trends, tools and best practices. This can involve regular updates to course materials and collaboration with industry professionals."
"More videos with students (Day in the life type videos or students walking around on campus, showing off the school)."
"More content from students about the program."
"More posts on Social Media."
"The program I am in is not so widely known."
"Raise more engagement, reach to young people, more videos and interactive visuals."
"Explain the several career opportunities."
"It seems that our master's program may not have been effectively communicated over social media. However, after reading some posts, I noticed a lack of clarity regarding the nature of the program. It's important to convey to students that they are not transitioning to an entirely new master's program but rather focusing general skills developed in the master into a more focused thematic that is medical field."

Do students and alumni use social media to further promote their Master's program?

Participants were asked if they would recommend their Master's program to others; 100% answered positively. Their specific recommendations are collected in Table 11.3.

Limitations and future perspectives

As mentioned by Ghahramani et al. (2022), evaluating the performance of social media in promoting an education program towards a sustainable outcome is a complex process. This chapter provides a modest approach, using three HEIs, in the search for new pathways for research into the impact of SMM in HEIs linked to recruitment.

As pointed out by Watermeyer et al. (2021), the future of student recruitment may strongly depend on the HEI's digital offerings. Online learning, teaching and assessment might reduce the appeal and holistic nature of education at HEIs. Nevertheless, online education is an attractive point when recruiting because it may eliminate the need for costly physical relocation. It seems that HEIs should not rely solely on their brand quality to attract students. They actually need to clearly demonstrate the quality of their digital offerings to stay competitive, especially given the challenge from more technologically advanced private higher-education providers.

Generation Z, expert users of social media, is getting prepared to attend higher education, but are HEIs fully prepared for a correct social media presence? Social media in higher education is undergoing an expansion, but not all

HEIs are using social media tools to build on their institutional reputation or foster a sense of engagement among prospective students. Candidate students depend on social media to help them make study decisions. Nonetheless, it is not enough to publish recruiting materials on higher-education social feeds. Using SMM and maintaining an active social presence capable of drawing continuous attention is a tactical game. Content communicated to the audience may fluctuate from fascinating to boring in a short period of time. Future research must include statistical tools that use the most important social media platforms (Facebook, X, YouTube and LinkedIn) to determine their further implementation for recruitment purposes. Given user affinity for these particular sites, they are the regulating hubs of Web 2.0, where SMM solely operates.

In general, more empirical studies are required to better understand the factors controlling the diffusion and adoption of SMM in HEIs. At the administration level, it would be important to know whether communication through social media platforms aligns with the mission and strategy of each HEI. By understanding this alignment, more effective communication strategies can be developed and would guarantee that the HEI's goals are effectively exhibited in its online presence. By embracing the findings of this research, HEIs can better leverage the potential of social media, enhancing their competitive advantages.

In addition to better recruitment opportunities, social media platforms provide HEIs with further possibilities for engaging with their (regional, national and international) communities, ultimately enabling them to promote fruitful dialogues and request stakeholder feedback. By actively participating in conversations, responding to suggestions and inquiries and addressing concerns, HEIs would be able to foster a sense of community and strengthen their relationship with followers.

Conclusion

Skills development by HEI leaders on SMM strategies for international Master's programs is mandatory. SMM allows prospective students to get a glimpse of the HEI and all potentially relevant programs (and not just one). The current students in Master's studies were born between 1990 and 2000. Because the prospective customers of higher education belong to Generation Z (born from 1997 until 2012), and given the ease of engaging them via social media, it is important for HEIs to continue implementing and enhancing SMM for recruitment purposes.

This chapter provides valuable insights for academic policymakers and administrators for optimizing and enhancing their SMM performance. Although social media greatly promotes HEI relevance in the academic landscape, many HEIs are not fully aware of the total potential that each platform offers. Some HEIs present challenges when implementing social media. Budgets are restricted, and personnel for these tasks are not always available, which sometimes leads to engagement of staff members (interns) who lack the proper experience in managing social media. Among other social media capabilities are improvements in information, including pictures, videos and interactive media, to enhance user motivation.

Information posted on the different social media by HEIs must always be comprehensive and user-friendly, and the social media presence should give potential students a different online means of communicating with HEIs. In general, HEIs still need to invest more time in monitoring user responses and interacting with the individual users to fully benefit from SMM strategies. SMM positively influences candidate students in their decision-making process to select a specific Master's program in Germany, and current students and alumni do positively encourage social media to further promote their Master's program.

Thus, SMM is causing a positive influence when candidates opt for a Master's study program (for the three German HEIs analyzed); furthermore, the same students support additional use of social media to keep promoting the program. These results should constitute an incentive for HEIs to assess and further develop the effectiveness of social media for student recruitment purposes. A proper regulation of SMM strategies is required to excel in recruitment. Moreover, in the general Pan-European educational context, further research possibilities in capacity building for business innovation, marketing and quality assurance in higher-education programs should be explored for adequate implementation. Additionally, funding agencies can also benefit from these aspects.

Indirectly, it was found that HEIs are still unable to see their social media users as senders of marketing communications. The continuous monitoring of conversations and content uploaded to blogs and social networks is not considered a priority yet. Communication tracking may lead to innovative perspectives and insights that could allow better management to improve SMM strategies.

The sole creation of a social media presence is important, but not enough to assure appropriate matriculation levels. Efforts in maintaining social media presence must be maintained to keep audiences (candidate students) and general stakeholders updated with current information. Evidently, Master's programs with SMM deficiencies belonging to HEIs that are either not well-ranked, are of recent creation or do not yet have established brand equity, are completely at risk of disappearing. On the other hand, the more specialized a Master's program is, the higher its uniqueness and the lower the risks that it will be shut down because a certain attractiveness remains.

Acknowledgments

I thank the collaboration of the M.Sc. HMDA community at the Friedrich-Alexander-Universität Erlangen-Nürnberg, especially to Dr. A. Jain for enabling the interaction with C. Barnickel, to M. Méjica and Dr. P. Carneiro. I thank Dr. H. Shamma, E. Nefen and the different cohorts from the MBA International Business Management at the *Hochschule für Wirtschaft und Gesellschaft*

Ludwigshafen, and the Master's program in Biotechnology from the *"Technische" Hochschule Mannheim*.

References

Abbas, J., Alturki, U., Habib, M., Aldraiweesh, A., & Al-Rahmi, W. M. (2021). Factors affecting students in the selection of country for higher education: A comparative analysis of international students in Germany and the UK. *Sustainability*, *13*(18), 10065. https://doi.org/10.3390/su131810065

Alalwan, A. A., Rana, N. P., Dwivedi, Y. K., & Algharabat, R. (2017). Social media in marketing: A review and analysis of the existing literature. *Telematics and Informatics*, *34*(7), 1177–1190. https://doi.org/10.1016/j.tele.2017.05.008

Aldahdouh, T. Z., Nokelainen, P., & Korhonen, V. (2020). Technology and social media usage in higher education: The influence of individual innovativeness. *Sage Open*, *10*(1), 2158244019899441. https://doi.org/10.1177/2158244019899441

Arici, H. E., & Arici, N. C. (2021). The role of social media marketing activities on international Students' brand preference: A study on English-speaking universities of Germany. In Shneikat, B., Cobanoglu, C. and Tanova, C., eds. *Global perspectives on recruiting international students: Challenges and opportunities* (pp. 51–64). Emerald Publishing Limited. https://doi.org/10.1108/978-1-83982-518-720211003

Bala, M., & Verma, D. (2018). A critical review of digital marketing. *International Journal of Management*, *8*(10), 321–339.

Birkinshaw, M., & World Health Organization. (1989). *Social marketing for health* (No. HMD/89.2). https://iris.who.int/bitstream/handle/10665/62146/HMD_89.2.pdf

Capriotti, P., Losada-Díaz, J. C., & Martínez-Gras, R. (2023). Evaluating the content strategy developed by universities on social media. *Profesional De La Información*, *32*(2). https://doi.org/10.3145/epi.2023.mar.10

Chaffey, D., & Ellis-Chadwick, F. (2019). *Digital marketing* (7th ed.). Pearson, Part 1, pp. 2–91.

Constantinides, E., & Zinck Stagno, M. C. (2011). Potential of the social media as instruments of higher education marketing: A segmentation study. *Journal of Marketing for Higher Education*, *21*(1), 7–24. https://doi.org/10.1080/08841241.2011.573593

Dias Proença, M. H. (2021). *The application of social media for marketing strategies in pharma healthcare* (Doctoral dissertation, ISCTE-Instituto Universitario de Lisboa, Portugal), pp. 1–272.

Durmaz, Y., & Efendioglu, I. H. (2016). Travel from traditional marketing to digital marketing. *Global Journal of Management and Business Research*, *16*(2), 34–40.

Dwivedi, Y. K., Kapoor, K. K., & Chen, H. (2015). Social media marketing and advertising. *The Marketing Review*, *15*(3), 289–309. https://doi.org/10.1362/146934715X14441363377999

Eastern Washington University (2022) *Using social media for public health education and outreach.* https://online.ewu.edu/degrees/healthcare/public-health/social-media-public-health-education/ (last consulted December 2024)

Freeman, B., Potente, S., Rock, V., & McIver, J. (2015). Social media campaigns that make a difference: What can public health learn from the corporate sector and other social change marketers. *Public Health Research & Practice*, *25*(2), e2521517. https://api.semanticscholar.org/CorpusID:45048242

Friedrich-Alexander-Universität Erlangen-Nürnberg. (2024) https://www.medical-engineering.study.fau.eu/prospective-students/joining-the-master-degree-program/ and https://www.medical-engineering.study.fau.eu/files/2019/11/HMDA-Welcome.pdf (Consulted December 2024)

Gatewood, J., Monks, S. L., Singletary, C. R., Vidrascu, E., & Moore, J. B. (2020). Social media in public health: Strategies to distill, package, and disseminate public health research. *Journal of Public Health Management and Practice*, *26*(5), 489–492. https://doi.org/10.1097/PHH.0000000000001096

Ghahramani, A., de Courten, M., & Prokofieva, M. (2022). The potential of social media in health promotion beyond creating awareness: An integrative review. *BMC Public Health*, *22*(1), 2402. https://doi.org/10.1186/s12889-022-14885-0

Gu, C., & Wang, S. (2012). Empirical study on social media marketing based on sina microblog. In: *2012 Second International Conference on Business Computing and Global Informatization* (pp. 537–540). IEEE. https://doi.org/10.1109/BCGIN.2012.146

Kaplan, A. M., & Haenlein, M. (2010). Users of the world, unite! The challenges and opportunities of Social Media. *Business Horizons*, *53*(1), 59–68. https://doi.org/10.1016/j.bushor.2009.09.003

Lamberton, C., & Stephen, A. T. (2016). A thematic exploration of digital, social media, and mobile marketing: Research evolution from 2000 to 2015 and an agenda for future inquiry. *Journal of Marketing*, *80*(6), 146–172. https://doi.org/10.1509/jm.15.0415

Li, F., Larimo, J., & Leonidou, L. C. (2021). Social media marketing strategy: Definition, conceptualization, taxonomy, validation, and future agenda. *Journal of the Academy of Marketing Science*, *49*, 51–70. https://doi.org/10.1007/s11747-020-00733-3

Manca, S., & Ranieri, M. (2017). Exploring digital scholarship: A study on use of social media for scholarly communication among Italian academics. In Esposito, A. ed. *Research 2.0 and the impact of digital technologies on scholarly inquiry* (pp. 117–142). IGI Global.

Orgilés-Amorós, M., Ruiz Moreno, F., Penagos-Londoño, G. I., & Tabuenca-Cuevas, M. (2024). Twitter killed the media star: A historical evolution of marketing communication used by Spanish universities. *Journal of Historical Research in Marketing*, *16*(1), 48–70. https://doi.org/10.1108/JHRM-07-2023-0033

Palmer, L. A. (2012). Understanding social media advertising in higher ed: A case study from a small graduate program. In *Proceedings of the 30th ACM International Conference on Design of Communication*, pp. 115–120. https://doi.org/10.1145/2379057.2379079

Ruangkanjanases, A., Sivarak, O., Wibowo, A., & Chen, S. C. (2022). Creating behavioral engagement among higher education's prospective students through social media marketing activities: The role of brand equity as mediator. *Frontiers in Psychology*, *13*, 1004573. https://doi.org/10.3389/fpsyg.2022.1004573

Sajid, S. I. (2016) Social media and its role in marketing. *Business and Economics Journal*, 7, 203. https://doi.org/10.4172/2151-6219.1000203

Scott, J. (2020). Recruiting international postgraduate researchers: Challenges and strategic alternatives. *Asia Pacific Journal of Marketing and Logistics*, *32*(1), 281–298. https://doi.org/10.1108/APJML-01-2018-0011

Shabur, M. A., & Siddiki, M. R. (2024). Investigating social media's impact on the new era of interactive learning: A case study of Bangladesh. *Heliyon*, *10*(4), e26234. https://doi.org/10.1016/j.heliyon.2024.e26234

Ventola, C. L. (2014). Social media and health care professionals: Benefits, risks, and best practices. *Pharmacy and Therapeutics*, *39*(7), 491. https://pmc.ncbi.nlm.nih.gov/articles/PMC4103576/

Watermeyer, R., Crick, T., Knight, C., & Goodall, J. (2021). COVID-19 and digital disruption in UK universities: Afflictions and affordances of emergency online migration. *Higher Education*, *81*, 623–641. https://doi.org/10.1007/s10734-020-00561-y

Conclusions

Jeff Wilkesmann

This book began by analyzing the importance of multidisciplinary education to support healthy lifestyles. This approach integrates knowledge from various disciplines (such as health sciences, nutrition, psychology, physical education, public health and social sciences) to promote and sustain healthy behaviors in individuals and communities. It emphasizes a holistic, evidence-based and collaborative learning framework to equip professionals, students and the public with the skills and knowledge to improve health outcomes. Health is not just the absence of disease but a combination of physical, mental and social well-being. This important concept has been adjusted and integrated for further research at the EIT Health Ageing PhD School. Traditional education often focuses on isolated subjects, but multidisciplinary education to support healthy lifestyles integrates knowledge from various fields into practical strategies for individuals and communities to adopt healthier lifestyles. Significant gaps were identified, and the Ageing PhD School proposes different approaches to bridge those gaps.

Noncommunicable diseases (NCDs), such as diabetes, cardiovascular disease and mental health disorders, are leading causes of mortality worldwide. A multidisciplinary approach helps design policies and programs to mitigate these risks at both local and global levels.

Multidisciplinary Education to Support Healthy Lifestyles is a transformative approach that integrates various fields to promote well-being, prevent diseases and empower communities. As technology advances and global health challenges evolve, this type of education will play a crucial role in shaping the future of healthcare, education and public health policy. More educational institutions are incorporating multidisciplinary health education into their curricula to equip future professionals with a comprehensive understanding of lifestyle medicine. It is foreseen that governments and organizations will increasingly adopt multidisciplinary education frameworks to design public health campaigns, workplace wellness programs and urban planning initiatives to encourage active and healthy living. The connection between healthy lifestyles and environmental sustainability (e.g., sustainable food choices, eco-friendly urban planning) will be a key focus area. Furthermore, as awareness of mental health grows, multidisciplinary education will

DOI: 10.4324/9781003568650-13

incorporate more strategies for stress management, emotional resilience and mindfulness practices alongside physical health education, as seen in Chapters 4 and 5.

In another context, the incorporation of extended reality (XR) in educational processes for the biopharma syllabus was documented in Chapter 2. Many syllabi in the biotechnology and bioengineering areas must include pharmaceutical production, which involves the manufacturing of medicines (including drug discovery, formulation for large-scale production, quality control, etc.). It also includes automation and innovation. By adopting artificial intelligence (AI), robotics and continuous manufacturing, efficiency is improved and costs are reduced. XR, including virtual reality (VR), augmented reality (AR) and mixed reality (MR), will enhance learning in pharmaceutical production. XR applications include virtual training environments, AR-guided operations, remote collaboration and troubleshooting. The example provided by the Technical University Mannheim using the cave automatic virtual environment (CAVE) assures a future of XR in pharmaceutical production, which will lead to an increase in the adoption of AI-driven XR for personalized learning experiences. By combining pharmaceutical production with XR-aided education, the industry can achieve greater efficiency, safety and innovation in drug manufacturing and workforce training.

An assessment of innovation in health education was delivered in Chapter 3. The integration of blended learning (a combination of traditional face-to-face instruction and digital tools to create a more flexible and engaging learning experience) and digital assessment (the use of online tools to evaluate student performance) was provided with a best-practice example from applied sport science at Deggendorf Institute of Technology. When integrated into program design, these approaches enhance accessibility, personalization and efficiency in education and training. The program is designed to prepare students for the complexities of modern health and sports professions and offers insights for educators in adapting to evolving educational needs.

Among the many advantages of this type of integration, it was clear that higher flexibility and accessibility for students were important (learning at their own pace, anytime and anywhere). The use of multimedia content, simulations and gamified elements improves engagement and interactivity. Another element is data analytics because it helps educators track progress and improve based on needs. Moreover, the setup reduces the time and financial costs associated with travel, which is especially advantageous for venues with remote geographical locations.

One could ask what the future of blended learning and digital assessment looks like. Clearly, AI-driven platforms, together with experts and educators, will tailor content and assessments to individual learners very soon. As seen in Chapter 2, immersive technologies (XR and VR) will provide adequate simulated environments that will enhance experiential learning. There is a clear tendency that schools, universities and corporate training programs will increasingly adopt digital-first learning models.

By integrating blended learning and digital assessment into program design, education becomes more inclusive, engaging and data-driven, shaping the future of learning and workforce development.

It is exactly this topic of inclusive education that is one of the main topics covered in Chapter 4. Advancements in technology are transforming healthcare accessibility, particularly for young people with intellectual disabilities. Mobile health apps provide personalized support, enabling users to track their well-being, medication, fitness and mental health. These innovations enhance independence, improve quality of life and foster self-care habits through user-friendly, adaptive digital tools. The authors introduce a new app called IDHEApp, which underscores the educational dimension, providing people with intellectual disabilities and their caregivers the needed resources to adopt and maintain healthier lifestyles through accessible and inclusive digital platforms.

By leveraging digital innovations, young people with intellectual disabilities can take greater control of their health, promoting inclusion, autonomy and lifelong well-being. There is a greater educational significance interlinked with this topic, namely, young individuals learn how to use an app to manage their health, fostering independence and confidence. Personalized learning approaches can also be implemented because apps are easily adaptable to support different learning styles and cognitive needs. Furthermore, a big impact will cause the integration into special education programs because teaching institutions can incorporate these tools into curricula to enhance well-being.

Chapter 5 guided us through the digital health innovations that are revolutionizing cardiovascular prevention by enhancing patient engagement through mobile apps, wearable devices, telemedicine and AI-driven health monitoring. These tools empower individuals to take an active role in managing risk factors such as high blood pressure, cholesterol and lifestyle habits (e.g., diet, exercise and stress management). Personalized digital interventions improve adherence to preventive strategies and facilitate early detection of heart disease. An important aspect of health is educating patients about their conditions and understanding how to handle and control symptoms and treatments, with the assistance of medical staff, on site and remotely. As exemplified by Rehab+, the future trends in digital cardiovascular prevention will follow a clear path involving AI-driven predictive analytics, allowing early identification of heart disease risk. The use of smart wearables and biosensors will contribute to further success in this type of approach. Personalized digital coaching will alternate between human and AI-powered virtual assistants for optimized and customized health guidance. Interestingly, the possible integration with electronic health records for a communication flow between patients and healthcare providers for proactive intervention will result in a generation of better and more sophisticated legal frameworks. By integrating digital health solutions into cardiovascular prevention, healthcare becomes more accessible, personalized and effective, ultimately reducing the global burden of heart disease and improving long-term patient outcomes.

Turning our attention from cardiovascular diseases to psychosocial health prevention in the workplace, Chapter 6 explained the strategies aimed at mitigating work-related stress, burnout and mental health disorders by improving work conditions, organizational culture and employee well-being. Small and medium-sized enterprises (SMEs), which often lack extensive resources for formal training programs, can benefit from digital solutions like massive open online courses (MOOCs) to enhance psychosocial health awareness and compliance with work standards. This is how "PsyHealth worXs! Psychosocial Health Prevention and Work Standards" came into life. This MOOC provides easily accessible digital training and increases awareness of employee mental health, bridging the policy, research and practice gap and paving the way for healthier and more innovative workplaces. By leveraging this MOOC, SMEs (among others) can systematically implement psychosocial health prevention strategies, ensuring compliance with work standards while fostering a healthier, more productive workforce. The future lies in AI-powered, interactive and integrated digital learning platforms that make workplace well-being education more effective and scalable.

As seen in Chapter 5, Chapter 7 also deals with patient engagement as a critical factor in improving healthcare outcomes, adherence to treatment and overall well-being. Advances in technology and web-based platforms have transformed patient education, making health information more accessible, personalized and interactive. The development of further education programs that attend to these needs is pivotal for the near future. Digital tools, including mobile apps, VR, telemedicine and AI-powered chatbots, empower patients to take an active role in managing their health.

As seen with the EUPATI example, integrating new technologies and web-based platforms, patient education becomes more engaging, personalized and effective, leading to better health outcomes and stronger patient-provider collaboration. The future of digital health education will rely on guided AI, interactivity and accessibility to empower individuals in managing their health proactively. Therefore, the creation of true equity in multistakeholder processes such as medicine research and development are key for establishing the new trainings to be offered.

Chapter 8 transports us to the fascinating world of AI and its impact on higher-education institutions (HEIs). Generative AI (GenAI) is reshaping international higher education by enhancing learning, research and administrative processes. Although AI-driven tools like ChatGPT, DALL·E and other content-generation platforms provide new opportunities for personalized learning and efficiency, they also present ethical, academic integrity and accessibility challenges. Indeed, the ease of generating AI-assisted content raises concerns about originality and ethical use. Danger still exists, especially because AI models may reinforce biases and produce inaccurate or misleading information. Therefore, educators and learners need to gain new skills to effectively use AI in teaching and research. It is therefore mandatory for HEIs to establish clear guidelines for AI use in assessments, coursework and research.

Because the topic is evolving so quickly, sometimes it is challenging to foresee the growth direction of AI in higher-education syllabi. Naturally, HEIs will need to integrate AI ethics, prompt engineering and critical AI evaluation into curricula. Furthermore, AI will be incorporated across fields, from the humanities to science, technology, engineering and mathematics (STEM), promoting a broader understanding of its applications. The development of frameworks for responsible AI implementation is an imminent mission of all HEIs.

A balanced collaboration between AI and human educators is expected to happen because AI will support, and not replace, traditional teaching, ensuring an equilibrium between automation and human mentorship. Consequently, GenAI is set to become a transformative force in international higher education. Although challenges exist, the future will see AI integrated into higher-education syllabi, focusing on ethics, critical thinking and interdisciplinary applications. With proper policies and training, AI will enhance learning experiences, improve accessibility and foster innovation in higher education.

Another important element that must be present when considering the development of a (health-topic-related) syllabus is the entrepreneurial mindset. Chapter 9 clearly establishes that a digital mindset behavior analysis tool can play a crucial role in helping healthcare students cultivate an entrepreneurial mindset by assessing cognitive patterns, adaptability, decision-making and problem-solving skills. Furthermore, these tools may use (and certainly will be ultimately coupled with) AI, data analytics and behavioral tracking to provide personalized insights, fostering innovation, resilience and leadership skills in future healthcare professionals.

With the SHINE Project, authors were able to prove that a digital mindset behavior analysis tool provides an active and personalized learning experience that helps a learner understand how the entrepreneurial mindset is of practical relevance in their own professional context and their individual goals, knowledge and skills. With the help provided, students can recognize opportunities in healthcare and develop solutions for industry challenges. Moreover, the use of interactive tools improves the teamwork, communication and leadership skills necessary for entrepreneurship. Entrepreneurial mindset development is essential for healthcare innovation, leadership and business insight. These tools bridge the gap between traditional medical training and the demand for innovation in healthcare.

A digital mindset behavior analysis tool offers an innovative way to nurture an entrepreneurial mindset in healthcare students, preparing them for leadership, innovation and problem-solving in the evolving healthcare industry. The future will see greater AI integration, immersive learning and interdisciplinary collaboration, ensuring that healthcare professionals are not just caregivers but also innovators and change-makers. Continuing with this tendency, Chapter 10 further examines the institutional approach of incorporating innovation and entrepreneurship guided by HEIs.

Bridging the gap between academia and the economy is essential for fostering innovation, commercialization and economic growth. HEIs can play a pivotal role by implementing an entrepreneurship funnel, a structured process that guides students and researchers from idea generation to the creation of successful spin-offs. This approach nurtures entrepreneurial talent, promotes knowledge transfer and enhances collaboration between academia, industry and investors.

Some essential components of the entrepreneurship funnel are good idea generation and research commercialization, which encourages students and faculty to explore business opportunities based on academic research. To achieve success, it is mandatory to incorporate business, leadership and innovation training into curricula. Furthermore, access to industry mentors, accelerators and funding opportunities should also be provided. Establishing university-backed venture funds, grants and partnerships with investors is also necessary, as is strengthening ties with businesses to facilitate real-world applications of research. The authors of Chapter 10 present the example of establishing the Gateway startup center as a successful story from the University of Cologne. The implementation of innovation scouts has enhanced the process of transference from academia to industry. Several best-practice cases were also explained, clearly indicating the importance of the overall process: boosting economic growth, as HEI spin-offs contribute to job creation, regional development and technological advancements, and in parallel, interdisciplinary collaboration and cross-sector partnerships are encouraged.

As discussed in Chapters 8 and 9, HEIs will need to further integrate digital courses on innovation, business strategy and investment readiness. Universities are consistently creating international startup ecosystems and are partnering with global investors. There is, indeed, a growing emphasis on startups focused on health, sustainability and social impact. Thus, implementing an entrepreneurship funnel, a crucial bridge between academia and the economy, fosters innovative startups and prepares students for the evolving job market. The future of higher education will increasingly focus on entrepreneurial skills, AI-driven incubation and cross-industry collaboration, ensuring that universities become key drivers of economic and technological progress.

Finally, Chapter 11 highlights the need for HEIs to maintain recruitment coupled with the newest technological tendencies of social media. Social media marketing has become a powerful tool for recruiting students into higher-education health programs, offering institutions a direct and engaging way to reach prospective applicants. Platforms like Instagram, LinkedIn, Facebook and TikTok enable universities to showcase their programs, share success stories and connect with a broader audience. Although social media marketing presents many opportunities, HEIs must address some challenges to maximize its effectiveness.

One of the major advantages of social media is that it allows HEIs to connect with a diverse and global audience. Compared to traditional marketing, digital campaigns offer a higher return on investment (ROI) and targeted outreach. Moreover, data-driven insights help optimize recruitment strategies. Yet, despite the clear advantages, many HEIs compete for attention, making it harder to stand out. Furthermore, negative comments or misinformation can negatively impact institutional perception. Because social media platforms are constantly evolving, HEIs must continuously implement new and adaptable recruitment strategies.

Social media marketing is an essential tool for recruiting students into healthcare programs and offers accessibility, engagement and cost-effectiveness. Success may vary depending on authentic storytelling, targeted campaigns and interactive engagement with prospective students. Clearly, HEIs must ensure content credibility, compliance with ethical guidelines and adaptability to digital trends. As seen in Chapter 2, implementation of VR and AR will allow interested candidates to perform virtual campus tours, and immersive experiences will attract more students. Social media marketing is a game-changer in recruiting students for higher-education health programs. Although it offers immense potential, universities must navigate competition, credibility and privacy challenges. Future trends will focus on AI, video content, VR experiences and influencer collaborations, ensuring that institutions remain innovative and competitive in the digital landscape.

Index

Note: Page numbers in *italics* indicate a figure and page numbers in **bold** indicate a table on the corresponding page.

FSC
www.fsc.org
MIX
Papier | Fördert
gute Waldnutzung
FSC® C083411

Kolibri 360 GmbH
Ferdinand-Jühlke-Straße 7
99095 Erfurt, Deutschland
produktsicherheit@kolibri360.de